# The Widow's Handbook

# The Widow's Handbook

## A Guide for Living

Charlotte Foehner and Carol Cozart

Fulcrum, Inc.
Golden, Colorado

Fulcrum, Inc., Golden, Colorado 80401

Design by Linda Seals

Library of Congress Cataloging-in-Publication Data

Foehner, Charlotte
The Widow's Handbook

    Bibliography: p.
    Includes Index
    1. Widows—United States—Life skills guides.
I. Cozart, Carol. II. Title

HQ1058.5.U5F64  1988     640'.240654       88-3619
ISBN 1-55591-014-9
ISBN 1-55591-023-8 (pbk.)

1  2  3  4  5  6  7  8  9  0

*In memory of*
Olin and Wayne

# Contents

# The Widow's
# Handbook

## The Authors' Message

# *For Widows and Friends of Widows*

When both of us were unexpectedly widowed in our early forties, we faced a barrage of problems ranging from whether the funeral had been done appropriately to planning our financial futures as far ahead as we could see. Each of us was left with a family, legal problems and worries about money. Within a year Charlotte's father had died, and her mother became a widow with a different set of problems. Charlotte's grandmother, at eighty-six, had been a widow for many years, but had additional concerns of advancing age and health.

At the beginning of our widowhood, we felt we had to be superwomen and experts in dealing with our own personal problems, being single parents and managing our financial and legal affairs. We attended widows' support groups and soon contacted other widows, both for mutual support and to learn about their widow-related problems and how they coped with them. Carol, as a suicide widow, found that the support groups for survivors of suicides focused on deaths of children, and she felt that her problems were different from those of the surviving parents; few books for widows describe the special problems that a suicide widow must face or how she might deal with them. Charlotte's husband disappeared in a scuba diving accident; there was no written guidance for how to get legal help and what problems to expect in this rare instance.

After the first year had passed, Carol suggested that we try to help other widows since we had learned to cope with many new situations. In bookstores and libraries we had found several well-written books for widows, dealing especially with the grieving process and how to handle it. Other books, written by financial experts and psychology professionals, focused on more practical aspects of managing your living environment and financial affairs. But no one book combined the two issues of dealing with emotions and practical affairs; thus the idea of a handbook for easy reference—a guide for living—was born. The Widow's Handbook is intended for use during progressive stages in the widow's recovery.

Being a widow isn't easy. It is probably the most difficult challenge of a woman's life. The aloneness and the sheer magnitude of additional responsibilities can be overwhelming. We also realize that few, if any, marriages are "made in heaven," that, indeed, some marriages are painful and widowhood may be easier. Yet the challenges remain to be met. Perhaps we can take heart from the bracing words of Prime Minister Margaret Thatcher: "The greatest driving force in life . . . is individual energy and effort." To grow from being wife to widow to woman takes enormous personal energy and effort.

We realize that although we have targeted this book for widows, many of the same problems may be felt by widowers. Facing grief, dealing with financial matters and being a single parent are as common to men as to women who have lost a spouse. Our practical guidance is appropriate for both men and women.

We could not have completed this book without the support and love of our families, especially our children. We appreciate the caring of our relatives, friends and neighbors and their confidence that we would recover and get on with our lives. We offer a special thanks to our widowed friends Marie Osse, Ann Jacobs and Mary Ann Beckley for sharing their personal experiences and to Carol's mother, Irene Cazer, for her contributing research about volunteering and getting involved with life. We especially want to thank our publisher, Robert C. Baron, and editor Patricia Frederick for continued encouragement and patience.

We are indebted to Susan R. Harris, attorney, for her contributing chapter on selecting an attorney. Professional reviews of selected chapters were generously given by William F. Buckley; Bruce Van Gundy; Alice G. Bullwinkle, certified financial planner; Daniel L. Stieren, financial planner; Dewayne Dunbar, certified insurance counselor; Arlene Osborne, Medicare service representative; Jerry Mahan, public information specialist, Social Security Administration; Dr. Roberta Goodman, psychotherapist; Linda Woodworth; Margaret Terrell Morse; Constance Hauver, attorney; and Bobbie Boldon, real estate agent.

—Charlotte Foehner
Carol Cozart
January 1988

P.S.

This book is written as though we, the authors, are sitting and talking with you, the reader. Most of the time our conversations address you and your concerns. We ask you questions and offer suggestions. We talk about widows in general, and at times we share our own experiences. We hope that our conversations with you will not end with this book and that we might continue our dialogue through your letters. If you feel so inclined, you may write and share your problems and solutions with *The Widow's Handbook*, P.O. Box 260786, Lakewood, CO 80226. In time, we hope to issue a revised edition.

# Chapter 1

## New Beginnings—Ready or Not!

*Life seems to be a never-ending series of survivals. . . .*
 —Carol Baker (1931– ), American actress and writer

For perhaps the first time in her life, the widow is a woman alone. No matter how many children, relatives and friends gather round in the aftermath of her husband's death, the widow will experience, off and on, the awful ache of feeling alone for some time to come.

One of every eight American women is a widow. In 1984 widows numbered about eleven million, with a half million more women becoming widowed each year. Almost no woman makes any preparation for this devastating, demanding time of her life. She hopes it will never happen to her—yet when it does her world is torn apart.

A widow is frightened, lonely and grieving. Life ahead is uncertain and now her full responsibility. Yet within a few weeks she will be expected to begin recovering and getting on with her life, ready or not. Well-meaning friends and concerned relatives will have put their grieving aside to some degree, getting back to their lives, and will unconsciously expect the same of her. The truth, though, for many a widow is that she fears that even after a few months she won't have fully recovered, won't be ready to begin a new life. She will still be feeling insecure and anxious coping with each day. How will she get through this one? What decisions should she have made yesterday?

To sustain herself initially, a widow needs the comfort and strength of family and friends, of flowers and funeral tributes. But when the friends and family begin to return to their own lives, she still needs emotional support and some goals on which to focus. Our hope is that this book will continue to provide sustenance long after the flowers are gone.

We know that no book can give you a guaranteed recovery formula. The process of healing and beginning to live again will come from within yourself. The widows we know who have made successful recoveries all have one thing in common: a hopeful, interested attitude toward life. Once again they have become positive about their "todays" and they have plans for their "tomorrows." Each of these women has put forth a great deal of effort to become a more interesting person by becoming involved with other people through volunteer work, full- or part-time employment, outside interests, hobbies or other creative endeavors. They have not been sitting at home turning inward and becoming reclusive.

Mingled with their tears has been the spirit or drive or gumption that has enabled them to gather small bits of courage and gradually gain the confidence that they can handle life alone. Their progress has been in repeated small steps, one thing at a time—but that has been the key to their success. In his book *Bereavement*, psychiatrist Colin Murray Parkes writes that taking on some of the responsibilities that your husband used to shoulder is part of the comforting process of keeping him alive within yourself. Charlotte felt her husband would have been pleased that she taught herself to prepare the income tax returns that he had always done, rather than hire an accountant. Her widowed mother, Marjorie, is successfully managing the stock portfolio that she inherited from her husband.

**Overview**

This book is a handbook to help you through the first months, and includes guidelines for dealing with the first two years as you begin to plan and get on with your life. We have included a master agenda, checklists, sample letters, a glossary of terms and the galvanizing personal experiences of many widows ranging in age from thirty to eighty-eight. Each chapter is short and deals with a separate subject—for easy reference. We know that the widow isn't ready to "study" or do "research" on how to solve all her problems at this juncture. Here you need only turn to a specific chapter to address the issue at hand. It is not necessary to read the entire book to be able to benefit from specific guidance.

The new widow is faced with a bewildering number of choices and decisions. Beyond her own emotions, she will have to deal with legal, financial and physical-environment problems. This book helps her to prepare for and deal with each of these areas. We tell her how to get organized, how to select professional help, how to work with the professional, how to monitor the status of her property and other assets, and how to do many things for herself. On the other hand, if the widow chooses not to manage her own affairs or if she isn't able to do so, she may use these guidelines in directing her advisors or overseer.

Making the first small decisions gives the widow the confidence to deal with larger problems. It is typical for her to have difficulty in concentrating on all she has to do and in becoming quickly knowledgeable about all her new responsibilities. The Master Agenda at the end of this chapter itemizes the more common details, tasks and responsibilities that you are likely to face in the first twenty-four months. It is arranged so as not only to remind you of what decisions are most likely to be required but also when, in this two-year time frame, they should be tended to.

Chapters 2, 3 and 4 deal with immediate issues a widow faces, such as planning the funeral, getting through the first days and recognizing that her grief emotions, no matter how unexpected, are normal. The funeral guidance in Chapter 2 also lists organizations to help the widow resolve problems. In Chapter 3 we discuss techniques for getting through the first few days. Keeping busy by organizing tasks and looking for important papers provides a sense of order. For the newly bereaved widow, Chapter 4 describes the phases of grief and how to work through them, and refers her to support organizations listed at the end of the book. Within a few months, many widows find it comforting to attend a support group. We guide you in finding one, or in starting a new group in your community.

Chapter 5 guides the widow in the important issue of selecting an attorney to help her settle the estate. It could be a mistake to assume that the attorney who handled your late husband's business affairs is the only person to probate the will. This chapter provides sample questions for interviewing an attorney, describes what to expect from a good attorney, and defines your responsibilities in working with the attorney. Most important, an attorney may be required to help you understand the transfers of title—that is, making sure you as a beneficiary now have title to all the property you are supposed to.

Many widows will need some sort of "financial advisory team," which may include an accountant, a banker, a stockbroker, an insurance agent or possibly a financial planner. In Chapter 6 we suggest strategies for getting highly qualified professionals. A banker can explain the advantages of different kinds of checking accounts and instruct you on how to purchase certificates of deposit or Treasury bills. If you need a stockbroker or insurance agent, this chapter describes how to select one and then how to work effectively with him or her.

Chapter 7 deals with the most complex legal issues a widow has to face—settling her late husband's estate. His estate doesn't have to include a mansion and vast acreage to require detailed, specific procedures for distributing his property and other assets to his heirs. This chapter outlines the steps you can expect to confront in the course of estate settlement.

Chapter 8 provides instructions, including sample letters, on how to file claims for insurance proceeds, pensions and annuities. We describe how to find out if your husband had life insurance through his employer, if he had insurance covering the outstanding credit card balances or your home mortgage, and what you can do with any stocks or bonds.

Chapter 9 tells how to apply for Social Security and Medicare benefits, and explains the basics of health and disability coverage. For the widow with dependents, health insurance and disability insurance should be of paramount importance! If you the widow are now the family breadwinner, you must be prepared for possible health care needs for yourself and your dependents. Disability insurance will cover you if you become injured and can't earn a living.

While the widow is waiting for insurance, veterans' or Social Security benefits, she must begin facing immediate financial reality. How do you determine how much income you have and what your monthly bills will be? Chapter 10, "Your Budget, Your

Checkbook and Your Credit," shows how to balance your check-book, how to create a budget and how to determine your income and expenses.

Chapter 11 covers home and auto maintenance responsi-bilities. Even if you are fortunate enough to have someone else in charge, you need to understand what you are paying for and when to have preventive maintenance performed. In the event you decide you want to sell your home or any other property you have inherited, we have included tips on what to expect from a good real estate agent. Different types of homeowner and auto insur ance coverage are clearly described.

Single parenting can be an awesome responsibility. In Chapter 12 we look at both the challenges and rewards of being "two parents," and address problems that a widow encounters as the parent of teens who have lost their father. We also discuss the "distancing" phenomenon that can occur as your late husband's family may drift away from you

In Chapter 13 we share the story of Mary Ann who nursed her husband during a lingering, terminal illness, and we share our own stories—Charlotte's husband disappeared while scuba diving and Carol's husband was a suicide victim. We discuss some of the special difficulties of widows in these circumstances.

The later chapters turn toward the widow's future. In Chapters 14 and 15 we focus on your social life and taking time for yourself. We talked to other widows and discovered it was okay to express feelings and discuss how to deal with them. We learned that no feelings are unique; other widows have them, too. We look at caring for yourself—understanding and dealing with your needs for a social life, and dealing with your friends' and relatives' reactions to your decisions. Your relationships with your relatives and friends will change. We discuss coping strategies and how to understand that their grieving and recovery may not proceed at the same rate as yours.

Working or having a career can be helpful in a widow's re-covery. Chapter 16 offers strategies for deciding what work skills you have and what you would like to do, especially if you are going out into the working world for the first time.

. In Chapters 17 and 18 we turn to planning for the future. The life insurance proceeds and other assets you inherited may have to last for many years. You can hire professionals to manage your money, but no one else will care as much about your financial affairs as you should. You don't have to become a financial expert, but the ideas and terms outlined in these two chapters will provide you with enough background so that you can ask questions and at least oversee your advisors. We talked to one widow of seventy-one who was ill one year and directed her broker to make all the buy and sell decisions in her stock portfolio. He initiated about $5 million in transactions, generating almost $60,000 in commissions for his firm, while producing only about $20,000 in additional income for her! The following year, she resumed control and made her own decisions.

**Master Agenda**     The Master Agenda that follows lists many of the issues you are likely to need to address, and links them to a likely time sequence. For certain legal issues, the time frame can be critical. The professionals you retain will guide you through the specifics, but you need to have an overall sense of what needs to be done and when.

Some other actions you might want to consider in the first few months:

• Plan for periodic expenditures, such as insurance premiums and property taxes;
• Determine the value of your assets and liabilities with your future in mind;
• Consider a financial plan for your future;
• Choose your own stockbroker, tax advisor and financial planner;
• Maintain your real estate and personal property;
• Review your banking practices and options with a bank officer;
• Consider participating in a support group.

Don't allow the burden of new responsibilities to overwhelm you. Take them one step at a time, and ask your friends and relatives for help. You can return the favor someday, when you're stronger. If you can afford it, hire professionals to assist you, at least in the beginning. Use this handbook as a tool to help you survive the early months of your widowhood and to get started on your new life.

## MASTER AGENDA

| Suggested Time | Action | Considerations |
|---|---|---|
| Immediately | Locate important papers. | Includes birth certificates for your entire family, marriage license, life insurance policies, Social Security numbers and military records. |
| | | Supports claims for benefits and death certificate. |
| | Notify friends and relatives. | For funeral attendance and as a courtesy. |
| | | List persons contacted in notebook. |
| | Retain all incoming mail. | Prevents loss of bills, checks, etc. If needed, get help to process. |
| | Photocopy all outgoing business mail. | Supports your position in case of confusion, during an emotional time. |
| Within first month | Get copies of death certificate. | Supports claims for benefits including insurance and Social Security. |
| | Review your health insurance. | Make sure you are still covered by calling health plan administrator where you or your husband worked. |
| | Select an attorney. | Probates and settles the estate. |
| | | Advises you of your legal and tax responsibilities. |
| | Apply for benefits. | Includes life insurance proceeds, Social Security, benefits, Medicare, Veterans' benefits, pensions and annuities. |
| | | Ask husband's employer if he participated in any company retirement plans. |

| | | |
|---|---|---|
| Before paying bills | Review immediate financial assets. | Determine resources in checking, savings, and money market accounts. |
| | Determine whether accounts are insured. | Includes home mortgage, auto loans, credit cards, savings accounts. |
| | Plan a short-term budget. | |
| First few months | Identify other assets. | Includes stock or bond portfolios, partnerships, real estate, personal property, bank accounts. |
| | | Provide this information to your attorney and accountant. |
| | Select an accountant. | Assists in estate fiduciary tax preparation. Advises you in preliminary financial planning. |
| | | Coordinates with your attorney on estate settlement. |
| Within three to six months | Review where you want to live. | Can you afford upkeep costs? Is the location appropriate for you? |
| | Review status of financial assets. | Make adjustments if necessary. Work with financial advisors. |
| By month six | Assess your emotional health. | Consider a support group. Treat yourself to something special. |
| | Plan property maintenance. | Review auto care and insurance and condition of home and its insurance. |
| By month nine | Complete estate settlement. | If required, file and pay estate and gift taxes. |

| | | |
|---|---|---|
| By month eighteen | Socialize. | Become involved, make new friends and commitments in such areas as volunteering, health and exercise, culture, entertainment, self-improvement. |
| | Network with other widows. | If you feel recovered, consider acting as a "grief support" person. |
| | Consider an estate plan. | For your financial future when you're older. |
| | | To save your heirs money and problems. |
| By month twenty-four | Look ahead. | Continue making plans to be involved with other people—travel, volunteer, work, take classes. |
| | | Give yourself credit for how far you've come! |
| | | Let your family and friends know you feel better about life. They'll celebrate with you. |

## Notes

# Chapter 2

# The Funeral

*There is no grief that time does not lessen and soften.*
—Cicero (106–43 B.C.), Roman scholar

Perhaps you won't see this book until long after your husband's
funeral, but in the event that you do need funeral planning guidance, we discuss here some of the typical decisions you will have
to make. Most likely, you will feel anxious and uncertain about
how to proceed, because in our culture aspects of death are largely
ignored until we are forced to deal with them firsthand. But, at this
early stage, while planning the funeral you are in such a state of
shock that you find yourself relying on the advice of others—the
clergy, your physician, the funeral provider and your family. Still,
though these people can help guide you through the prescribed
steps, you have the ultimate responsibility for choosing the burial
site, casket, pallbearers, music, biographical information for the
memorial card and obituary, and for deciding whether you want
a graveside service. These choices are influenced by personal,
religious and regional preferences, as well as by your state laws.

We are assuming that funeral arrangements were not made
in advance and that you, the widow, are making decisions about
purchasing funeral goods and services while experiencing intense
grief and time constraints. Perhaps the greatest pressure will come
from yourself as you strive to make the "right" decisions while
trying to please everyone else. In order to make a good impression or because you are confused, you may tend to agree to
whatever is suggested and then, consequently, overspend. Funer-

als can be expensive, and it is easy to be persuaded to buy more than you intended.

To help you, the federal "Funeral Rule" from the Federal Trade Commission, effective since 1984, makes it easier for you to select only the goods and services you want or need and to pay for only those you select. The Funeral Rule requires disclosure of the funeral provider's practices and fees, but does not override state laws.

As required by the Funeral Rule, a funeral provider may quote prices over the telephone. If you inquire in person about funeral arrangements, the funeral provider can supply a general price list. This list, which you can keep, contains the cost of each individual funeral item and service offered. You can use this information to help select the funeral provider and funeral items you want, need and are able to afford.

The price list also discloses important legal rights and requirements regarding funeral arrangements. It must include information on embalming, cash advance sales (such as newspaper notices or flowers), caskets for cremation and required purchases.[1]

Certain services, such as "cash advance" items, are paid by the funeral provider on your behalf. These generally include honoraria to clergy, limousines, funeral escorts, memorial cards, newspaper obituary notices, musicians' fees, flowers and copies of the death certificate. In some cases, the funeral provider will charge you a service fee in addition to the actual cost of these items.

## Difficult Decisions

In addition to planning the formal services for your husband's funeral, you will face other difficult choices. We mention some of these in an attempt to prepare you mentally for the emotional stress you may feel when you are required to make urgent and "final" choices.

*Autopsy.* If the cause of your husband's death was uncertain, the law may require an autopsy. If you are unsure about whether the autopsy is necessary, ask your family attorney. However, in many cases it is a matter of family choice. This may be an emotionally difficult decision. Seek guidance from your family and clergy.

*Burial Site.* Private cemeteries each charge different prices. If you have a choice of sites, compare prices and maintenance practices. If your husband was a veteran, he may be eligible for burial in a National Cemetery free of charge, including a headstone or marker and a United States flag to cover the casket. To qualify, you must provide supporting documentation to show he was a veteran. These documents include his honorable discharge papers, Social Security number, rank, branch of service and dates of entrance and discharge. If, instead, you choose a private cemetery, you may apply for a burial allowance, a flag and partial reimbursement toward the plot and marker. For further details, see our discussion of veterans' benefits in Chapter 8, "Filing Claims for Life Insurance and Survivor Benefits."

*Funeral Service.* The funeral provider will ask what funeral arrangements you want and guide you in making decisions. Ask a member of your family, the clergy or close friends to help you make these choices; their support will help stabilize and console you.

- The funeral is generally a ceremony held in connection with the burial or cremation of the dead. A graveside service may be included. A memorial service, while similar to the funeral, is performed in remembrance of the deceased, but does not incorporate the burial or cremation. In addition to or in lieu of the funeral you may have as many memorial services as you choose, even in different states. For heads of state, memorials are sometimes held on an anniversary of the death.
- Embalming the body before burial or cremation is determined by health and state laws as well as religious practices. Embalming is commonly ordered, but is *not* required in every instance. The funeral provider must disclose in writing that embalming is not required by law, except in certain special cases. The funeral provider cannot charge you for an unauthorized embalming.
- The issue of whether to have an open casket for viewing the body is determined by religious practice, your own preferences and local custom. In some cases the viewing and visitation are arranged at a mortuary, without a viewing at the funeral. Sensitively prepare young children for this experience in advance. Gently describe what they can expect to see and take time to talk about their feelings.

• Cremation is frequently chosen as an alternative to burial. For the funeral service, if you wish, a casket can be rented to accommodate the body and allow a viewing. Under the Funeral Rule, if you choose direct cremation, you have the right to buy an unfinished wood box or an alternative container, rather than a casket.

• You will be asked to provide the burial clothing to be worn by the deceased: street clothes, special religious garments, or perhaps a uniform or other clothing that had special meaning for your husband.

**The Obituary**

The obituary is a notice of death, usually including a biographical history of the deceased. Ask your funeral provider or clergy to help write the obituary and submit it to a newspaper for publication. Use the following list to help organize the information.

• Names of:  Deceased _____

Surviving Spouse _____

Children _____

_____

_____

Other Relatives (siblings, parents) _____

_____

_____

• Number of Grandchildren _____

• Date and Place of Birth _____

• Education/Degrees _____

• Profession/Career _____

• Honors/Distinctions _____

• Other (membership in organizations, community service, etc.)

_____

You will need to provide a copy of the death certificate to substantiate each claim for life insurance proceeds, various widow's benefits and to transfer assets from your husband's estate. Some institutions will require a certified copy to retain in their files, while others will photocopy the document and return the certified copy to you. Your funeral provider can order as many copies as you need. For completion of the original death certificate, you must supply biographical data about your husband, and your husband's parents' full names, *including his mother's maiden name*. Examples of assets for which you may need a death certificate include:

**Death Certificate Requirements**

- Life insurance benefits,
- Social Security survivor benefits,
- Veterans' survivor benefits,
- Retirement or pension plan survivor benefits,
- Financial accounts at banks, savings and loans, brokerage firms and safe deposit boxes,
- Property insurance proceeds,
- Auto (vehicle) registration,
- Health insurance policy proceeds,
- Credit card companies,
- Real estate title transfers,
- Stock and bond title transfers.

If you need additional copies at a future date ask the funeral provider for assistance, or order them yourself from your state's vital statistics or health agency.

If you have a problem about the funeral arrangements, discuss it first with your funeral director. If you are still dissatisfied, contact your state licensing board. Two additional sources of help include the Conference of Funeral Service Examining Boards, 520 East Van Trees Street, P.O. Box 497, Washington, IN 47501, (812) 254-7887; and ThanaCAP, 11121 West Oklahoma Avenue, Milwaukee, WI 53227, (414) 541-7925.

**Concerns and Problems**

As distasteful as it may be, homes have been robbed during the funeral service. You may want to have someone stay in your home to prevent a possible burglary. It is easy for thieves to read the obituary notices to determine when your house will be empty.

Dealing with the funeral can be emotionally difficult and stressful. It helps to be able to discuss your funeral choices with relatives and friends. You may need their reassurance that your decisions are appropriate. With the guidance from this chapter, we hope you will feel more comfortable with your selections.

# Chapter 3

# *The First Days*

*When it is dark enough, you can see the stars.*
    —Ralph Waldo Emerson (1803–1882), American writer
                                              and philosopher

The first days of one of the most traumatic experiences of your life may pass with a sense of unreality. You can function pretty much by rote through the funeral or memorial services by following the prescribed rituals. Your clergy, family and friends may be there to support you and help you make the first decisions. This chapter addresses the special problems of those unrelieved, pain-filled days, with suggestions that may help you focus on small tasks to give you a sense of purpose, and to help you accept consolation and share your grief. We discuss how to feel comfortable about accepting offers of assistance, and what friends might do to help. If you have young children, consider that they will need to be reassured that you, too, won't leave them.

## Accepting Condolences

In the beginning, visitors—family, clergy and friends—surround you to hold and comfort you, to express their sadness and to share your grief. They sincerely want to help. Some may say, "If you need anything . . . just call me." Others may simply take command, organizing the kitchen, receiving food offerings and bringing visitors to greet you. Try to accept their love and caring gestures. Until now, as a wife and perhaps a mother, you were in the position to nurture and comfort others; you may have put their needs ahead of yours. Now is a time for you to let your and your husband's families and friends show you how they care. Allowing them to express themselves and do things for you will not only buoy you up but will help them deal with their grief.

**How Friends Can Help**

There are several things friends can do to help, depending on your needs. If you're uncertain about whether accepting an offer is appropriate, just imagine whether you would feel comfortable making the same offer to a friend if the situation were reversed. For example, a neighbor may offer to mow your grass or shovel the snow off your walk. If that's something you or a member of your family would do for them in a time of need, then accept it. Remember, these gestures are tributes to your late husband and you. Your friends will feel better for having been able to give, even in a small way.

The Widow's Network in California has developed the following tips for friends and family of the newly widowed:[2]

• Get in touch. Call and go visit the newly widowed.

• Be a good listener. Let the survivor express his or her feelings. The widowed person needs to release strong feelings openly and with a trusted friend or relative who will not be judgmental.

• Do not give advice. Each person has to be given the chance to work out her own problems. Be a sounding board for the widowed person to bounce ideas off you, but always leave the decision up to the widow.

• Mention the deceased spouse. The spouse was a living human being and the survivor will be happy to hear some good and interesting stories about the deceased spouse. Many times no one will talk about the deceased spouse, as if that person never existed.

• Social activity. If the surviving spouse was in your social circle, continue to include that person in your social plans.

• Keep in touch. Continue to be supportive. Remember birthdays, anniversaries, even the date of the death anniversary. Continue to phone, and invite your widowed friend to lunch or dinner.

• Just be there to listen.

Often friends want to help you, but have no idea what needs to be done. In many areas of the country it is common for friends to bring food to the widow's home. You'll need help in keeping track of who brought what so you can thank them later. Don't be reticent about asking a friend or two to stay on top of that. And don't be shy about accepting offers from others to stay with you or to clean the house, change the bed linens, do the laundry, go to the grocery store, cook, run errands, wash the car and fill it with gas, act as chauffeur, feed the pets or tend the garden. Farm widows will need more immediate and substantial help with livestock and crops.

A friend can assist by offering to notify out-of-town friends and relatives of the death. Sometimes family members need to have clothing cleaned or purchased to wear to the funeral. If there are no close relatives or clergy available, a friend can offer to help with funeral arrangements.

If there are children still living at home, a relative or friend could take them aside for some individual attention. Carol's friends asked to take each of her children for a walk or for lunch. Charlotte was pleased when her young daughter was invited for an overnight stay with a best friend; it allowed the child a chance to escape the intense grief for a brief time. This form of personal reaching out seems to help children understand that their whole world hasn't ended, that there is still laughter and diversion. Let your child decide whether to accept or decline any invitations.

In an attempt to be helpful, friends may urge you to immediately relocate or dispose of your husband's clothing and personal belongings. Don't rush this process. Wait until you are comfortable with your own feelings about moving his clothes. If you receive comfort from touching, smelling or just looking at his belongings, then keep them intact for the time being.

## Reassuring Your Children

For young children, death may be something they've experienced only through television or the loss of a pet. They may not understand what has happened to their father, only that you are upset and nothing seems normal. They may be frightened and uncertain about what will happen to you or to them. They may fear that you'll die, too. If your husband was ill and in a hospital, they may associate hospitals with death.

They'll need to feel your love and reassurance constantly. Perhaps you'll want them to sleep in the same room with you. If they want to go out to play with friends, let them have a brief respite. Their ability to grieve is in short bits of time.

If the younger children wish to attend the funeral or burial service, explain to them what will happen—what they'll see and what they might hear. Describe how grieving persons might behave. Reassure them that although this is a sad time, it is also a special and important occasion, and that you'll all be together.

Older children and teenagers may wish to help with the funeral arrangements. Sharing in choosing music, flowers or readings may help them feel they've done something special for their father. One children's psychologist recommends asking older children if they wish to participate in the funeral service by being a pallbearer, musician, reader or by presenting part of the eulogy. This should be at the child's wish, and never forced. The most important issue for your children before and during the funeral observance is that they understand they can count on your continued love and support.

## The Early Tasks

During the first few days and weeks, even before you begin working with your attorney, you can attend to some small but important tasks that can save you confusion and pain later. These organizational activities may help you get through this difficult period by keeping your mind occupied and by filling your days. These include notifying relatives and friends of your husband's death, keeping track of your mail, making notes about phone messages and beginning to locate important papers.

## Keeping Things Organized

Even the seemingly insignificant chores will be easier if you organize them with a friend's help. Follow these suggestions:

- Make notes of who should be notified about your husband's death. Besides family, friends and the funeral providers, you may want to include his business associates and his attorney. If your children are school age and still living at home, call their principal and ask that each teacher be notified. You may even wish to notify the parents of some of your children's friends.

- Keep a small spiral-bound notebook near the telephone so you can take notes on all incoming and outgoing messages. Don't discard any notes; simply draw a diagonal line through the old ones. You'll be surprised at how often you may need to refer to an earlier phone call. It's difficult to remember whom you spoke to, what you talked about or when. Small, loose notes are more easily lost.
- Use small index or note cards to organize the name and address of each person who contributes food. You could also jot down what item was brought, the container description, and how it could be or was returned. These details will be invaluable for your thank-you notes.
- To organize incoming mail, ask a friend to purchase a few dozen manila folders. Sort the mail and file it in a labeled folder for your later attention. Don't discard anything you haven't reviewed personally. Folders could be labeled by category, such as Medical Bills, Household Bills, Insurance Information, Attorney, Bank Statements, Social Security and so on. Or, consider time expiration labels such as Immediate Attention—Today, By the fifteenth, By the thirtieth, Hold, etc.
- Condolence cards and letters may continue to arrive for weeks. If a folder is not large enough to contain them, perhaps a basket or small box near the front door would suffice. You may want to reread these messages when you have more time to yourself. Preserve the return addresses for thank-you notes.
- For future reference, record your family members' Social Security numbers on one small card to tuck in your wallet. Include your late husband's number, too. Under stress, you may not be able to recall even your own number. You'll be needing these frequently during the next few months when you file claims for benefits.

LOCATING IMPORTANT PAPERS

Almost immediately, you'll need to begin searching for "important papers." Some are required in the beginning days; others may
not be needed for a few months. Search in your safe deposit box,
your husband's desks at home and work, file cabinets, dresser
drawers. Your family attorney may have a copy of the will. The
initial documents to locate include:

- The will and any prearranged funeral plans,
- Life insurance policies,
- Military records, which include honorable discharge pa-
pers showing branch of service, dates of service and rank,
- Social Security numbers for each family member. In some
states, this is shown on the motor vehicle operator's license. Look
on last year's income tax return or in your husband's checkbook.
Call his employer.

You may want to file each document in a separate manila
folder. If you're concerned that they might get lost, make photocopies. Within a few months you will need to locate property
deeds, home and auto insurance policies, last year's income tax
returns, and asset records such as stock or bond certificates.

These beginning days are excruciating, but later there may be
some comfort in being able to recall what you experienced and the
strength you gathered. The simple tasks of organizing your mail
and searching for important documents will give some element of
continuity to your days. Accepting help and sympathy from family
and friends helps them deal with their grief. Already, in the midst
of your bereavement, you've begun again to give love to friends
and to heal yourself.

# Chapter 4

# Emotional Support During Grief

*It is natural to interest all in our grief.*
*The deeper the griefs, the greater the joys, when restored to health*
*and favor.*
> —Samuel Richardson (1689–1761), British writer

The dictionary defines grief as "mental suffering and pain." Yet, this concise understatement can't begin to convey the depth of the emotional turbulence you'll typically experience on the long, difficult road to recovery. In this chapter we discuss the feelings a grieving person may have and the working-through-grief advice we've encountered. Only a person who has experienced the loss of his or her spouse can understand fully what you may be feeling. We review the medically defined "phases of grief," recommend what to do about professional counseling, and suggest where to look for emotional support.

**Grief and Grieving**

It's widely known that losing a spouse is one of the most traumatic experiences one can ever have. Psychiatrists at the University of California at Los Angeles and San Diego have reported there is a common thread linking grief, illness and death in new widows. The bereaved woman's immune system response to illness is significantly decreased. In addition to the emotional pain, grief can manifest itself in a variety of physical symptoms. For example, the initial physical response may be felt as a sense of cold numbness or faintness, with ringing in the ears. Our minds often react to stress by focusing on our emotional pain, while ignoring our physical needs. Hunger may be forgotten; stress often results in a total loss of appetite; eating or swallowing may become almost intolerable. During this period of intense grief, you may experience chest pains, rapid breathing, chills, dryness of the mouth, or a lump in the chest or throat. These are normal. However, should they persist, contact your physician.

Perhaps the most common physical ailment is insomnia. Your physician may prescribe a sleeping aid or tranquilizer, but take these medications only when absolutely necessary. The decisions you make now could have far-reaching consequences, and later you may want to recall these first days.

During acute grieving, your reaction time and concentration abilities may be decreased. Although you may expect to function normally, for the first few days of widowhood you may be in shock, which can impair your driving ability. If possible, wait a few days or weeks before driving yourself and rely on others to get you around. Tears can come easily in the privacy of your car, but they obscure your vision and alertness.

There are three concerns of the grief process that worry every widow. The first is "How long does it take to recover?" or "Will I ever get over this?" Grieving is unique to each individual. It can take from several months to years to run its course; it can even last the rest of your life, though to a far less excruciating degree. With time, the intense, piercing pain of grief abates and the frequency of remembering diminishes. But you never totally forget or get over that part of your life. Instead, you go forward, building on the strength you gained during your married years.

The second concern is "Are my feelings normal?" or "Am I losing my mind?" During the first months (and sometimes longer) of widowhood, you may feel that on occasion that you are actually losing your mind. You sometimes can't remember what you said or did. You can't always control your emotions, and the tears may begin for no apparent reason. Something as simple as a color, a sound or a smell reminds you of what you have lost. We set a place at the table, then remember that he isn't coming for dinner anymore. Charlotte was surprised that, even after two years, it was painful to announce her husband's death to one of his acquaintances who hadn't known of it. No matter how unfamiliar, uncharacteristic or just plain bizarre your feelings sometimes seem to you, be assured that they are normal under the circumstances. You are experiencing one of the most painful, devastating, stressful events that can occur in a human lifetime.

The third concern is "How do I know whether I should get professional counseling?" A qualified professional will not designate a specific time frame within which you should seek counseling. The need for counseling varies with each individual. Speaking from personal experience, we feel that if after two years of being a widow you are not looking ahead and making plans for your own life, but are still dwelling on what you had and what you lost, then you need some guidance in sorting out your feelings. Professional counselors won't tell you what to do specifically; instead, they'll help you to articulate what you are feeling and guide you in identifying for yourself what you want to do and how you intend to resolve your problems.

If private therapy with a psychiatrist or psychologist is beyond your financial means, consider a grief support group. These groups allow persons with common problems to air their concerns, at no charge. With the guidance of a group leader, usually someone trained in counseling, the members share their strategies for coping with problems. In addition to counseling, some support groups plan social occasions and promote friendships.

The term widow has many connotations. You have heard of the *merry widow*, who appears to enjoy her new status and may be eagerly looking for her next mate. On the other hand, in many regions and cultures, the widows of the community are set aside and respected but socially isolated—left alone to deal with their misery. Today, though, we have choices; we can find answers, understanding and guidance for dealing with our grief through therapy and support groups.

## Phases of Grief

Grief begins with death or with the knowledge of an impending death. You may already be familiar with the "stages of death" identified by Dr. Elisabeth Kubler-Ross in her work with dying patients.[3] She has defined five stages that *precede* death, with hope persisting through all of these: denial, anger, bargaining, depression and acceptance.

Similarly, when we experience the actual death of a loved one, we feel some of these same emotions, which then become *phases of grief*. They usually include shock, denial, anger, guilt and recovery. Collectively, the feelings of denial, anger and guilt are felt as suffering. Recovery follows slowly and gradually, with acceptance and growth. Together, all these phases comprise grief. Grief is a process whereby we move from intense pain caused by loss to a recovery based on personal growth.

For the purposes of treating patients or writing about grief, it is convenient to assume that each person progresses through these stages in an orderly, step-wise fashion—one stage after the other. However, in real life, this is not likely to happen. Most grieving persons move erratically back and forth, progressing ahead one or more phases, then temporarily regressing to an earlier phase. Nor do people spend an equal amount of time in any two phases of grief. For example, one woman said she felt that she had passed through all the grief phases within the first day of her widowhood. Other widows have mentioned they experienced several grief emotions simultaneously. For example, shock and denial seem to meld. We are shocked or stunned in trying to comprehend the full impact of what has happened, while at the same time we are denying the event. Our mind recoils and seems to cry out, "No, this hasn't happened. It's just a bad dream!" Yet another woman was distressed that she did not experience these grief emotions in the neat orderly way she had seen them identified; she was surprised that she could skip certain phases, but then experience them at a later time. So the point is, in the grieving process, nothing you feel is really abnormal.

To help you more clearly understand the grieving process, we briefly describe each of the phases of grief, focusing on the feelings and behaviors commonly experienced by widows.

**Shock and Denial**

Shock is defined as "something that jars the mind or emotions, as if with a violent unexpected blow." Shock also occurs after an accident, or when we perceive a threat to our physical or emotional selves. Our body reacts as though preparing for battle. Indeed, we are preparing for a tough, prolonged battle—to accept and recover from perhaps the most devastating loss in our life. Physical symptoms are very real and can include faintness, heart palpitations, dry mouth, dizziness, loss of appetite, gastrointestinal disorders and insomnia. We may move and act in a mechanical robotlike fashion, cushioned by shock.

The occurrence of death is always unexpected and traumatic, even though we might have had time to prepare for the event. No matter how long someone is ill, when death happens, it is over in an instant. You feel shock and disbelief no matter whether death is anticipated or comes out of the blue. If your husband's death was expected, friends who want to comfort you may mistakenly assume that you don't feel disbelief. They knew you had time to mentally prepare yourself and may not understand your shock. But in fact all death is sudden, even though not all death comes as a surprise.

Feelings may vacillate between denial and acceptance. In our state of shock, we may recall, "Only yesterday he was alive." If we doze, we may slowly awaken feeling quite normal for a moment; then, with a start, we remember our pain and we grieve. For a moment, in our slumber, we have been able to deny our grieving and to postpone acceptance.

In our culture, the funeral and burial rituals help us deal with our denials. Seeing a casket or viewing the body reinforces the awful reality. One of Carol's children stood next to his father's open casket and quietly sobbed, "I just knew that when I looked, it would be someone else. I wanted it to be a terrible mistake." Regarding her father's death, Carol recalls that she knew he was dying and that he had died, but until she saw him lying in his coffin, she had denied the death. As difficult as the funeral service may be, it helps us resolve our denials and begin the process of acceptance.

Denial is one stage that keeps coming back again and again in small, subtle ways. Do you answer the telephone at a certain time of day expecting to hear your husband's familiar voice? Do you hear his car in the driveway or expect him to walk in the door at the end of the day? If you have dreams that he has returned, or that you are searching for him, realize that these are normal experiences. The avoidance of sorting through your husband's belongings is also a form of denial. It may be best to leave your husband's closet untouched for a few months. If you give away his clothes at too early a stage, you may be plagued by feelings of disloyalty.

Another early reaction to shock and denial is disorientation, or inability to make decisions. Some widows blindly follow well-meaning guidance, while others determinedly resist all advice. In her grieving state, Carol developed a strong case of following the "shoulds"—advice from family and friends that she should do this, or should not do that. Carol became so persistent in following her "should" compulsions that her concerned sister taped a note on the refrigerator: "Have you should on yourself today?" Later, as Carol worked through her grief and became stronger, she recalled that she had performed like a dutiful little robot, to the extreme of appearing for a job interview, emotionally unprepared, only a month into her widowhood.

**Anger**

Anger and guilt are normal emotions each grieving person is expected to feel. How or when they are experienced varies with each individual. The first emotion, anger, is sometimes equated with rage, fury or resentment. This normal human reaction to death can be felt by a child or an adult. We may feel anger that our father or husband has left us, even though we realize he had no control over the leaving. We can still resent his abandoning us and not meeting our needs.

After a death you may feel anger toward the doctor for not doing more to save your husband's life, at the policeman who brought you the bad news, or at your husband for not taking better care of himself. Typically, this anger may be suppressed or denied for a time. We don't like to think of ourselves as capable of feeling anger at our dead spouse or at friends we care about. We like to excuse their faults and recall their best qualities. Yet, when the plumbing clogs, the car breaks down, or the bank sends an overdraft notice, you may resent even having to consider the problems. After all, if your husband had routinely taken care of these responsibilities, you may very well feel anger that he left you alone and helpless. If he left his financial affairs in disorder, you will most likely feel intense frustration on top of resentment.

Anger is danger without the "d." If you had a dangerous hole on your front porch, you would not ignore it. You would resolve the problem by getting the hole repaired. The hole doesn't disappear by itself. Similarly, your anger doesn't go away by itself. You must not ignore or suppress your anger, but constructively express it. Several months after she became a widow, Carol received a letter from a former neighbor. She too had recently become a widow and was seeking Carol's sympathy. Although she knew of Carol's circumstances, she had never acknowledged that Carol was a widow, not then or now. Carol was angry, and expressed it by standing in the living room screaming and tearing the letter to shreds. Then, ashamed to have behaved in such a manner, she began to apologize. Her brother, who had witnessed her tirade, said, "Don't apologize. This is the first time I've seen you express any emotion. I'm happy and relieved to see that you are beginning to feel again."

When you begin to emerge from numbness, shock and denial and begin entering the feeling world again, you may feel anger. We are taught from childhood that anger is bad. We are taught not to express anger. However, in the grieving process, you must express anger to get rid of it so you can get on with acceptance and recovery. You have every right to feel angry about what has happened to you—losing your husband and being alone. Although death is nearly always beyond our control—that is, it occurs in spite of our every effort to prevent it—we feel anger at the unfairness. The platitude, "Life isn't fair," doesn't help the feelings of anger to dissipate.

God can be another target for our anger, but most people are uncomfortable acknowledging this anger. We are taught that God is loving and forgiving. It is not right to be angry with God. However, Detrich and Steele, in their book *How to Recover from Grief*, point out how we might reconcile our feelings of anger toward God: "God is big enough to take our anger and not fall apart! Sometimes in order to realize how big and great and good and loving God is, we need to get angry with him and confess that anger to him. Jesus cried out on the cross, 'My God, why have you forsaken me?' Certainly that's the same cry of anguish and anger we sometimes feel. The psalmist cried out and wrestled with God, letting go of his feelings of hurt and anger. When we go to God and explain how angry we are with him, he listens, understands, accepts, loves and wraps comforting arms around us. And when we've finished flailing our arms and our anger is spent, God wipes away our tears—and is still there. Listening to our anger is one of God's ways of helping our healing."[4]

RESOLVING ANGER

It is normal to be frustrated or angry at having to assume additional unfamiliar responsibilities. Some therapists recommend directing your anger toward objects rather than other people. Some tactics you may find helpful are to scream or cry while sitting in (not driving) the car, punch or kick some pillows, or shovel the snow or mow the grass at a furious pace. Do something physical to expend your negative energy and partially exhaust yourself. If possible, put the problem aside for a while. Then try to calm yourself with soothing music, a slow walk outdoors or a cup of tea. It is better to take your anger out on objects rather than family and friends. If you kick the door the only thing hurt is your toe. Angry words cannot be taken back.

If expressing your anger at inanimate objects doesn't offer relief, find someone with whom you can talk freely. One choice for resolving anger is to become involved with a widows' support group. These groups are designed to let people come together to talk over their problems and suggest solutions. It helps to learn that you are not the only person who feels angry about what has happened to you. It also helps to hear about how other widows deal with their anger. Sometimes the best therapy to relieve anger is simply to be able to talk about it with someone who is non-judgmental. We need to have our anger accepted as normal, not unreasonable. If you do not feel comfortable with a support group, remember that your minister, priest or rabbi are trained to counsel grieving and angry persons.

**Guilt**

Guilt is defined as "being responsible for an offense or wrongdoing." In our grief, we may easily feel we are guilty or responsible for doing or not doing something that led to our husband's death. Guilt is the most difficult phase of grief. It is sometimes felt as anger toward ourselves. It can be the most painful, the most self-destructive and the most difficult to resolve. It is hard to be angry at a dead person and easy to be angry with yourself.

Perhaps you feel guilty for not making your husband go to the doctor sooner, for not realizing that the pain in his chest was not just heartburn, or for not being more sensitive to his depression. The spontaneous sense of relief felt after death from a long-term illness may immediately be perceived as guilt. How could anyone feel relief, even though a loved one's suffering has ended? One of Charlotte's friends devotedly attended her young husband, who was suffering with a brain tumor, through his final days. In this case, the woman's religious faith and nursing background spared her feelings from turning to guilt.

In dealing with your guilt, you need to understand that you cannot be responsible for another person's decisions and actions. The "if onlys" and the "should haves" are common expressions of guilt. We haven't met a widow yet who has not mentioned these phrases. If you had an argument with your husband, ending with his storming out of the house, and that was the last time you saw him alive, you might berate yourself with, "If only I hadn't said that. I should have stopped him. It was all my fault." Probably during your marriage the two of you had other arguments, but you would later kiss and make up. This time, however, the argument went unresolved and perhaps you are placing the blame on yourself. Every couple has conflict and disagreements. This is part of life. We grow through problem solving.

If you have unresolved anger or guilt, try writing a letter to your late husband. Tell him what you are feeling. Describe what you wish you had done or said. Write about your anger at yourself. Ask for his understanding, and try to forgive yourself. Some women keep journals or notebooks by their bedsides. Rereading these personal entries later can serve as an index to show yourself how you are progressing.

Guilt does not just go away. It does not take care of itself. You may choose to live with your guilt and continue your own self-imposed punishment for what you think you have done wrong. You may decide you are not worthy of being loved, that you should remain alone, filled with pain and suffering. When you realize that you cannot get on with your life because you are living with your guilt, your grieving time becomes abnormally long. What can you do about it? How can you resolve your guilt?

RESOLVING GUILT

Widows' support groups may provide the forum where you can talk about your "should haves" and "if onlys." You are not alone, and every widow can identify with some of your pain. The other widows may have "tried and true" solutions that worked for them.

You can never undo the events of the past, but you can find support and guidance for dealing with your guilt in the present.

Additionally, professional counseling may help you to clarify your feelings. A trained counselor can help you in sorting out your feelings and can guide you in letting you decide how you want to proceed. Some advantages of seeing a professional counselor are: he or she is certifiably trained and qualified, you receive his or her undivided attention, and you retain your privacy.

## Acceptance and Recovery

The grief process is not bounded by any specific amount of time. Some widows claim it never really ends; it just abates or recedes in intensity. You never forget that part of your life. At unexpected times and in peripheral or fleeting ways, your grief returns now and then. You may not realize when acceptance and recovery are beginning. There is no sharp delineation, no clear starting point. Acceptance may begin with the funeral planning, but then be overwhelmed by denial. Acceptance comes in fits and starts, in brief flickers—perhaps when you rearrange or redecorate the master bedroom, and then again when you clear out your husband's belongings. Acceptance gradually commingles with hope. From early on you hope that somehow things will get better, that you won't recall his death every hour.

Recovery is a fitful process, proceeding on one front, then receding on another. On one hand you may feel proud that you have recovered enough to manage your finances, yet on the other hand feel devastated when you are reminded of your "single" status. Recovery is not a discrete, tidily contained package but a slow process occurring in tiny, sometimes even obscure triumphs as you cope with daily living. You cannot recover emotionally one day and then get back to practical living the next. Recovery means not only learning the healing process but also, simultaneously, struggling with everyday problems and deciding how to handle them.

A pitfall to recovery is to idealize or promote the deceased to an image of "sainthood." This happens most frequently with the death of a child, but can also happen with the death of a husband. If you recall only your husband's finest qualities, forgetting he had any faults, no one else (not even your children) will ever be able to measure up to your memories of him. The helpful efforts of others may never meet the perfect results you feel your husband could have accomplished. Avoid the sainthood label for your husband if you really want to recover and be able to develop accepting relationships with other people.

In recovery, you begin to look ahead more than you look behind. When you begin to think of yourself as an individual person, not just as a widow, you are beginning to emerge from your grief. Ordinarily, you don't recognize any progress until some time has passed. Then, after a few months, you may look back at yourself and realize how far you've come. Friends may comment about how much better you're looking.

The second time you get through a holiday or anniversary, you may notice a difference in your feelings. Carol now realizes that she is no longer the same person as when she was a wife. She wonders if her husband would recognize her now. Carol, formerly a career homemaker and volunteer, has met the challenges of getting a full-time job and developing new friendships. She has accepted her widowhood as a source of strength and as a foundation upon which to build her new identity.

## From Suffering to Growth

Sages and philosophers have long written that life is a mosaic of contrasts. If you think about it for a moment, it makes sense that without pain, there can be no joy. Without dark, no light. Without suffering, no growth. There would be only a monotonous sameness. You are proceeding through the dark and pain to light and some level of joy. Only by turning your suffering into strength can you move forward and grow. Focus not on what you've lost; instead, rise above your grieving and take pride in how far you've come.

Don't try to always shoulder your burdens alone. Even Superman has to have his cape to fly to the rescue. When you are feeling overwhelmed or when you have a success to share, consider that you can get help or give support to another widow by becoming involved with a support group. On pages 296–298 we list the headquarters of nationally known support groups that help widows.

**Support Groups**    Your friends and family can be a great source of emotional support and comfort during the initial period of your grief; but as time passes, they have to go back to their own families and their own lives. At this point you may be emerging from shock and beginning the process of grieving. Just when you realize how much you need the continued help and guidance of your personal support group, it seems to disappear.

However, you don't have to "keep a stiff upper lip and go it alone." There are many organized groups to help you with your grief. Most groups are supported by professionals trained in the grief process. Others are run by widows who have experienced the same kind of loss you have. They understand how you feel and can help you work with your grieving. You may develop new, lasting friendships in a support group. These may also provide bereavement counseling, or workshops on finance, running your house alone, coping with loneliness, and travel opportunities.

How do you locate a support group? Ask your doctor or call a local hospital. Call senior citizen service organizations, community social service agencies or your county mental health center. Some churches sponsor various kinds of support groups.

When you decide to attend your first support group meeting, call to ask if you can be escorted by a current member. When you are grieving, it is difficult to approach a group of strangers to talk about your personal life. It helps to meet another member ahead of time, and possibly to just sit and listen at the first meeting. If you are uncertain that one group meets your needs, try a second meeting or visit another group.

If you live in a community where there are no widow or grief support groups, consider starting one yourself. Call or write the national organizations listed at the end of this book to ask for guidelines on how you might find a group or get training to start one. It is never too late to seek help from a support group, even though you may have been widowed for years.

# Chapter 5

# *Enlisting Legal Help*

Do you, as a widow, need an attorney? The answer is usually "Yes!" A good estate administration attorney can solve many problems for you in much less time and with far fewer headaches than if you try to solve them yourself.

For example, you may be facing the following questions:

- Am I entitled to Social Security, Veterans' Administration or worker's compensation benefits?
- My husband wrote a will. How do I carry out his wishes?
- My husband did not write a will. Who is entitled to his property?
- How do I find out if my husband wrote a will?
- My husband wrote a will and left me out of it completely, in favor of (a) his children of a previous marriage, (b) other relatives, (c) friends, (d) charity, or (e) other. What can I do?
- My husband never got around to changing his will after we got married and his former wife is named as beneficiary and executor. What can I do?
- My husband had a safe deposit box in his name alone. How do I get our property out of it?
- Do I owe any estate or inheritance tax? How will my husband's death affect my income tax situation?
- How do I take care of my husband's business interests/life insurance policies/stocks/bonds/real estate/other property, and how do I have it sold or transferred?
- I have children who are not yet of legal age (minors). What will happen to them if I die too?

• I am facing hospital and medical bills/funeral bills/an accident lawsuit which will deplete my husband's estate. Can I keep any portion of the estate for myself or do the creditors get it all? Is any part of my own property liable for these debts?

The answers to most of these questions can depend on where you live. State laws vary widely. If you are faced with any of these issues or similar problems, a good probate attorney can do a lot to help you. If you have never been to an attorney, you may be wondering how to select one in the first place.

## Selecting Your Attorney

Your attorney should have experience in estate administration (most lawyers do not) and should know how to deal with the property transfers, tax problems and human issues that often accompany the death of a loved one. An experienced probate lawyer is familiar with the territory.

You may or may not feel comfortable using your husband's business or estate-planning lawyer. This lawyer may appear to be a logical choice at first, because he or she is presumably familiar with your husband's business and property matters. But the real question is whether you feel that the lawyer can represent your interests as a widow—not those of your husband's business partners, his children by a previous marriage, or other persons whose interests may be different from yours. You may feel more comfortable entrusting your affairs to a lawyer you yourself have selected.

The best way to find a suitable lawyer is via "word of mouth," getting solid referrals from reliable contacts. If you don't have such sources, call the local probate court, which may have a list of lawyers who handle probate matters. Metropolitan areas have lawyer referral services. And your yellow pages may have a sublisting of probate lawyers. However, if you use the yellow pages or other listing services as a resource, you should interview several listees before making your decision. It pays to choose a probate lawyer carefully!

Perhaps you have a friend who is a lawyer; even if he or she does not specialize in probate matters, ask that friend for a referral. Lawyers have access to specialized information services that contain confidential ratings of other lawyers. And, generally, they are part of an informal network in which information is exchanged about the competency and personal sensitivity of other lawyers. Your lawyer friend may also, in the course of practice, have observed various probate lawyers in action and may be able to give you a knowledgeable recommendation on that basis.

There is only one way to find out how much your probate lawyer will charge for his or her services. Ask beforehand! Ask if you may have an initial no-charge meeting to mutually consider your case. Ask what the hourly rates are. If your case is complex, you may be able to negotiate a flat fee.

**What Will It Cost Me?**

Ask if a retainer (down payment for future services) is required. Ask if the lawyer you are interviewing charges by the hour or uses another method, and determine how you will be billed for telephone consultations.

Fees vary a great deal from location to location. Your lawyer may quote a fee anywhere from $50 to $300 or more per hour. This fee is determined by local economics, the lawyer's level of experience, and the legal or research libraries and government agencies to which your lawyer has access. Alternatively, some states permit probate lawyers to take as a fee a stated percentage—usually averaging 4 percent—of the value of the estate.

If you need a lawyer's help, but cannot afford legal fees, where can you go for help? Check your local phone directory to find out if legal assistance services are available in your community. The federal government helps fund Legal Services Corporation offices across the country to assist low-income clients. To locate the nearest office call their headquarters at (202) 863-1820 or write them at Virginia Avenue, SW, Washington, DC 20024. Or call your district attorney's office, the local courthouse or any lawyer referral service and ask for help.[5] The American Association for Retired Persons suggests that, if you live near a law school, find out if it has a legal clinic serving the community. Local bar associations often have "pro bono" programs in which participating lawyers handle cases for low-income clients without a fee or for a reduced fee. The bar association in your area may be helpful in giving you information about available programs.

Be aware that lawyers who quote higher fees are not necessarily "more expensive." Many lawyers, particularly well-established ones, hire paralegals who are willing to do routine work, such as preparing court documents, for $40 to $50 an hour.

In general, the more complicated an estate, the higher the legal fees. However, a good lawyer can bring long-term savings and peace of mind that will more than justify the cost of the legal services. And estate administration fees are often tax deductible, even though the 1986 Tax Reform Act eliminated many income tax deductions.

If you have an unusual estate settlement case, ask the attorney if he or she has experience in handling similar cases. How frequently will you be informed as to the status of your case? You should be kept up to date on what is happening. Ask how long it should take to complete all matters. Request that all bills be itemized and sent to you on a regular basis.

## What Can My Attorney Do for Me?

A lot! If your husband left a will, you may have to attend a local probate court hearing at which your lawyer will ask the judge or registrar to admit the will to probate. This means your lawyer will ask the court to rule that the will is valid and that your husband's property be distributed according to its terms. If no one is contesting the will, the law in your state may permit the court to admit the will to probate without requiring a court appearance.

Once the court admits the will to probate, it will usually officially appoint as executor (or "personal representative" in some states) the person named in the will to fulfill that function. That person may be a bank, a lawyer, a business associate or you! Married persons often, but not always, name their spouses as their executors.

It is the executor's duty to marshal the deceased's assets, pay debts and taxes, administer the property wisely, prepare accountings and distribute the property according to the will. If you are named as executor, your lawyer will be invaluable to you. He or she will advise you about legal and accounting requirements, property transfers and sales, documents that must be prepared or filed with the court, compliance with tax laws and myriad other legal and practical issues. Your lawyer will strive to make the administration of your husband's estate as smooth and free of technicalities as possible.

The duration of estate administration depends on how complex the estate is. If your husband left a business that must be liquidated or assets that are difficult to sell, collect or transfer (such as oil and gas interests, artwork, accounts receivable and real property), the estate may be open for two or more years. If, on the other hand, your husband owned very few assets in his own name or owned only easily transferred assets such as cash and publicly traded stocks, his estate may be closed within a year. In fact, if most of your husband's assets were held in joint tenancy with you or in a trust, you may be able to have only minimal administration because, depending on local law, at least most of those assets may be transferred automatically at death, without the need for probate or complex transfer work. (Caution: *This does* not *mean you should keep all your property in joint tenancy with relatives. There are pitfalls as well as advantages to joint tenancy. Ask your lawyer!*)

What if your husband did *not* leave a will? Your lawyer will ask the court to appoint an administrator, who has the duty to distribute the estate to the "heirs at law." The "heirs at law" include the spouse, children, descendants and relatives of the deceased. The share that each heir receives varies and depends on state law. Your lawyer will advise you about estate distribution in the absence of a will.

What if your husband left a will that you feel is not favorable to you? Then your lawyer's abilities and loyalty to you become very critical. If you want to contest the will, you will want to hire a different lawyer than the one who drafted it! In those circumstances, your lawyer will advise you as to whether a "will contest" is the best alternative; in many cases, state law will provide less expensive and more effective alternatives. In most states, for example, a widow has a right, if she asserts it, to a share of her husband's estate, no matter what the will says. She may also be entitled to a monthly allowance from the estate as well as to certain items of personal property, such as an automobile or household furniture. State laws vary widely on this issue. A good probate lawyer has an arsenal of legal weapons to protect your interests if need be.

Your lawyer can be invaluable to you in matters other than those relating to the estate. She or he can refer you to various resources, including counseling services, appraisal services, reliable real estate agencies, and a variety of other services you may need. Your lawyer should be able to help you determine whether you are eligible for Social Security, veterans', or worker's compensation benefits. If your husband died because of someone's negligence or intentional misdeed, your lawyer can help you assess your chances of recovering damages in a wrongful death action. Finally, your lawyer can suggest appropriate ways to plan your own estate and your children's future.

**The First Meeting**

Bring as much documentation as you can to the initial interview, including any wills that your husband might have left, even if you believe some have been cancelled. (Be sure to bring the originals. Courts will not admit photocopies to probate.) Sometimes there are defects in a will that can prevent probate; in that case, an older will may be the valid one.

You should also bring one or two death certificates (which the funeral home can supply to you on request) as well as life insurance policies and a list of assets owned by both you and your husband. The list should include real property, stocks, bonds, cash, limited partnership interests, business interests, valuable personal property such as artwork or fine jewelry, and anything you can think of that could have value. You will save your attorney time (and yourself money) if you come to the initial meeting prepared! If you have a difficult time determining what assets you and your husband have, enlist your lawyer's help in inventorying the estate. Your list of assets will help your attorney decide whether a federal estate tax return or state estate or inheritance tax return must be filed. Under the Tax Reform Act of 1986, generally only estates valued at $600,000 or more (as of 1986) are required to file federal estate tax returns. Depending on the state you live in, you may have to file a state inheritance tax return even if you don't have to file a federal estate tax return.

If you are in a financial bind, your attorney can ask the court for an emergency order to provide you with a living allowance from the estate until the will is probated or an administrator appointed.

While you are administering your husband's estate, you may need to look at your own estate plan. If you do not have a will, the state in which you die or in which you have property will write one for you, with consequences you may not have intended.

**Your Children and Your Future**

For example, does your will name a guardian in the event that you die before your children are adults? If you have no will or your will does not name a guardian, a court proceeding is generally necessary so that a guardian can be appointed for a child both of whose parents are dead. In that case, your children may not have the guardian you want them to have. Courts generally honor the nomination of a guardian in a will, unless there is a substantial reason they should not do so.

If you have received valuable assets from your husband's estate or you have a substantial estate of your own, will your children be able to manage the property in the event of your death? If not, your will should create a trust with a named trustee to manage your assets on behalf of your children until they come of age. If you choose, the trust can come into being only if you die before your children are able to manage your assets. If you have a disabled child, the trust can provide for that child's needs for life.

What if you remarry? Many people who remarry want their estates to pass to the children of their first marriages. You may need a prenuptial agreement with your betrothed to assure that this happens. Your attorney can help assure that your estate passes to the desired recipients. If you have no prenuptial agreement, your new spouse may defeat your estate plan, at your children's expense, by contesting your will or by electing (choosing) a share of your estate under state law.

Not only can your attorney effect the smooth transfer of your estate upon your death, but he or she can help you plan the rest of your life as well. If, for example, you are an older widow anticipating retirement, your attorney can help you plan for a financially comfortable retirement or for certain contingencies such as moving to a nursing home or setting aside money for extended health care. Or your attorney can draft a trust to enable a bank or your adult child to manage your property for you if you become disabled. If you anticipate that your estate will have to pay estate taxes, your attorney can arrange a program of lifetime gifts to your children or grandchildren, to minimize estate taxes and save your family money.

A good estate attorney can be a very helpful ally to you in dealing with the practical consequences of your husband's death. Later on, the attorney can arm you with the information and long-range planning needed to manage your own life and future as well as your children's security.

# Chapter 6

# *Your Financial Advisory Team*

Within a few months after your husband's death, you may need advice from several financial experts, both for settling the estate and for your own immediate and long-term financial and estate concerns. These may include a lawyer, a banker, a trust officer, a tax accountant, a stockbroker, insurance agents and perhaps a real estate agent and a financial advisor. To help you take control of your own money matters, you need to know when and where to go for professional help. Shop wisely to avoid paying for unnecessary guidance. In other chapters we offer suggestions on how to select a lawyer and work with real estate and insurance agents. Here we review strategies for how to choose and work effectively with selected professional "finance and security" advisors and institutions.

Where do you start looking for these professionals, especially if you live in a small town or rural area? In your interviews with them, what kinds of question should you ask? Is it acceptable to talk about fees before you contract their services? How can you make your wishes clearly known? How can you work effectively with these professionals?

**Where to Start**

It is only natural to first ask your friends for advice about getting financial expertise. This sometimes works well—if your friends are strongly positive about the results of the financial experts' advice. However, if their responses are off-handed or lukewarm, that may indicate that their advisors are less than desirable. Ask how long they have worked with their financial experts and why they selected this particular person or firm. Your attorney, if you already have one, should be a good source of recommendations; he or she is likely to have an informed idea as to who can best help settle your husband's estate and advise you about your finances.

Another approach is to ask your bank what financial and estate settlement services they offer. Many banks have trust departments that can administer property from an estate. Large, full-service banks have access to tax accountants, real estate agents to evaluate the estate property, portfolio management experts and administrative specialists to file claims for insurance and pension benefits and to keep track of the funds going into and out of the estate account. Smaller banks may have fewer in-house services but can often recommend other professionals within your community. You can employ specialists for as few or as many services as you wish, but understand clearly that the more you have them do, the more fees you will have to pay.

The general questions to ask any financial expert you may employ include:

- May we arrange a no-charge initial interview to discuss my needs?
- What do your services cost? Do you charge for phone call consultations?
- Are your fees negotiable? (When one woman received what she considered to be an exorbitant bill from her attorney, she appeared in his office with her checkbook in hand and declared she was prepared to write a check for what she thought was reasonable—20 percent less than the total shown on the statement. Her attorney accepted the negotiated price.)
- What special payment plans can be arranged to fit my budget?
- What credentials do you have to support your professional status?
- Which professional organizations do you belong to?
- Will you put our agreement and estimated costs in writing?

If any professional responds with vagueness or is hesitant to answer your questions, talk to someone else. Your money should always matter to you, and you want the best advice you can buy.

If your late husband handled the bank accounts, you may be unfamiliar with what a bank can do for you. Years ago banks offered only checking and savings accounts and loans, but nowadays they can be complete financial service organizations.

**Bankers and Banks**

When you go to the bank, ask the new accounts or customer service section to describe what services the bank offers. Ask them to explain clearly what choices you have for checking, savings and money market accounts. If you don't understand how to balance a checkbook, ask them to explain. For further reference, in Chapter 10 we give detailed instructions on how to balance a checkbook. Other questions to ask include the following:

- What is the minimum opening deposit?
- If this account earns interest, what is the rate and how does it vary?
- What is the monthly service charge, if any, for handling this account?
- Is a minimum monthly balance required to avoid any monthly service charge?
- What are the "item" charges, i.e., charges for processing each check or deposit?
- If overdraft protection is available, how can it be obtained?
- How is an account insured and up to what level? Most accounts are insured, per person, up to $100,000 by the Federal Deposit Insurance Corporation (FDIC), or by the Federal Savings and Loan Insurance Corporation (FSLIC).

Other insurance plans may be risky. Banks in a number of states, insured by state-approved organizations, have failed recently and depositors' funds have been frozen for long periods; most depositors in these banks will not recover their deposits completely, if at all.

If you are a person who forgets to record what checks you wrote, ask about checks with carbonless copies. The new accounts representatives are generally patient and used to answering questions. You should expect them to guide you in getting the most service for the least cost.

Full-service banks can offer many other personal financial services, such as loans, international banking, investment banking, credit cards, safe deposit boxes and automated tellers. Often, many of the same services are available from a credit union, savings and loan, or thrift and loan institution.

**Trust Institutions**    Some widows are fortunate because, while their husbands lived, trust arrangements were made to provide for future estate asset management. At their time of greatest need these women have access to expert legal and financial counsel. Although a trust arrangement may not have been made in advance, you may want to consider hiring a trust institution to help you settle your late husband's estate, provide you with investment counsel and custody services, and establish and administer any trusts you might set up for your own estate.

There are misconceptions that trust departments or trust institutions are formal, somewhat impersonal organizations. Not so! A good trust officer must be capable of dealing with people and not be just a specialist behind the scenes working with facts and figures. Desirable qualities for a good trust officer include empathy, tact, patience, accuracy, positiveness and a sense of humor or a sense of flexibility. You will never have a sense of what a trust institution is like until you get to know the people there. To find out, arrange a no-charge meeting with a trust officer to discuss your needs, your financial concerns and your personal estate plans.

You do not have to be a millionaire to hire trust management services. However, before most trust organizations will accept your account, they may require that the net worth of your assets be in the six-figure range. Trust services are performed for a fee, usually a small percentage of the assets managed or income collected. In many states the fees for settling an estate are set by law, while in others they are limited to "reasonable compensation" as determined by the courts and competition.

Trust institutions, similar to banks, must obtain a charter from the federal or state government in order to manage assets belonging to others. Most trust organizations are affiliated with banks or are associated with a bank holding company. However, some of the more than 4,000 trust institutions in this country have no banking connections and operate independently.

**Tax Accountants**    According to IRS regulations, within nine months of your husband's death, you may be required to file an estate tax return. You should be working with your tax accountant or tax preparer by the fourth month. Your attorney or bank trust department can recommend a tax accountant to assist in settling the estate, but if you wish to make the selection yourself, go to a certified public accountant. Make sure he or she has experience in filing estate fiduciary tax returns. The accountant you employ should be familiar with the final *U.S. Individual Income Tax Return* (Form 1040), (the *U.S. Fiduciary Income Tax Return* (Form 1041) and the *United States Estate Tax Return* (Form 706). You may not be required to file all these returns, but make sure your accountant understands the requirements for each one. Few tax preparers specialize in fiduciary returns. (The term *fiduciary* refers to someone who is in a position of trust and is responsible for property or money held in trust for others.)

The accountant should expect to cooperate with your attorney in settling the estate. Inquire about fees and when they will have to be paid. Financial professionals respect your concern about money. A good tax accountant can give you valuable advice throughout the year to keep you from paying more taxes than you should and about sheltering some of your income from taxes.

If you decide that you need a certified public accountant who specializes in estate settlement tax preparation, shop carefully. As when selecting an attorney, ask about professional credentials and what you will be charged for services. Some accountants charge by the hour, while others may need to study your case to give you an estimate. Ask who will respond to IRS inquiries, if any occur. In estate settlement cases, often the accountant and your attorney will work together, or your attorney will review the accountant's work. A tax attorney is probably the most expensive professional option, yet if you have a dispute with the IRS, a tax attorney may be your best choice.

**Free Tax Assistance**

There are at least two programs for persons who do not have many tax problems or a lot of money to spend on tax advice. (Caution: *The following programs are intended for routine tax preparation and may not be suitable for the complex requirements of estate settlement. No matter who prepares your estate tax return, the Internal Revenue Service holds you responsible for its accuracy!*)

TAX COUNSELING FOR THE ELDERLY

This is an IRS-funded program that sponsors free services to older taxpayers who need help filing their tax forms. Tax counseling centers are located in senior centers, libraries, banks, savings and loan institutions, and other central sites in cities and towns around the nation. The staff are trained volunteers. Tax counselors also make housecalls and visits to nursing homes and other locations to help persons unable to travel. Many of the tax counseling centers are organized by the American Association of Retired Persons and are called Tax-Aide Centers.

VITA

This Volunteer Income Tax Assistance program also is sponsored by the IRS. It trains volunteers working in VITA centers around the country. VITA workers provide free tax preparation services, primarily to low-income, elderly, non-English-speaking or disabled individuals who file simple tax returns. You can learn more about the VITA or tax counseling programs through your local IRS office.[6]

**Stockbrokers**

Chances are, if you're dealing with a stockbroker early in your widowhood you have inherited a portfolio of securities from your late husband. You may have never met your stockbroker and have little understanding of the stock market, but you may now need to make decisions whether to hold or sell certain securities. Many widows continue to rely on their husband's broker for advice. However, if for any reason you should decide to choose another broker, the following considerations may help you select a highly qualified professional.

A registered stockbroker is required to have completed formal training and have passed a qualifying exam in order to be able to execute your buy and sell orders for securities. A broker is a commissioned salesperson who does nearly all his or her work by telephone. For buy and sell orders on listed securities, the broker's firm charges a sales commission on the total dollar value of the transaction. The brokerage firm usually retains the larger part of that commission, and the individual broker gets a smaller part. The commission rates vary from firm to firm. You should ask what they are and how they compare to others.

Stockbrokers may work for full-service brokerage firms or as discount brokers. For the beginning investor, the full-service brokerage firm will offer the most assistance. To find a reputable firm, ask your financial advisors and friends for recommendations, then call about opening a new account. Call more than one firm to discuss your investment goals. Select a firm based on their reputation, their general attitude about your call and on their advice to you. A full-service brokerage firm can offer advice about how to get started investing, will recommend which stocks to buy, and send you written information about stocks and the corporations issuing them. For this research and advice you pay a sales commission on each buy or sell transaction.

A discount broker, on the other hand, will perform the buy or sell transactions for a lower sales commission, but does not offer advice or provide research reports. A discount broker does not provide "hand-holding" services and can consequently execute buy and sell orders for lower rates. If you are somewhat more sophisticated about investing and prefer to do your own research, a discount broker may meet your needs.

• Choose a broker who works for a firm registered with the New York Stock Exchange. There are other qualified firms, but the NYSE has the most stringent requirements for membership.

• What kind and how much training has the brokerage company provided and was some of it at the securities exchanges in New York? Every reputable broker is required to have a registered representative's license.

• How long has the broker been in the business? At least two to three years' experience is recommended.

• What is his or her background? The specialty areas should match your investment needs—stocks, mutual funds, bonds, limited partnerships, etc.

• Your broker should be able to clearly describe different types of investment products, such as stocks, commodities and options, government securities, corporate and municipal bonds, mutual funds and tax investments. He or she

**Considerations for Selecting a Broker**

should be relatively up-to-date and knowledgeable about the economy in general and current market trends.

If you become dissatisfied with your present broker and you select a new firm, ask the new broker to arrange to transfer your account from the old firm to the new. There should not be a fee.

If you want to call your broker, have your most recent statement available, with your account number and a list of your questions. If you are not making a buy or sell order, call later in the afternoon after the stock exchanges close at 4 p.m. in New York, so that your broker will have more time for explanations.

**Responsibilities of a Good Broker**

A good full-service broker should first help you assess your financial goals and objectives in the context of your overall financial status. For example, do you need safety or security for your investments? Or can you afford to take some risk with your money in order to earn a greater return? Do you need regular monthly income from your investments?

Your broker should offer to:
• Provide information about the brokerage firm,
• Explain clearly how to read your monthly statement,
• Make buy and sell recommendations,
• Arrange to send you quarterly and annual statements on any issues (shares of stock in a particular company) you own,
• Send you recommended buy lists, and
• Call you if something unusual is happening to a company in which you own shares.

You may also want to request brochures that explain stock market terminology.

How much time should the broker spend on your account? That depends on how large your account is and how many transactions you request. On smaller, conservative portfolios valued at $50,000 or less, your broker may call you as frequently as once a week or as infrequently as every few months. The frequency of buy and sell orders you initiate, your enthusiasm in learning about the market, and how often you call him will influence how much time your broker spends evaluating your account and making recommendations to you. A broker has to divide time among many clients, and the interested, active clients will get more attention.

If you are a novice investor, remember that a stockbroker, like any commissioned salesperson, earns his or her living by making buy and sell transactions. If you feel your broker is pressuring you to make overly frequent purchases or sales, then your broker may be "churning" your account to generate commissions! Ethical, competent brokers will not pressure you with urgent, frequent requests to buy and sell.

In addition, with a full-service brokerage firm, your broker can offer buy-and-sell advice, review your portfolio status at your request and explain investment jargon. You may never meet your broker face-to-face. It doesn't matter, so long as he or she monitors your account to your satisfaction. Good brokers do not need to pressure you to make hasty decisions or urge unnecessary transactions that would generate additional sales commissions. You should not expect your broker to make "right" recommendations all the time. No one can predict the future. A good broker will not promise quick or huge profits and will not push only one issue. A good broker respects your concerns and helps allay your fears.

## Financial Planners

Perhaps the newest professional in the realm of money management is the financial advisor or financial planner. With the myriad choices in financial products, few people are willing to devote the time and effort to be their own financial managers. It is easier to leave funds in a money market account earning a relatively low interest rate than to try to analyze where to invest your money to earn a higher return. But if you don't need immediate access to part of your ready cash, you may want to begin to work with a financial planner to invest the money in other alternatives. Some people like to learn about investing so as to make their own decisions, while others prefer to hire someone to advise them.

A financial planner works with you to define your present and future financial needs, to evaluate how much you have to invest, and to help you decide how much and whether to invest in stocks, bonds, life insurance, mutual funds, savings or retirement plans. The planner considers your entire financial picture and makes recommendations about how much to invest and when. Some industry experts claim that people earning as little as $20,000 a year should consider seeking some financial advice. Investment terms and objectives are discussed in Chapter 18.

Be wary, however. There are no licensing or registration requirements for financial planners, and almost anyone can claim to be one! If you decide you want to employ a financial advisor, ask your attorney, accountant, banker and friends for recommendations. The person you choose should be either a certified financial planner (CFP) or a chartered financial consultant (CHFC), if not already licensed as an accountant, attorney or insurance or securities broker. The Registry of Financial Planning Practioners lists (but makes no recommendations) professionals who offer financial planning guidance and who meet stringent requirements for inclusion. Write or phone the International Association for Financial Planners (IFAP) for a copy of the directory. (The address and phone number are shown on the following page.)

Be prepared to pay fees for plans or services, and expect to pay commissions for financial products. Be careful about who is giving you advice. Unethical planners will push one product with a sense of urgency and a get-rich-quick scheme. If it seems you can't lose, then you probably can! Do not accept "one-solution" plans.

All financial advisors charge a fee for their services. Some charge a flat fee, others receive a commission for products sold to you, and yet others charge a combination of both. In choosing the flat fee, you know the amount up front, you pay it in the beginning, and you don't feel the pressure to buy more insurance, annuities, mutual fund shares, real estate investment trusts, or whatever other products they might be selling. "Commission only" planners, on the other hand, tend to sell products such as insurance rather than develop a comprehensive plan. The planner charging a flat fee often offers more objective, balanced recommendations, but may be more expensive. Some people prefer to work with a planner who charges a combined flat fee and commission. They feel the commission keeps the planner interested and committed to your interests after the plan is implemented.

In any case, you can best work with a financial advisor if you understand what the advisor will need from you and should discuss with you. Here is what you should expect:

  • Be prepared to list all your assets and liabilities, current income and monthly expenses, and other investments. The planner will need to have a clear idea of your complete financial picture.

- Be prepared to discuss your immediate and future cash needs.
- Do you need some monthly or quarterly income from your investments, or can the income be accumulating for reinvestment, to be distributed at a future date?
- What is your tolerance for risk? That is, how much chance can you take on losing part or all of your investment? Usually the greater the risk, the more the borrower is prepared to pay in return for using your money.
- You should be asked how or if you plan to contribute more capital to your investments as time goes on.

You may need to provide copies of previous tax returns to help plan for tax advantages from your investments.

If you want further information about financial planners and their credentials, write to one of the following professional organizations:

International Association for Financial Planners
2 Concourse Parkway, Suite 800
Atlanta, GA 30328
(404) 395-1605

Institute of Certified Financial Planners
Two Denver Highlands
10065 East Harvard, Suite 320
Denver, CO 80231-5942
(303) 751-7600

## Keeping Records

You may feel secure keeping important papers in safe deposit boxes and copies of your will lodged with your attorney. However, in dealing with financial and legal professionals, you should also keep additional records at home where you can refer to them to avoid confusion and to compare them to the services for which you are charged. These may include:

- Notes of all telephone calls made and received between you and your advisors. List the date, time, to whom you spoke and what you talked about. (As we mentioned in Chapter 3, a steno notebook near the phone works well for

telephone messages.) Keep notes of face-to-face meetings.
• Retain all bills, receipts, estimates and written correspondence regarding financial, tax and legal affairs. File folders are helpful for organizing numerous papers.
• Photocopy all letters you write and send to your advisors, retaining a copy for your files. Occasionally documents are misplaced, and this way you will have a copy to protect yourself. Libraries and supermarkets usually have photocopy machines available for public use. You can send important documents by registered or certified mail to ensure their receipt.

## Resolving Problems

Most financial, legal and tax experts are ethical and will genuinely try to help you with your financial affairs. However, if you become dissatisfied with your advisor, begin by discussing the problem with him or her. If you kept copies of contracts, receipts and other important papers, you can document your complaint. The next step is to talk with the firm manager or your advisor's supervisor. If you can't clear the problem with negotiation, the AARP suggests the following strategies for resolving disputes.

## Lawyers

Contact your city, county or state bar association and register your complaint with the grievance committee. Fee complaints are usually handled by the state bar association's arbitration committee. Additional help may be found through a local consumer protection agency.

## Tax Preparers

If your tax preparer is a certified public accountant, you can contact your state board of certified public accountants. If your accountant is not a CPA, or is a lawyer, you can contact the Internal Revenue Service. For complaints about commercial tax preparation firms, contact the IRS, the Better Business Bureau or your state, county or city consumer affairs office.

If your financial planner is a licensed stockbroker, contact the **Financial Planners** Securities and Exchange Commission. If your planner is a lawyer, contact the bar association. The two organizations that certify financial planners—the International Association of Financial Planning and the Institute of Certified Financial Planners mentioned earlier in this chapter—respond to complaints from consumers and investigate disputes involving their members.[7] If you selected a non-certified financial planner, contact the Better Business Bureau or a consumer affairs office.

If you have problems with your bank, assuming you have kept re **Banks** cords and receipts to document your claim, talk with a department head or even a vice president. If you are still dissatisfied, ask who has regulatory power over the financial institution and then submit your claim in writing. Banks, savings and loans, credit unions and finance companies may be chartered by either federal or state regulatory agencies. Not all banking practices are regulated.

We have discussed only some of the many kinds of financial services available to help organize and plan your financial investments. You can select a one-stop financial service center such as a full-service bank or the Sears Financial Network, or you can shop around for an expert in each financial discipline. The professionals you employ will vary according to what you need to settle your late husband's estate and to begin getting control of your own financial affairs.

## Notes

_____

_____

_____

_____

_____

_____

_____

_____

_____

_____

_____

_____

_____

_____

_____

# Chapter 7

# *Settling the Estate*

The major burden of settling a husband's estate usually falls on his wife, the surviving spouse. She is often named the executor or personal representative, responsible for carrying out the terms of his will. If you are the person responsible, you may want to hire professionals, as described in Chapters 5 and 6, to undertake some or all of the complex procedures involved in estate settlement. But even so, you alone may be the only person who can assist your attorney or bank trust department in locating important papers, determining the validity of creditors' claims, and making sure your husband's estate is distributed as he wished.

Estate settlement procedures apply not only to large, complex estates but to almost every instance of a death—with or without a will. You may find the legal and tax jargon confusing and the time requirements alarming. It is easy to unquestioningly comply with your attorney's requests to provide information or sign forms without understanding exactly what is happening. To help you prepare for your responsibilities, this chapter discusses exactly what estate settlement is, explains how to begin the procedures, and defines common terminology. You cannot settle an estate satisfactorily without some degree of legal advice. However, you will be less overwhelmed, and you may even be able to perform some of the tasks yourself, if you have some knowledge of at least the basic steps involved.

If your husband died without a will (intestate), you still need to follow some of the estate settlement procedures to ensure that you and his other heirs determine what assets he had, settle any debts, pay taxes and ultimately distribute the remainder of his estate.

**Estate Settlement Overview**

Generally the estate settlement procedures begin by determining if your husband had a valid will that directs how his estate is to be distributed and that designates the responsible party (individual or corporate trustee or both) to carry out the terms of the will. If there was a will, it must be filed with the probate court, often within a few days after death. If there was no will, the laws of the state where your husband resided and died, or where he owned property, will mandate how his assets will be distributed. In effect, when there is no will, a state institutes default procedures to handle property distribution.

Whether or not there was a will, a court (often called the probate court) designates a person or institution to be responsible for overseeing the distribution of your husband's property and possessions. The responsible person or institution is called an executor, administrator or personal representative, depending on the laws in your state. After appointment, the executor is required to "administer" the will; that is, to determine in exact detail what is included in the estate, manage and take care of the estate, determine what claims and debts are owed by the estate, and make various types of reports to interested parties. These "interested parties" may include the federal Internal Revenue Service, for possible estate and income taxes; the department of revenue in your late husband's home state or a state in which he owned property, for possible inheritance taxes; persons who may be owed money by your late husband; and relatives and heirs who expect or feel entitled to receive part of the estate.

We are assuming that your late husband left an estate of some sort and that you will become involved in helping settle it. Even though a bank, friend or relative might have been named executor or administrator of the estate, you should be aware of the overall process—what is expected and when. If you have been named as the executor or personal representative, you have even more need to understand the steps and terminology.

The numerous estate settlement procedures can extend from several months to years, depending on the complexity of the estate. The more detailed explanations that follow may be unnecessary if you retain an attorney or bank trust department to complete all these tasks for you. And, in states where the attorney's fee for estate settlement is a percentage of the estate, letting him or her do most of the work makes good sense! But even if you yourself have taken on much of the burden, you will need an attorney to direct and review the work you've done, to make sure it complies with the applicable laws.

We present the following detailed explanations to familiarize you with the terminology you will encounter; this will be useful particularly *if you choose to take part in the estate settlement and do some of these steps yourself!* In some cases you can help close the estate sooner and save yourself money by doing some of the groundwork for your attorney. Ask how you can help and what is required. The procedures we outline are not all-inclusive. Each state has different laws, which may require either more or fewer steps, depending on the size and complexity of your husband's estate. Your attorney will guide you. The most common estate settlement task a widow performs is to locate and describe all her late husband's assets. At the end of this chapter we provide inventory worksheets for his estate assets and liabilities.

## The Executor, Administrator or Personal Representative

For guidance in settling an estate, it is common to hire a lawyer or the services of a bank trust department. Check your husband's will to see if it specifies a particular trust department or person to act as executor or personal representative. You may need to coordinate your choice of legal assistance with what is specified in the will.

When you begin, don't be awed by "legalese," or legal jargon. The terminology used in legal documents must be very specific to avoid misinterpretation. Indefinite pronouns like "he," "she," "it," or "they" are not appropriate. Instead, the Latin terms, specific for gender and function, are used. For example, an *executor* is the designated male person who is responsible for carrying out the terms of the will. A woman is the *executrix*. When there is no will, the responsible male person is called an *administrator* and the female is an *administratrix*. To simplify, some states use the term *personal representative* for either sex. The deceased person is often termed the *decedent*. Legal documents are also extensively enumerated or contain paragraph designations and sometimes have the date on every page. This is to help locate a particular word or point that may need to be discussed or questioned.

**Duties of the Executor, Administrator or Personal Representative**

The executor has four major areas of responsibility in settling the deceased's estate:

- Inventorying and safeguarding the assets,
- Overseeing and managing the estate while settlement procedures are ongoing,
- Paying taxes and debts, and
- Distributing the assets to the proper beneficiaries.

The executor, administrator or personal representative is legally responsible for seeing that the estate settlement procedures are completed. There can be co-executors, such as an individual and a bank who work together on an estate. The executor need not perform the tasks alone and may hire an accountant, attorney and other professionals, who are all entitled to reasonable fees and, in some states, may receive a percentage of the value of the assets.

**Estate Settlement Steps**

Estate settlement is sometimes called estate administration. We have grouped the executor's major responsibilities into six areas, each followed by a list of specific tasks. There is a space for checking off each task as it is completed. The order may be varied and some steps may not be required, depending on state laws and guidance from your attorney. The executor, personal representative or administrator is ultimately responsible for seeing that, when appropriate, these steps—there can be as many as sixty or seventy —are accomplished. Several can be performed simultaneously.

*Funeral*

☐ Make funeral arrangements, if this has not already been completed. Sometimes these are stated in the will or a written memorandum. See Chapter 2 for details.

*Attorney*

☐ Retain an attorney. See Chapter 5 for guidance.

*Protect Assets*

☐ Determine whether your husband had assets that need immediate protection (such as livestock, crops, pets or perishables) and take steps to provide care and security. In an emergency, the probate court can appoint a temporary special administrator to perform these functions if necessary, or you can ask a family member or friend to help.

*Locate Will*

☐ Locate the will and life insurance policies by searching desks, cabinets, closets, safe deposit boxes (requires your husband's and the bank's keys), office files and drawers—any places your husband might have stored private papers. If you or an attorney can't locate the will in any of the logical places, then it is possible that there is no will or that the will is lost. Contact your husband's attorney, who may know when the will was written and who may have a copy, if not the original.

*Expendables*

☐ Note quantities of expendable or consumable assets, such as animals and their food supplies, or crops.

*Record Keeping*

☐ Immediately begin keeping detailed records of all expenses and income regarding the estate. Keep all receipts. You'll have to provide this record for the closing of the estate.

*Death Certificate*

☐ Obtain as many copies of the death certificate as may be needed (perhaps fifteen), to be used in filing claims and to facilitate transfer of assets. Some funeral providers will order the copies for you at a small additional charge. Or you can apply in person to

**Getting Organized and Gathering Information**

the appropriate state agency, such as the bureau of vital statistics (it may take several weeks!), and pay a fee for each certified copy.

### Bank Accounts
☐   Find out if checking accounts are still open so you can have access to funds if needed. If they are joint accounts, change them to your name. You may have to show a death certificate to do this.

### Estate Account
☐   Establish an "estate account," a separate checking account to receive funds earned by the deceased before death but not received until after death. You will need a separate taxpayer identification number for this account (rather than your own Social Security number). You can apply for one using a Federal IRS form SS–4. (This identification number will be needed for paying estate taxes, so you will need to apply for one eventually in any event.) Ask your attorney, accountant or the bank trust department for help.

### Living Allowance
☐   Determine your present and near-future cash needs. In some cases, your attorney can help you apply for an immediate living allowance from the assets of the estate while the estate is being settled.

### Probate and Appointment
☐   Apply to (petition) the probate court to admit the will to probate and ask that the named executor be appointed. Usually your attorney does this for you, but you may apply yourself. The court will respond with a special document called "letters testamentary," which gives the executor authority to begin settling the estate. Ask the attorney if the will can be informally probated, or if you can use any simplified estate settlement procedures to avoid the need for a court hearing.

*Probate is the procedure or process by which specialized courts prove that the written will of the deceased is valid, before authorizing the distribution of a deceased person's property according to the will's provisions.* Through practice, the settling of an estate under the terms of a will has become known as probate. The mere word "probate" can conjure up images of expensive teams of lawyers. This isn't necessarily true, but in complex estates, the procedural steps can become costly because of the professional skills and time involved in estate administration and in satisfying tax requirements.

*Family Records*
☐ Locate birth certificates for each member of the family (including your husband), any military documents, your marriage certificate, any divorce or annulment records, Social Security numbers for each family member and beneficiary, and income tax records for the past three years. These will be needed to file claims for Social Security and veterans' benefits.

*Life Insurance*
☐ File claims for life insurance benefits. (See Chapter 8 for guidance.)

*Social Security*
☐ Apply for Social Security and veterans' benefits, if applicable, and for pension and other retirement survivor's benefits. (See Chapter 9 for specific guidance.)

*Health Insurance*
☐ Review your husband's health insurance coverage. Determine if there is a time limit for filing claims for benefits. (See Chapter 9 about continued coverage for yourself and dependents.)

*Auto Insurance*
☐ Ask your auto insurance agent to check your auto insurance coverage for accidental death and dismemberment benefits. Change the name of the policy holder as needed.

*Credit Cards*
☐ Review credit and bank cards for any insurance on outstanding credit card balances. If there are none, you may decide to pay valid charges as usual or write to the creditor explaining the death and requesting a delay, or arrange for lower payments until the estate is settled. Some companies automatically cover accidental death if the deceased was traveling when he died and bought his ticket by credit card.

*Pensions*
☐ Notify your husband's employer, or pension or retirement fund manager of his death. Then ask the personnel department how to apply for survivor benefits or any other benefits that might be distributed. If he was still employed, ask if there is any group or other life insurance on his life.

*Inventory*
☐ Locate and begin to inventory assets by describing physical (tangible) assets or by collecting documents. These assets should include all bank accounts, stocks, bonds, life insurance policies, annuity or pension accounts, ownership of business interests, partnership agreements, real estate titles and abstract descriptions, lease contracts, collections of coins or stamps, and titles to personal property such as automobiles. In their book *Survival Kit for Wives*, Don and Renée Martin advise looking for assets listed on the most recent income tax return.[8]

*Addresses*
☐ Get current addresses of all heirs and persons who will receive property or cash from the estate.

*Asset Values*
☐ Value each asset as of the date of death, or, if you are required to pay federal estate taxes, then on another allowable date called the "alternate valuation date," which is usually six months after the date of death. In calculating these valuations, you may encounter the following terms:

*Fair market value.* For valuation purposes, this is the price at which the property would change hands between a willing buyer and seller in a free and open market. A qualified personal property appraiser can help you arrive at the appropriate values. The fair market value is used for silver, antiques, jewelry, furs, art, coins and other collectibles. Do not use dealer prices; they are too low.

*Real estate valuation.* Get property appraised by a real estate agent or appraiser.

*Oil, gas and mineral interests.* Ask your attorney or bank trust department for expert appraisals on these properties.

*Farm estates.* Since 1981 farms or other businesses considered major assets may be valued at "current use"—meaning the use they were put to during the deceased's lifetime—providing they remain in the family. There are several special rules and conditions for using the current-use valuation; for example, you can prevent farmland next to a town from being valued as if it were to be a shopping center or at "highest and best use." Consult with your attorney.

*Stocks and bonds.* Prices for these securities on the date of death, or on the alternate valuation date, can be found in the financial section of the newspaper. Check at the library or ask your broker to determine these values.

*Autos.* At the library, consult the *CPI Value Guide*, the *NADA Official Used Car Guide* or the *Kelly Blue Book.*

*Business interests.* The bank trust department or your attorney will assist in reviewing the terms of agreements, value of your husband's share and your rights as a survivor.

**Managing the Estate**

The executor or personal representative has a *fiduciary* obligation, or position of trust, in managing the property and financial affairs of the deceased for the benefit of others. The executor is not to favor the interests of one party over another, is not to put her or his own interests in conflict with those of the estate, and is to administer the estate carefully and prudently.

The executor must keep records and make reports or accountings to interested parties. The following checklist can be done by the widow, if she chooses.

*Record Keeping*

☐ Continue careful bookkeeping of all income and expenses pertaining to the estate, including income in respect of the deceased (income earned before death, but not paid until after death).

*Inventory*

☐ Within about three months, or at specified times, prepare an inventory of assets (noting changes in live assets such as livestock and crops) and a detailed accounting of estate transactions. Consult with your attorney as to whether the inventory or accountings need to be filed with the court.

*Accounting*
☐ Periodically submit to the beneficiaries a report and detailed accounting of estate transactions.

*Insurance*
☐ Examine all insurance documents as to adequacy of property insurance coverage and status of taxes and assessments.

*Property*
☐ Collect rents, obtain tenants, make repairs—be the rental property manager. Arrange for management of "live" assets such as animals and crops.

*Title Transfer*
☐ Change the names on all stocks and bonds to the designated executor or beneficiary, and arrange for collection of dividends and interest. Send the broker a certified copy of the death certificate and a copy of the will, if requested.

*Investments*
☐ Review all investments for safety versus risk and make changes as necessary. See Chapter 18, "Finance and Investments," for guidance on dealing with a broker.

*IRAs*
☐ Notify managers of IRA and other retirement funds in the deceased's name of his death so the account can be transferred to the beneficiary designated at the time the account was established.

**Determining Debts and Claims Against the Estate**

In addition to assets, the estate usually has debts—funeral expenses, medical bills, balances on mortgages and loans, etc. The executor is responsible for determining the validity (truthfulness) of claims against the estate and for paying estate debts. You may wish to ask your estate attorney to do any or all of the tasks below.

*Pay Bills*
☐ Determine current bills—such as rent, utilities, medical, credit card balances, etc.—and arrange to pay them.

*Death Notices*

☐   Publish required notices of death to creditors. This is usually done in the local newspapers. In most states, this allows creditors about four months in which to file claims. Publication is not required in all states, but, if a notice is not published, the risk is that creditors could have up to one year or longer to file claims.

*Estate Assets*

☐   Re-register (change the name on) estate assets to your name as personal representative. For registered stocks and bonds, submit your authorization to the broker, along with securities if you have the actual documents, and a statement of legal residence.

*Estate Expenses*

☐   Keep track of estate administration expenses that may be deductible on estate or income tax returns, such as legal and accounting fees for work done to settle the estate. These may still be deductible even though the Tax Reform Act of 1986 sharply curtailed available income tax deductions.

Estate, inheritance or fiduciary taxes to be paid on the deceased's estate are usually calculated by an accountant working with your attorney. The federal estate and state estate and inheritance taxes are commonly called "death taxes." Additionally, "fiduciary income taxes" may have to be paid on income earned by the estate during its administration. Death taxes and fiduciary income taxes are perhaps the most distressing aspect of estate settlement. No one enjoys paying them! These taxes are complex, and you would be well advised to leave this responsibility to the experts.

**Filing Returns and Paying Estate Taxes**

By the time taxes are due, the estate assets have been valued, most administration expenses have been recorded and debts have been determined. We urge you to employ either an estate tax accountant or one who is experienced in filing these returns to work with you and your attorney. Hire this accountant by about the second month after the death. If you understand the jargon, concepts and time deadlines for death taxes, you can assist the professionals and save yourself some money.

Listed below are the types of tax returns involved in estate settlement and the procedures that your accountant will most likely perform. You may have to pay up to several different taxes following your husband's death, depending on federal and state laws.

Continue to file your *U.S. Individual Income Tax Return* (Form 1040) as usual, showing your income and deductions for the entire year, but showing your late husband's income and deductions only until the date of his death. This will be your husband's "final income tax return." As a surviving spouse, you may file a joint return for the year of death and be entitled to special benefits for the two following years, if you meet the IRS requirements for qualifying widows.

The *Fiduciary Income Tax Return* (Form 1041) is usually filed if the gross income to the estate is $600 or more during the taxable year (at the time of this writing). Income earned before death, but not received until after death, is called "income in respect of a decedent [deceased]." For tax purposes, you may think of your late husband's income that arrived after his death as "estate income." This income is reported on the estate's income tax return, Form 1041, not on your late husband's personal Form 1040. It is as though he became two tax-paying entities in the year he died—the first (while he was alive) filing a joint 1040 along with you, the second (the estate) filing a 1041 and recording income and expenses realized after he died. This splits the income into two parts, which may or may not result in a lower tax bill. The fiduciary return, Form 1041, is used to pay income taxes for the estate. In some cases where the estate is open for more than one year, a fiduciary return is filed each year.

The *United States Estate Tax Return* (Form 706) is not filed for every estate, but only when the gross estate is worth more than $600,000. This return is due within nine months after death, unless an extension is granted. The estate tax concept is based on the notion that if the deceased was wealthy enough to have assets, his estate is wealthy enough to pay taxes before those assets are transferred to heirs and beneficiaries. These taxes must be paid before those disbursements. The estate tax is calculated on both the assets of the estate and certain gifts made to beneficiaries before death. First, a total dollar value is determined for the deceased's gross estate, including the gifts. Then allowable debts, expenses, losses and charitable contributions are deducted to leave the *taxable estate*. Taxes are assessed against the taxable estate.

A *federal gift tax* may be levied on gifts that exceed the current annual excludable limit of $10,000. Twenty-five percent of the *states* have a *gift tax* and sixty percent of the *states* levy an *inheritance tax*.

In addition to the assets being valued for tax purposes, the estate can realize exemptions and deductions, thus reducing the overall tax bill. Minimizing taxes is as American as apple pie, and your accountant and attorney will help reduce your tax liability. Two major tax savings can be realized by using the unified tax credit and the marital deduction.

## UNIFIED TAX CREDIT

In the past, a vast number of estates, including estates of people of modest means, were burdened with the requirement to pay federal estate taxes. To alleviate this problem, especially for the surviving spouse, a federal law enacted in 1981 provides that a "unified tax credit" is allowed for each person's estate. In effect, this means that the estate tax will be lower because part of the estate is not taxed. You get a "credit" on your tax bill. The tax credit on the estate and the tax credit on gifts are combined or "unified."

For example, if your husband died in 1987, the unified tax credit would apply to $600,000 of his estate. That is, there would not be a tax on the first $600,000 of the taxable estate. You should not even have to file this tax return (Form 706) if your husband's taxable estate was less than $600,000. However, if his taxable estate were worth more than $600,000, say as much as $750,000, then the estate might be liable for taxes on $150,000.

## MARITAL DEDUCTION

The next most important tax savings for you as the surviving spouse is the "unlimited marital deduction," which allows you to deduct 100 percent of the value of the gross estate—or all of the portion of your husband's estate that is given outright to you under the will or under state law—thus possibly saving you from any federal estate tax bill whatsoever. However, there are qualifying circumstances that must be met. Ask your attorney and accountant to explain in detail. Also, in some cases overeager use

of the marital deduction may not be in your future heirs' best interests. This varies with each individual estate plan and must be
carefully considered with guidance from your tax accountant or estate planner.

The following table outlines features of the three most
common death taxes paid on an estate. Consult with your attorney
for specific guidance regarding your tax liabilities. Keep in mind
that the taxes are paid only when base levels are exceeded.

## TAXES PAYABLE AFTER DEATH

(Death Taxes or Unified Transfer Taxes)

| Name | Estate Tax | Inheritance Tax* | Fiduciary Income Tax |
|------|-----------|------------------|----------------------|
| Reported on form | U.S. Estate Tax Return 706 | State forms | Fiduciary Income Tax Return 1041 |
| Paid to | Federal government | State government | Federal government and state (if applicable) |
| Based on | Both the estate and inheritance tax are each calculated on the value of the gross estate, which may include jointly owned property and gifts. | | Income received on non-probate assets, such as certain trusts, earned by the estate after death. |
| Reason levied | Paid on right to transfer wealth. | Paid on right to received wealth. | Paid on income earned in respect of the decedent. |

*Note: 60% of states have an inheritance tax and 25% of states have a gift tax.

## TAX FILING AND TAX PAYING DUTIES

The checklist below outlines the tax filing and tax paying duties of
the estate's executor or personal representative. The executor is
legally responsible for paying the estate taxes, but should be able
to delegate the preparation tasks to an attorney or accountant. The
list below is provided to help the widow as executor understand
what steps are required.

• Apply for a tax identification number using Federal IRS
Form SS–4, *Application for Employer Identification Number*.
This is required because the estate is considered to be a

different taxpayer than the deceased.
• File a written notice with the IRS (Form 56) of the person named to act in a fiduciary capacity, that is, to be the executor or personal representative.
• Complete the final 1040 tax return for the deceased and file by the required deadline date.
• Determine the proper valuation date (for assets for federal estate tax purposes).
• Determine whether estate administration expenses should be deducted from the 1041 income tax or from the 706 estate tax return. Ask your tax accountant for guidance.
• Determine which funds will be used to pay taxes.
• If necessary, complete and file estate tax return, Form 706, which is due nine months after death. Include a certified copy of the will (if there was one), a death certificate and Form 712, *Life Insurance Statements*, to be obtained from and completed by the life insurance companies for each policy listed in the estate tax return.
• File and pay state estate tax returns, as required.
• Estate and fiduciary income taxes must be paid when the returns are filed. You may need to apply for an extension of time to pay or arrange for installment payments. The 1986 Tax Reform Act requires some estates to make estimated quarterly payments of income taxes.
• Pay personal property or real estate taxes (if any).

While the estate settlement procedures are ongoing, the executor may make a partial distribution of assets to the beneficiaries and, if there are enough assets remaining, also pay taxes and debts. It isn't necessary to wait until the estate is closed. The exact order of distribution may vary, according to state law. The assets are distributed in each state according to statute. Generally, funeral costs are paid before debts and taxes, with the "residuary estate" (what remains) being distributed to beneficiaries and heirs last.

**Paying Claims, Settling Debts and Distributing the Estate**

The executor must also provide an explanation of "income tax basis" to beneficiaries receiving non-cash assets, so that these beneficiaries have the tax information needed when the assets are resold. For example, suppose John is the beneficiary of the family summer cottage, which his parents bought in 1955 for $11,000 and which for estate tax purposes in 1986 was valued at $89,000. If ten years from now John decides to sell the cottage for $95,000, his capital gain will generally be calculated on the basis of $89,000, not on the deceased's original purchase price. "Basis" is the term that describes the recently determined value of the inherited property.

**Termination—
Closing the Estate**

When administration is complete, the executor must file with the court or give the beneficiaries a final accounting for all income, expenses and administration of the estate. If formal proceedings for closing the estate are required, the court will issue a decree that approves the accounting and proposed distribution and discharges the executor. In informal proceedings, your attorney may file a closing statement, signed by the executor, that the estate has been fully administered.

Settling an estate can be an extremely complex, time consuming and legally specific process. For the widow, it customarily requires her attention for at least one year, sometimes two or more. Hiring professionals, understanding some of what they do, and overseeing the administration of your husband's estate will protect and preserve the assets you are to receive.

## ESTATE ASSETS WORKSHEET

*Cash* (bank, credit union, savings & loan, checking, money market, CDs, Christmas club, etc.)

| Financial Institution Name/Phone | Type of Account | Account No. | Ownership Sole —Joint | Amount |
|---|---|---|---|---|
| | | | | $ |
| | | | | $ |
| | | | | $ |
| | | | | $ |
| | | | | $ |
| | | | Total Value | $ |

*Life Insurance*

| Company Name/Phone | Policy No. | Beneficiary(ies) | Cash Value* | Face Amount |
|---|---|---|---|---|
| | | | $ | $ |
| | | | $ | $ |
| | | | $ | $ |
| | | | $ | $ |
| *(accumulated dividends, credit for unused premiums, etc.) | | | Total Value    $ | |

*Real Estate*

| Description & Location | Purchase Date—Price | Ownership Sole—Joint | Cost Basis | Appraised Value |
|---|---|---|---|---|
| | | | $ | $ |
| | | | $ | $ |
| | | | $ | $ |
| | | | $ | $ |
| | | | Total Value | $ |

*Securities—Stocks, Bonds, Mutual Funds, Unit Trusts, Government Securities*

| Institution-Broker Name/Phone | Account No. | Ownership Sole—Joint | Cost Basis | Value at Death or Alternate Date |
|---|---|---|---|---|
| | | | $ | $ |
| | | | $ | $ |
| | | | $ | $ |
| | | | $ | $ |
| | | | $ | $ |
| | | | Total Value | $ |

*Pensions, Annuities, Retirement Plans, Profit Sharing, IRAs, KEOGHs*

| Description & Location (firm name) | Account No. | Value of Survivor Benefits (if any) |
|---|---|---|
| | | $ |
| | | $ |
| | | $ |
| | | $ |
| | Total Value | $ |

*Business Interests* (corporations, partnerships, sole proprietorships)

| Firm Name/Address/Phone | Type of Business | Cost Basis | Appraised Value |
|---|---|---|---|
| | | $ | $ |
| | | $ | $ |
| | | $ | $ |
| | | $ | $ |
| | | Total Value | $ |

*Debts Due Your Husband's Estate* (notes, mortgages, royalties, patents, etc.)

| Name of Person/ Firm Owing | Address/Phone | Ownership Sole—Joint | Date Due | Amount |
|---|---|---|---|---|
| | | | | $ |
| | | | | $ |
| | | | | $ |
| | | | Total Value | $ |

*Personal Property* (collections such as coins, guns, stamps, vehicles, art, furniture etc.)

| Description | Location | Approximate Current Value |
|---|---|---|
| | | $ |
| | | $ |
| | | $ |
| | | $ |
| | Total Value | $ |
| | TOTAL OF ALL ASSETS | $ |

**ESTATE LIABILITIES WORKSHEET**

*Funeral and Estate Administration Expenses*

| Description | Date Incurred | To Whom Paid | Amount |
|---|---|---|---|
| _____ | _____ | _____ | $ |
| _____ | _____ | _____ | $ |
| _____ | _____ | _____ | $ |
| _____ | _____ | _____ | $ |
| | | Total Value | $ |

*Mortgages, Liens, Property Taxes*

| Description of Property | To Whom Owed | Date Owed | Amount |
|---|---|---|---|
| _____ | _____ | _____ | $ |
| _____ | _____ | _____ | $ |
| _____ | _____ | _____ | $ |
| _____ | _____ | _____ | $ |
| | | Total Value | $ |

*Loans* (auto, personal, insurance, etc.)

| Description | To Whom Owed—Address/Phone | Amount |
|---|---|---|
| _____ | _____ | $ |
| _____ | _____ | $ |
| _____ | _____ | $ |
| _____ | _____ | $ |
| | Total Value | $ |

| | TOTAL VALUE ALL LIABILITIES | $ |
|---|---|---|

# Chapter 8

# *Filing Claims for Life Insurance and Survivor Benefits*

One of the earliest concerns for any widow is life insurance. How much life insurance did my husband have? With which companies? How do I get the proceeds and how soon will they be paid? Did he have any retirement pension or annuity? How do I find out about them? Am I entitled to veterans' benefits?

This chapter provides common-sense guidance about where to begin and how to apply for these benefits yourself. We show an example claim letter and guide you in getting started. An overall safeguard for all claims is to photocopy every letter you send. However, if you live in one of the states where an attorney receives a percentage of the estate to settle all these matters, you may wish to have him or her submit the claims.

**Life Insurance Claims**

Look for the life insurance policies among your important papers. If you cannot find them, look in your late husband's checkbook to see to which insurance companies he made payments. If he was still employed, call his supervisor or the personnel office to ask if his company had insurance on his life. Some people have life, health, auto and homeowner's insurance coverage with the same company.

Once you have determined which policies covered your husband's life, you can write a letter similar to the sample shown below. You need to know the policy number, and you must enclose the policy and a copy of the death certificate with the claim letter. Address it to the attention of the claims department. If you cannot locate the policy, you must contact the insurance company and request a "lost policy form." Then complete the lost policy form and submit it along with your claim letter and death certificate. *Life insurance proceeds are not automatically paid following a death. You must file a claim for them!*

**Example Claim Letter**

March 4, 1988

New York Life Insurance Company
Claims Department
Street Address
City, State, Zip

Reference: Policy No. 12345-XYZ

Dear Claims Adjustor:

My late husband, John Doe, died on February 1, 1988. I am filing a claim for the life insurance benefits as described on Policy No. 12345-XYZ.

I am enclosing the policy and a copy of the death certificate. Please explain in detail how you determine the amount of payment. I will appreciate your prompt attention to my request.

Sincerely,

*your signature*
your typewritten name

Enclosures

If your state law provides for interest to be paid on the insurance proceeds from the date of death until the payment is made to the beneficiaries, make reference to that statute in your letter. This lets the insurance company know you are well informed! If by coincidence you paid premiums on any life insurance policy between the date of death and the date of the claim, ask for reimbursement.

Even if the death was a suicide, you may still have a claim in some states. If the policy was in effect for the minimum time required by your state law, you may be eligible for benefits, unless the policy specifically states that no benefits will be paid in the event of a suicide. The major insurance companies usually require that the policy be in effect for two years. Some state laws require less time. Be aware that in suicide deaths, no accidental death benefits are ever paid. Some persons may have separate "accidental death and dismemberment" or accident policies; these benefits are payable only in case of an accident, not for death by illness or suicide.

You will need an explanation of the payout for estate settlement purposes. Depending on the type of life insurance, the amount of payment may include the death benefits, or "face amount," plus credit for unused premiums, accumulated dividends and possibly interest on the proceeds from the date of death to the date of payment, less deductions for outstanding loans.

## Pension Claims

A pension refers to a special type of benefit account to which your husband and/or his employer may have made regular contributions. This money is to be wisely invested, then in the future paid out as a retirement or disability benefit. Your late husband may have had one through his employer or a labor organization. Depending on several conditions, you may or may not be eligible for survivor benefits.

• Did my husband participate in a pension fund? First, ask his employer (or former employer). If he belonged to a labor organization, look in the yellow pages and call or write them. Ask how you might apply for survivor benefits.

• Am I eligible for any survivor pension benefits? Many men, in anticipation of larger pension checks, choose to waive the option for survivor benefits if they should die. Some pension funds don't permit survivor benefits at all.

• How much will my survivor benefits be? If they are available at all, they will be smaller than the amount that would have been payable to your husband.

• When will they begin? They may not begin until your late husband would have been sixty-two, or at retirement age for that particular pension.

• How long will they continue? Probably they will be paid only for a few years, not for your lifetime.

• How frequently are cost-of-living increases applied?

A recent concern about private pension funds is that some of them are now underfunded or bankrupt. This year in the steel industry and a few others, some companies have not met their retirees' pension or health insurance payments. A surviving widow is no more secure—and, in many cases, even less secure—than her husband was.

## Annuity Claims

An annuity is a contract that guarantees an agreed-upon payment at some future time—typically at retirement—to an individual called an annuitant. Insurance companies sell annuities and some employers have annuity programs. Check with his employer, stockbroker and insurance agent to see if any annuities were purchased.

Call your late husband's employer or the insurance company for information about how to apply for survivor annuity benefits. When you apply, you will need a copy of the death certificate and Social Security numbers for yourself and your husband. Be sure to get a written explanation of the estimated benefit calculations for yourself and any other dependents.

In annuity programs, as in pension programs, the primary recipient (your late husband in this case) may have chosen to receive the full monthly payments—and therefore not have left any survivor benefits. Since 1984, when the Spouse Equity Act, Public Law 98-615, was passed, if the survivor annuity is to be less than 55 percent of the retiree's annuity, then the spouse's signature must be notarized and on the document! If your husband set up his annuity or pension program before 1984, he was not required to inform you of his choice.

In the Civil Service Retirement System for survivors of federal government employees, it can take months to receive the first annuity payment. Special conditions apply for children over eighteen to qualify for benefits. If the amount of payment is different from what you expected, photocopy the check and deposit it to your account. *Do not return the check*. Returning the undeposited check just causes confusion. The system is huge and it takes time to process thousands of claims. If you were overpaid, the government will let you know; be prepared to write a personal check to return the amount of overpayments at their request. If you feel you were undercompensated, it is up to you to write a letter requesting an adjustment. Include your reference or claim number, the amount you feel you are entitled to, along with clearly stated reasons, and list the dates and amounts of each check received. Photocopy all checks and keep careful records for tax purposes and to document any adjustments you request.

**Veterans' Benefits**

Survivors and dependents of veterans may be eligible for certain Veterans Administration (VA) benefits. The benefits usually include burial in a national cemetery, payments toward burial expenses, a headstone or marker and an American flag to drape the casket. There are 110 national cemeteries, and the VA may pay for transportation of the deceased to the cemetery nearest his last place of residence. There is no charge for burial of a deceased veteran in a national cemetery. If a qualified deceased veteran has already been interred in a private cemetery, either by preference or because the funeral provider wasn't aware of or didn't advise you of the national cemetery alternative, you can still apply for burial reimbursement and other benefits. Your application must be made within two years of the date of death.[9]

Other benefits include educational assistance for dependents, dependency and indemnity compensation (DIC), non-service-connected death pension and reinstated entitlement program for survivors. In some cases medical care is available to the surviving spouse or child. Divorced widows may also apply for benefits.

**How to Apply for Benefits**

In every telephone directory there is a toll-free number listed for the Veterans Administration assistance in your state. They will send you a packet of instructions and forms you need to complete in applying for benefits. Or you can apply in person at any VA office. If you live in a rural area or small town, telephone or visit your local Disabled American Veterans (DAV) or Veterans of

Foreign Wars (VFW) office. These service organizations can help you apply for widow's benefits.

If you apply in person, be sure to take the following documents:

- Certified copy of your husband's death certificate;
- Military records, especially the *Form DD 214*, the *Certificate of Release* or *Discharge from Active Duty* (also called separation papers);
- Certified copy of your marriage license (if you need a certified copy, just write or visit the county clerk's office where the marriage license was issued and pay for a copy);
- Certified copy of birth certificate for each child;
- If applicable, divorce or annulment agreements;
- Social Security number of deceased and of yourself;
- Name and address of any guardian for minors (children under legal age);
- Name and address of executor or administrator, if any, appointed by the court to settle the estate of the deceased.

Filing claims for life insurance, pension, retirement and veterans' benefits can be emotionally troubling. We spoke with one young widow who felt the insurance proceeds represented a kind of perverse reward connected with her husband's death. In her grief, she had forgotten he wanted to provide for his family, should he die. These benefits are a part of your husband's estate and can make the difference between eking out an austere existence or comfortably enjoying your future well-being.

# Chapter 9

# *Social Security, Medicare, Health Insurance and Disability*

In addition to life insurance proceeds, survivor's pension benefits and monthly salaries, a widow often has other sources of income in the form of Social Security benefits, including a one-time funeral payment, monthly support for herself and her children, retirement income and disability or medical insurance.

*A widow of any age, no matter how young, may qualify for Social Security benefits.* Even divorced surviving spouses or non-U.S. citizens may be entitled to benefits. Women age sixty-five and older can save money by having Medicare health insurance in addition to a private health plan. If your husband died after July 1, 1986, you may be eligible for three additional years of health insurance under his plan.

In this chapter we review how to apply for Social Security payments and Medicare. Additionally, we outline criteria for comparing health insurance plans and discuss the seldom-considered aspects of disability insurance.

**Social Security**

If you are a widow—no matter of what age, for how long, or even if you are a common-law widow or a surviving divorced spouse—you may be eligible for Social Security survivor benefits. However, these benefits are not bestowed automatically; you must apply for them either now or later in your life. If you don't know whether you are eligible for Social Security benefits as a widow—apply and find out! The only universal requirement is that your late husband or mate contributed to the Social Security system for the specified minimum qualifying time, which depends on his age at the time of death. If you have dependent or disabled children or grandchildren, they could be eligible for benefits too. But you won't know until you apply.

**If You Are. . .
You May Be
Entitled to. . .**

• Almost every widow is entitled to a one-time funeral payment (the lump sum death payment) of $255. That amount is set by law and is the same for every qualified widow. The claim must be made within two years of her husband's death.

• A widow of any age with dependent children or grandchildren qualifies for mother's benefits and children's benefits.

• Even if you have never worked yourself, you may be entitled to benefits based on your late husband's account.

• A disabled widow age fifty or over is often entitled to disability benefits.

• Widows as young as age sixty may be eligible to receive reduced Social Security benefits.

• If you are a widow age sixty-five or over, you will likely be entitled to either full survivor's benefits or your own retirement benefits and medical insurance through Medicare.

*If you feel you may be entitled to Social Security benefits based on your own work record and present age, ask if you would receive higher benefits on your own or as a widow. Then apply for the greater benefit amount.*

These conditions also apply to divorced surviving spouses and common-law widows.

**Locating Your
Social Security
Office**

No matter how small or remote your hometown is, every telephone directory in the United States has a listing for a Social Security office. It is usually in the government section of the directory, and may be listed under the Department of Health and Human Services. If a local number or toll-free "800" number is not listed, you can make the initial contact by calling collect. At the present there are more than 1,300 Social Security offices in the United States, Guam and Puerto Rico.

Call in advance for an appointment in person or on the phone, requesting one during their least busy hours; that way you will have sufficient time for questions. Ask which documents you will need to provide for your claims. You will most likely be making claims for (1) the Lump Sum Death Payment, (2) Widow's Insurance Benefits and possibly (3) Child's Insurance Benefits. If you are within three months of age sixty-five or older and eligible for Social Security benefits at that time, you may also apply for enrollment in (4) Medicare. We discuss Medicare later in this chapter.

To initiate your claims you'll need the following documents and any other items the Social Security representative requested when you made your appointment: **The Initial Application Interview**
- Your late husband's death certificate,
- His Social Security number,
- Your marriage certificate,
- The divorce decree, if applicable,
- Each child's birth certificate (if applying for children's benefits),
- Knowledge of your combined earnings last year (as shown on the W-2s) and estimated earnings this year and next year.

If you have a personal interview, the claims representative will assist you in completing the claim forms. In addition, he or she should advise you about how long the claims process will take. This may range from a few weeks to several months, depending on how complex your case is. Charlotte's case was complex, requiring additional documentation and interviews that took six months to complete. Carol's experience in filing claims for Social Security benefits was more typical, taking only a few weeks. Ask how long your case should take. Get a phone number and name to contact in case you have questions later.

WHAT IF . . . ?

- You haven't applied for any widow's benefits and you've been a widow for years? There is no time limit within which you must apply for survivor's benefits, but it is to your advantage to apply as soon as possible; some are retroactive for only a limited period of time. For example, if you waited until three years after your husband died before applying for benefits for your dependent children, it might be too late! Each case is determined on an individual basis. As previously mentioned, you *must* apply for the lump sum death benefit within two years of the date of death.

• You can't find your late husband's Social Security number or the marriage certificate? Ask the claims representative for assistance in locating the Social Security number. To apply for a duplicate marriage certificate, simply write to the county in which the marriage was performed and request a copy.

• You aren't sure whether or for how long your late husband contributed to the Social Security system, and therefore whether you are eligible for any benefits? File your application and let the Social Security Administration look for these answers. You could qualify for partial or full benefits, immediately or later.

• You were not married to your mate? In some states, the common-law widow is recognized as a legitimate claimant to the deceased's Social Security benefits, if you can prove to the satisfaction of the Social Security Administration that you lived together as husband and wife, and that you held yourself out to the community as his wife. The Social Security Administration determines whether you are qualified.

YOUR RESPONSIBILITIES

Ask to review your late husband's Social Security records. They will show posted earnings and contributions. Verify that they are accurate, based on your husband's personal records and your memory. Your future benefits will depend on this accuracy. Always keep a record of his Social Security number. You will need it to apply for survivor benefits when you are old enough.

Keep yourself educated about what is available to you and about changes in the law. This is no different than keeping yourself informed about changes in income tax laws. Each year the Social Security Administration updates its publication *A Woman's Guide to Social Security*, which is available from your local Social Security Administration office. Completing forms for government benefits can be tedious and frustrating. But for some widows the benefits may make the difference between worrying about not having enough money and being free to meet other challenges in their changed lives.

The federal Supplemental Security Income (SSI) program provides a minimum monthly income and other social services to the aged, the blind or the disabled. You must qualify based on low monthly income and a low asset value. Assets are any resources you own that can be turned into cash, such as property, jewelry, collectibles, securities or other valuables. Your main residence and its land, part of the value of your car, and certain personal property are not counted as assets.

**Supplemental Security Income**

   Don't make the mistake of assuming that your assets are too valuable for you to qualify for Supplemental Security Income. Ask your claims representative. If your income is low, by all means call the Social Security Administration to find out how to apply for these benefits. And if you know of any widow who may qualify for these services, tell her about them.

If you are a widow aged sixty-five or older you may apply for health insurance through Medicare. This is a federal government health insurance program that provides some coverage for entitled persons over sixty-five and for certain disabled people.

**Medicare Health Insurance**

   Medicare has two parts—Hospital Insurance Part A and the optional Medical Insurance Part B. The *hospital insurance*, Part A, can help pay for inpatient hospital care, inpatient care in a skilled nursing facility, home health care and hospice care. Part B, the *medical insurance*, can help pay for medically necessary doctors' services, outpatient hospital services and a number of other medical services and supplies that are not covered by the hospital insurance part of Medicare. Medical insurance also can pay for home health services. Medicare does not pay the full cost of some covered services. For details about what Medicare does and does not cover (the list is long), consult *Your Medicare Handbook*.

   For eligible persons, Social Security taxes pay the monthly premiums for hospital insurance while the individual is responsible for paying the premiums for medical insurance. At the time of this writing, the medical insurance coverage costs only $24.80 per month!

To find out about Medicare, just phone or write your local Social Security Administration office, listed in each phone directory in the country. Ask for a copy of *Your Medicare Handbook*, published by the Government Printing Office. It explains what Medicare is and how it works, listing which expenses it does and which it does not pay for.[10]

**To Apply for Medicare**

You may be automatically eligible for Medicare, but you won't receive any benefits unless you apply for them. There are two ways to apply for Medicare, assuming you are within three months of being sixty-five or older and you feel you will be entitled to Social Security benefits. You can call the Social Security Administration and make an appointment to complete the *Application for Enrollment in Medicare* (Form HCFA-40B). Or you can indicate your desire for enrollment by using the same forms as when you apply for either *Widow's Insurance* (Form SSA-10BK) or your own retirement benefits (Form SSA-1F6).[11]

You are *automatically* eligible for Part A Hospital Insurance of Medicare at *no monthly premium* if any of the following conditions applies to you: (1) You have reached age sixty-five and you are eligible for Social Security benefits, even if you are not drawing such benefits because you're still working. (2) You have received disability payments for twenty-four months. (3) You are a sixty-five-year-old widow or widower or spouse of a worker who is or would have been entitled to Social Security benefits.[12]

If you are sixty-five or older and for any reason you are not entitled to monthly Social Security benefits, you may not be eligible for Medicare Hospital Insurance, whose premiums are paid from Social Security taxes; but you can purchase it on a voluntary basis. If you choose voluntary enrollment you'll be required to pay monthly premiums for both hospital and medical insurance.

**Medicare-Participating Doctors and Suppliers**

In choosing health care, you may want to go to a Medicare-participating doctor or supplier. They have agreed to "accept assignment" on all Medicare claims. To accept assignment means the doctor or supplier agrees that the total charge for the covered service will be the charge approved by the Medicare carrier, and that he or she will send the bill to Medicare for reimbursement. You may be charged for the part Medicare does not cover if you do not have other insurance to cover the difference. Ask or look for the "Medicare-participating" displayed emblem or certificate.

In addition to Medicare, you may want to buy a supplemental health insurance plan or keep a reduced level of your existing health insurance. It may pay the $75 annual deductible for Medicare as well as nonrecognized charges. Be especially careful when shopping for a supplemental plan, noting whether it limits coverage on doctors' bills to "approved charges." You already have that on Medicare! Carefully compare the supplemental plan to see that it supplies additional benefits and doesn't duplicate the Medicare benefits. The free pamphlet, *Guide to Health Insurance for People with Medicare*, is available from a Social Security Administration office. This pamphlet describes the various kinds of supplemental insurance available and explains how they relate to Medicare coverage. Several major insurance companies offer special Medicare supplemental plans.

**Supplemental Health Insurance**

In his book *The Complete and Easy Guide to Social Security and Medicare,* Faustin Jehle describes four features to look for in a supplemental health plan.[13]

- Does the policy pay any medical expenses that are not considered "approved charges" by Medicare?
- Does the policy exclude pre-existing illnesses or other physical ailments?
- How much coverage does the policy provide for the expenses it covers that Medicare does not cover?
- Are there limits on your reimbursement for such expenses?

Note that, although Medicare is a government health program, payments to hospitals, doctors and nursing facilities are handled by private companies (carriers) under contract to the government. For example, in Denver, Medicare payments to doctors are processed through Blue Cross and Blue Shield.

The federal Medicare health insurance program is enormous, and you may occasionally experience delays or errors in processing claims. However, the low cost of medical insurance for persons entitled to Medicare hospital coverage more than offsets any problems.

## Medicaid

Medicaid is an assistance program to provide health care for persons with very low incomes. It is administered by your state government. Call your state social services office for information.

## Health Insurance for Your Family and Yourself

Within a few days after her husband's death in 1984, Carol called his employer, worried that health insurance coverage for herself and her children would end. With four sons, she didn't want to take the risk of being uninsured. In her case, Carol learned that while she remained a widow, she would continue to be eligible for health insurance through her late husband's group plan. Until recently, many widows didn't have this option and could expect only a thirty-day grace period during which their spouse's health insurance would continue for them. After that month, they were on their own.

Today, fortunately, that problem has been resolved for many widows. Some major health insurance companies, sometimes called "carriers," now offer survivor's benefits or continuation of dependent coverage for up to a year without charging any premium. To qualify, the deceased husband and surviving family members must have been insured at the time of his death.

Since July 1, 1986, many women who became widows and would have lost their group health insurance coverage because of the death of their spouse, now have the choice of continuing that insurance for up to three years.[14] If this applies to you, the coverage can continue if (1) you are the widow of a worker who had group health insurance through an employer of twenty or more persons, (2) you were already covered when he died, and (3) you agree to pay the entire monthly premiums, both the employer and employee portions. Dependent children may also be covered. This coverage ends if you fail to pay your premiums, become covered by Medicare or by other group insurance as an employee or spouse, or if the employer ends group health insurance for all workers. In some cases, continuing these premiums can be more expensive than finding your own group policy.

No matter what kind of health insurance you choose, make sure the company has a good track record of writing health insurance. Look for the big-name companies that have been selling health insurance for years. Some small companies that offer unbelievably low premiums may discontinue coverage at any time.

## GROUP HEALTH INSURANCE

In looking for health insurance for yourself and any dependents, check first with your employer about getting coverage through a group health plan. Group plans usually offer better coverage for a lower price. If you don't work, look for a group plan through a membership organization. The Older Women's League suggests you try the following groups:[15]

- American Association of Retired Persons (AARP), 1909 K Street, NW, Washington, DC 20049; (202) 872-4700
- National Council of Jewish Women, 15 East 26th Street, New York, NY 10010 (women of any denomination may join NCJW); (212)532-1740
- Co-Op America, 2100 M Street, NW, #310, Washington, DC 20063; (800)424-2667.
- Other national organizations you might consider are the American Association of University Women, National Organization for Women, Business and Professional Women's Clubs, and National Council for Senior Citizens. In addition, there are numerous local and national professional organizations in which you must maintain membership to be eligible for group health plans, such as those for nurses, teachers, public administrators and so forth. Most people find that group health insurance is less expensive and provides better coverage than an individual policy.

## INDIVIDUAL OR PRIVATE PLANS

Individual or private health plans usually are either more expensive or provide less coverage than a group plan. They may exclude any pre-existing conditions and require evidence of insurability, such as a physical exam. If this is your only alternative, ask about an interim or short-term plan while you join an organization and look for a group plan. Private companies are listed under "Insurance" in the yellow pages. Carefully compare premiums, deductible amounts and coverage using the comparison outline later in this chapter.

## PREPAID PLANS

Prepaid plans such as health maintenance organizations (HMOs) may cost less than a private plan. They offer comprehensive medical services for a monthly payment, but may require that care be provided by or arranged for by their physicians and hospitals. Call your state medical association or look in the yellow pages to see which prepaid plans accept individuals.

## HOSPITAL INDEMNITY

This type of policy pays you a daily "hospital income" to help with expenses such as intensive or extended care, outpatient surgery, child care, long-distance telephone and transportation. Indemnity insurance is offered by major insurance companies, some membership groups and direct mail advertisements. Avoid the similarly named "hospitalization only" coverage, which does not cover outpatient surgery or follow-up care.

## MAJOR MEDICAL OR CATASTROPHIC MEDICAL EXPENSE

This coverage is purchased generally as a rider policy that goes beyond basic medical coverage. It usually has a deductible amount of $1,000 or more and an upper maximum limit, perhaps a $1 million lifetime benefit. Some insurance experts feel this is the most important coverage you can have.

## SPECIFIC DISEASE OR
## SUPPLEMENTAL HEALTH INSURANCE

Specialized policies can be purchased to cover illnesses such as heart, kidney or cancer disease. Supplemental coverage might be used with Medicare. Some major insurance companies advertise coverage specifically to complement Medicare.

When you compare costs of health insurance to benefits, in two instances a higher price now may mean savings in the long run. In the first instance make sure your insurance company uses a "reasonable and customary" charges table, such as that developed by the Health Insurance Association of America, as the basis for how much it will pay toward each procedure you claim, e.g., medical treatment, hospital stay, surgical procedure, etc.[16] Some health insurance companies offer lower-cost insurance, but allow a lesser amount toward each claim, leaving you to pay the remainder out of pocket. Avoid any company that claims its reasonable and customary rates are confidential or any company that pays "scheduled" amounts toward claims. The scheduled amount may be significantly lower than the actual charges, and you will have to pay the difference.

The second instance of higher premiums now versus lower costs over the long haul has to do with how the health insurance company adjusts your future premium rates after you submit claims. For example, if you submit a claim for knee surgery this year, you don't want a company that dramatically increases your premiums in the future. A better plan is one that considers all claims by the "group" as a whole, then decides whether to moderately increase the premiums for the entire group rather than increase individual premiums based on individual claims.

As you shop for a health insurance plan, remember that the one you choose should include five common areas of coverage:
- Medical services that include physician diagnosis and treatment, laboratory tests, x-ray, office visits,
- Surgical procedures both in and out of the hospital,
- Hospital and extended care to cover full daily rate of a semi-private room and care, hospital supplies, medications, laboratory tests, X-rays and specialized care such as cardiac or intensive care units for a minimum of 30 consecutive days (120 is preferable),
- Emergency service such as ambulance or treatment in another facility if you have a prepaid HMO plan,
- Other—one or more of these: treatment for mental health, substance abuse (drug or alcohol), eye care, dental, prosthesis, maternity, hospice, nursing home, home health care, physical therapy and speech therapy.

**HEALTH PLAN COMPARISON GUIDE**

Name _____    Type _____

(group, prepaid, indem, priv, major)

Eligibility (Y/N) _____   _____   _____   _____   _____

       Self  Child to 19   Student to 23   Child Not Home   Other Dependents

       Physical Exam Required? Y/N _____ (to clarify "pre-existing condition" issues)

Monthly Premiums        Self  $ _____        Family  $ _____

Deductible Amount       Per Person  $ _____       Per Family  $ _____

       (per calendar year)

Days Continuous Hospital Care Covered _____

Out-of-Hospital Surgery Covered?   Y/N _____

Nursing Care Included?      Y/N _____
Nursing Home Included?    Y/N _____
Maternity?                       Y/N _____

Major Medical Included?    Y/N _____
     Per Claim Upper Maximum Limit?      $ _____
     Lifetime Limit (not less than $250,000) $ _____
     Annual Restoration of Benefits?      Y/N _____
     Deductible per Person   $ _____       Per Family  $ _____

What Is Excluded? _____
_____
_____

ALSO CONSIDER . . .

*Exclusions.* These could include dental care, eye care and prescription lenses, congenital defects or illness and mental illness.

*Basic Surgical.* Does it keep up with increases in surgical rates to the usual and customary fees charged in your area? Does it pay the physician's fees for surgery performed in or out of the hospital?

Does it include office visits directly related to the surgery both before and after? Would you be reimbursed for a second surgical opinion?

*Hospital.* What miscellaneous expenses does basic hospital cover? After the limit of fully covered days in hospital is exceeded, what do you pay?

*Nursing Home.* How does it cover hospital outpatient care, convalescent care, nursing home and home health care?

*Maternity.* How are maternity benefits included? How does it handle complications with pregnancy?

*General Policy.* Is your policy guaranteed renewable? Under what conditions could you be cancelled? What is the maximum percent of premium increase allowed? Does it have a maximum limit per illness or injury?

*Conversion.* Can you convert your group insurance plan, without evidence of insurability (physical exam), to an individual plan if you leave your job?

In spite of the difficulties in making a health insurance decision, you can't afford to be without some kind of coverage. Medical costs have skyrocketed and insurance benefits continue to change. If you have inherited coverage from your late husband, request an up-to-date policy and read it carefully to understand how your plan works. After you purchase a new policy, review it annually. If you have problems paying premiums, call your agent or service representative and try to work out a payment schedule. Don't let your policy lapse and don't terminate an old one before you get new coverage.

**Disability Insurance**

We never expect to be disabled and unable to work. We assume that our health and willingness to work will sustain us. However, if you are a widow and the main source of support for your family, what would happen to your children if you became disabled? Where would you find ready cash to tide you over until the disability insurance began? Where can you learn about disability insurance? What are the differences in disability coverage? The purpose of this section is to explain what disability insurance provides, how to decide if you need any and where to get it.

**Where to Find Disability Insurance**

In preparation for the day your paycheck might stop due to disability, consider all your sources of income. If you have other ways to pay your bills, you may not need this insurance. First check with your employer to see if you have or can get disability insurance through your group health plan. A group policy will be less expensive than a private plan. Sometimes the employer will pay for it. Second, find out if your state provides any worker's compensation if you become ill or have an accident as a result of work. You may qualify for Social Security disability benefits, but they won't begin until about the fifth month after you are disabled. The federal Social Security program provides disability checks for any qualified worker who becomes severely disabled before age sixty-five. The coverage includes mental and physical illnesses. Another choice is a private insurance company. One company offers "mortgage disability" income to cover house payments, even up to three years, while others offer "credit disability" to pay your monthly charge card payments while you are disabled.

Other possible sources for disability income are:
- Veterans Administration,
- Civil Service disability benefits for government workers,
- State vocational rehabilitation benefits,
- State welfare benefits for low-income people,
- Aid to Families with Dependent Children,
- Group union disability benefits,
- Automobile insurance that provides benefits for disability from an auto accident.

**Disability Insurance Considerations**

- Does the insurance cover disability due to both illness and accident, or only one? Some policies pay only for accidents. Some policies are good for a lifetime if the disability is due to illness; if an accident is the cause, the payments sometimes last for only one year. How long will the payments continue?
- What does the plan define as "disabled?" Must you be unable to do any work at all, or only the same kind of work you were doing when you were disabled?

- How disabled must you be before you qualify to collect any disability income? Totally, partially or residually? Ask the company to explain with an example of when and how its policy works. Make sure a company representative clearly defines the differences.
- How long must you wait before receiving any payments? In some policies, people disabled by accidents may receive partial payments from the day of the accident. For illness, it may vary from thirty days to several months.
- How much disability income would you get from this policy? Some pay a maximum of up to 75 percent of your weekly income.
- Must you be totally hospitalized or stay at home to receive benefits? If you must, find out how often a physician's statement of disability is required.
- Will other sources of income, such as state workmen's compensation or Social Security, jeopardize or reduce your disability benefits? Usually they don't, but find out.
- How often and how much can the premiums be raised?
- Ask about renewability, or extending the policy beyond the expiration date.

Don't buy more insurance than you need. If you are a widow without dependents and your home is paid for, you may not need disability insurance, other than what you may qualify for in a government program.

One of the more tedious chores of being on your own is researching and deciding if and where you should spend your money on protection that you hope you will never need but can't afford to be without. Social Security and Medicare benefits may make the difference between scrimping or feeling safe and comfortable about your future.

**Notes**

# Chapter 10

# *Your Budget, Your Checkbook and Your Credit*

Money is an early and urgent concern for a widow, especially if her husband's death was sudden and unexpected. Some women carry little cash and if the checking accounts are in his name only or require both signatures to withdraw funds, she may have difficulty making purchases or paying immediate bills. If your husband paid the monthly bills and generally managed the finances, you may have no idea how much immediate cash or long-term resources are available, nor any idea what your living expenses are. Further concerns for any woman on her own for the first time include:

- Do you have access to immediate cash? You may need this for food, gasoline, prescription drugs, etc. If a friend or relative offers to lend you money, sign a promissory note that you will repay the funds. Make a duplicate as a reminder for yourself and keep it with your important papers.
- Do you have an idea of how much money you will have coming in each month? Your monthly income has most likely decreased, perhaps drastically and perhaps for the rest of your life.
- Do you have a clear picture of what your monthly expenses will be? Are you aware of any occasional expenses that may come up, such as auto or other insurance premiums?
- If your husband managed the bank accounts, do you know how to balance a checkbook and why it is important?

• What happens if all the credit cards are in your husband's name? Will you still be able to use them, and for how long?

If you are uncertain about the answers to any of these questions, this chapter is intended to guide you in understanding how to estimate your costs of living simply by reviewing your checkbook registers, learning how to develop a plan for spending (a budget), and learning how to balance a checkbook. We discuss the pros and cons of cancelling your husband's credit cards and establishing your own credit.

Almost immediately Carol knew that money would become a major factor in her life as a widow. She knew her monthly income had dropped and that it wasn't likely to change much, even if she went to work. Her first reaction was, "Oh, how I hate money!" A friend asked, "Is it really money itself, or your dependence on money that you hate?" With a little thought, Carol realized it was her anxiety about not having money and not knowing if she could make it on her own that she feared. She had been a career home-maker and had never worked to support herself, let alone a family!

It is normal to be worried about your financial circumstances. Besides the fear of not having enough money, one widow friend of ours stated she felt guilty about receiving the life insurance and other benefits from her husband's death. Even though you may feel uneasy and uncertain about what to do with these funds, apply for the proceeds. Your husband wanted to provide for his family, and you may have helped him accumulate the premiums by forgoing other expenditures.

If you don't immediately need the insurance money, place it in a federally insured passbook savings or money market account to earn some interest, while you take as much time as you need to make decisions about your financial future. Don't be pressured into investing these proceeds until you know what you're doing. We discuss investment decision making in Chapter 18.

**Immediate Cash**

Often the first money worry is where you will get immediate cash. There are several alternatives:

• First, depending on your state laws, if the checking accounts allow either your husband's or your signature, the account should remain open allowing you access to the funds. If the account is in his name only or requires both your signatures, it will be closed.

• Determine if you have access to any savings or money market accounts.

• If your husband had a will, ask your attorney for help in applying for a living allowance from any funds that may be available in his estate.

Our next two means of getting money involve borrowing. We urge you to use borrowing as a last resort! If your costs of living exceed your income, you'll only compound your problems by borrowing. Eventually you have to pay the money back—with interest. If you must borrow money, then get as little as possible for as short a time as possible.

• If your husband had a stock portfolio, with you as a joint owner and "rights of survivorship" (that is, the survivor inherits the account when the other owner dies), you can borrow money based on the value of the account. Your broker may say something like, "We can margin your account for the money you need." What he means is the brokerage firm can loan you the money, using the value of the portfolio as security. They have little risk, because if you can't repay the loan the brokerage firm can always sell your securities to get their money back. Therefore, they can loan you money at a much lower rate than through a personal signature loan at a bank.

If your late husband owned the account in his name only, you can still borrow the funds after submitting a copy of the death certificate and will, allowing the brokerage firm time to confirm your right to the portfolio assets.

A word of caution is in order about borrowing money by "margining the account." If the value of the account were to drop below the amount you borrowed, you could be in trouble, because you would immediately have to pay the difference—in cash! For example, if you borrowed against part of the value of your late husband's (now your) portfolio, say $20,000, and the total value of the portfolio dropped to $15,000, you'd have to pay the brokerage firm $5,000—now!

• Banking and financial institutions offer personal signature loans, but at relatively high interest rates. Often no collateral is required, just your signature and good credit rating. Loans backed by some form of security are available at slightly lower interest rates.

If you simply cannot get immediate cash, contact your creditors and explain that you are a recent widow in the process of settling your late husband's estate. They will expect an estimate of when and how much you'll be able to pay to settle your debts, but usually they are understanding and prefer to work with you, rather than lose the money in the long run.

## A Personal Budget

The first place to begin getting control of your immediate financial situation is to determine your "cash flow." Typically, for each household, income or cash "flows" into checking accounts or pockets each month, then "flows" out to pay the bills. When your income exceeds your expenses, you have a "positive cash flow," with a little cash left over to be used as you choose. When your expenses are greater than your income, you have a "negative cash flow." This may be a new problem for you if your monthly income is now lower than it was when your husband was living.

To determine your cash flow you need to look first at how much and where you have been spending your money. Next, you have to consider what your income is likely to be—both monthly income and occasional income such as stock dividends or interest from bonds. Then you can compare your income to what it costs you to live, and plan for your future expenditures.

This plan for how you will spend your resources compared to your income is called a "budget." A budget doesn't necessarily mean scrimping and penny pinching. But it can indicate that you may have to reduce your spending. Most widows realize a drop in monthly income when their husbands die. Some women become fearful and frugal, not spending money on anything—even food or medical care. Others splurge on shopping sprees to console themselves. Carol found a simple, relatively inexpensive way to lift her spirits—redecorating the master bedroom. She didn't have to buy expensive new furniture. She just painted, bought a new spread and curtains, and rearranged the furniture. She still had the comfort of familiar belongings, but they looked fresh and new.

Don't be anxious about preparing a personal spending plan or budget. No bookkeeping experience is necessary. It is simply an estimate of how you will manage your income and expenses. It can be an exciting challenge, rather like the first dinner party you and your husband had as newlyweds. You may have postponed the experience until you could gather the courage to plan who you would invite, what you would serve and how to get all the parts of the meal ready at the appropriate time. Even though you might not have been perfect, your mistakes weren't fatal, and entertaining was easier the next time. Similarly, examining your spending habits and sources of income takes careful thought, coordination and some attention to detail. It needn't be perfect, and it becomes easier with practice.

**Four Steps to a Spending Plan**

There are four steps in developing a budget: (1) analyzing how much you've spent in the past for a particular category, such as food, (2) determining how much income you can expect from your earnings, survivor annuity, retirement or other benefits, (3) making estimates about how much you can afford to spend in the future for clothing, shelter, health care and so on, and (4) using the estimates to create your budget. This first budget effort should be short-term, for perhaps the first year, and should cover everyday living. At this point, you may not know what you will receive in life insurance proceeds after the estate is settled. Later you may wish to consider major expenditures and long-term investments for your future.

WHAT YOU HAVE BEEN SPENDING

To determine how you have spent money in the recent past, look in your checkbook registers, the part of your checkbook where you have entered to whom and for what checks were written. Be sure to examine the registers from all your accounts for the past year, considering even occasional checks written on money market accounts or cashier's checks drawn on savings accounts. If you can't locate the registers, use the cancelled checks or tissue copies.

Next, purchase a budget workbook or ledger, or make rows or columns on ruled notebook paper and label each with headings like those shown shown on page 105. Use a separate sheet for each month. You may want to develop headings to suit your own lifestyle. (An easier strategy is simply to purchase two inexpensive budget workbooks and complete the expense portion in one for the past year. Then use the other notebook for the coming year.) Call your bank or savings institution to ask if they can provide you with budget or cash flow worksheets. Household budget record books are available from office or business supply stores for only a few dollars.

List each check amount in an appropriate space. If you aren't certain which category it should be in, just guess. Correctness isn't critical, but try to be consistent. This first step is the most tedious and may take a few days. Take enough time to be careful. To save time, group your expenses under the headings; don't detail all last year's information. You just need a clear idea of how you used to spend your money so you can plan for the future.

Total each month's entries, then on a separate sheet enter the grand total for each category for the past year. You may notice that recent expenses for food, clothing and entertainment have decreased, but that home and auto maintenance expenses have gone up. Unfortunately, the fixed expenses such as rent, loan payments (those that weren't insured), property taxes and others won't go down. Your health insurance premiums may go up if you have to get new coverage.

## EXPENSE RECORDS FOR THE MONTH OF _____ 19 ___

| Category | Entry | | | | | | | Line Total |
|---|---|---|---|---|---|---|---|---|
| | *1* | *2* | *3* | *4* | *5* | *6* | *7* | |
| Food: | | | | | | | | |
|   groceries | | | | | | | | |
|   eating out | | | | | | | | |
| Housing: | | | | | | | | |
|   rent/mortgage | | | | | | | | |
|   water/heat/lights | | | | | | | | |
|   alarms/phone | | | | | | | | |
|   maint./repairs | | | | | | | | |
|   insurance | | | | | | | | |
|   property taxes | | | | | | | | |
| Clothing: | | | | | | | | |
|   purchases | | | | | | | | |
|   clean/repairs | | | | | | | | |
| Medical: | | | | | | | | |
|   insurance | | | | | | | | |
|   doctor/dentist | | | | | | | | |
|   prescription drugs | | | | | | | | |
| Transportation: | | | | | | | | |
|   gas | | | | | | | | |
|   auto repairs/maintenance | | | | | | | | |
|   tires/battery/etc. | | | | | | | | |
|   parking/bus | | | | | | | | |
| Education/development: | | | | | | | | |
|   tuition | | | | | | | | |
|   books, supplies | | | | | | | | |
|   organization dues | | | | | | | | |
|   subscriptions | | | | | | | | |
| Entertainment: | | | | | | | | |
|   tickets | | | | | | | | |
|   sports/hobbies | | | | | | | | |
|   travel | | | | | | | | |
|   toys | | | | | | | | |
| Other: | | | | | | | | |
|   beauty/sundries | | | | | | | | |
|   gifts | | | | | | | | |
|   charitable contributions | | | | | | | | |

Total Expenses for Month _____

### YOUR INCOME—SOURCES OF FUNDS

The next step is to determine all your sources of income, both monthly and periodic. Monthly income may include salary, wages, tips, survivor annuity payments, Social Security benefits, your own retirement payments, rent from tenants, etc. Periodic income may include interest from bonds, dividends from stocks, payments on debts due you, one-time benefits you may receive as beneficiary of your late husband's estate. Using a budget workbook, ledger sheets or ruled sheets, make rows and columns with headings similar to the following.

**SOURCES OF INCOME**

| Source | Monthly | Quarterly | Semi-Annual | Annual |
|---|---|---|---|---|
| Salary/Tips | | | | |
| Retirement Annuity | | | | |
| Social Security | | | | |
| Dividends | | | | |
| Interest | | | | |
| Bonds, CDs | | | | |
| Royalties | | | | |
| Other | | | | |
| | x12 | x4 | x2 | x1 |

Total Annual Income (TAI) _____

TAI/12 = Average Monthly Income = $ _____

### COMPARING INCOME TO EXPENSES

The next step is to compare income and expenses. This comparison shows whether your cash flow is positive or negative. If your monthly expenses are greater than your income, you will have to decide where to reduce your spending, or how to increase your income.

Eating meals at home costs about half that of eating out. Generic food products offered in the plain black and white packages offer wholesome nutrition without the more attractive but expensive brand-name labels.

To reduce housing costs, consider renting a room to a student (if zoning laws permit). Be sure to check references carefully before letting a stranger move into your home. Prepare a written contract with the terms and conditions for rental before admitting any boarder.

If you and your husband had two cars, consider selling one.

To reduce health insurance costs, if you're almost sixty-five, call your Social Security office and inquire how to enroll in the Medicare health plan. If you're younger, ask if you are eligible to continue health insurance coverage through your late husband's plan. Compare these costs to getting your own health insurance through a group. See Chapter 9 for detailed discussions on health insurance. Ask your bankers for advice on how to reduce expenses.

If you're fortunate enough that your monthly income exceeds your expenses, you will be able to consider savings or investments for your future. In Chapter 18, "Finance and Investments," we describe investment strategies.

## COMPLETING YOUR SPENDING PLAN

Now that you have examined how you typically spend your money and you have a sense of your future income, you can prepare a budget or household spending plan. This personal, informal document is for your use only. It is a plan or estimate of how much and where you will spend your resources. It is flexible; you can change it as many times as you wish. We illustrate with a sample budget below. You may customize yours to suit your circumstances. Notice that for simplicity we have used the categories as shown on the expenses worksheet.

**BUDGET PLAN FOR YEAR  FROM** _____ **TO** _____ **(DATES)**

Date Prepared: _____

| Category | Average Monthly Expenses Last Year | Available Expenditures This Year | Actual |
|---|---|---|---|
| Food: groceries, eating out | | | |
| Housing: rent/mortgage, water/heat/lights, alarms/phone, maint./repairs, insurance, property taxes | | | |
| Clothing: purchases, clean/repairs | | | |
| Medical: insurance, doctor/dentist, prescription drugs | | | |
| Transportation: gas, auto repairs/maintenance, tires/battery/etc., parking/bus | | | |
| Education/development: tuition, books, supplies, organization dues, subscriptions | | | |
| Entertainment: tickets, sports/hobbies, travel, toys | | | |
| Other: beauty/sundries, gifts, charitable contributions | | | |

After you have developed this plan, remember it is just a guide to help you stay in control of your finances. It isn't cast in concrete! If you overspend or "go over the budget" in any one category for a month, try to reduce your expenditures in another category to even things out. Look for categories in which you may not want to spend anything and shift those dollars to a preferred category. For example, if your husband attended several sporting events, the dollars spent for tickets could be moved to something you like, such as the theater.

If you need to economize, consider cutting back in the entertainment category. Finally, remember this is your personal plan and may be adjusted as you see fit, as often as you wish. Once you have a sense of where your resources are going, you may be able to monitor your budget plan in your head.

## Balancing Your Checkbook

If you have had your own checking accounts or been in charge of paying the household bills, you're probably familiar with "balancing" a checkbook. However, if your husband traditionally took care of the checkbooks and finances, this new responsibility may seem difficult and mysterious. Balancing a checkbook is simply reconciling the amount you believe you have in your account to the amount the bank statement says you have. We take you step by step through the process.

The first time Carol successfully completed a "balancing" after becoming a widow, she jubilantly cheered, "I did it! I did it!" During the years of their marriage, Carol's husband had traditionally balanched the checkbook each month, sometimes with frustration. Carol confesses that she did not volunteer to take over this tedious chore. But, when she had to, with strength and determination, Carol taught herself to reconcile her checkbook and the bank statement.

## Reading the Bank Statement

To begin, you'll need your checkbook and the most recent bank statement, which may include your cancelled checks. Study your bank statement. Each bank prints them in a slightly different format or arrangement. But essentially each statement should tell you:

• The dates for which the statement is prepared—including the date of the previous statement and this statement, and a summary of the deposits and withdrawals and the ending balance,
• The forward balance, or amount of money in your account as shown on last month's statement,
• The total amount of deposits,
• The total withdrawals, and
• The ending balance, or amount shown in your account, which does not include withdrawals and deposits made after the statement date.

The statement also shows each transaction that was made—that is, each check processed, each deposit, any interest earned, each automatic debit and any fees shown (by check number and date). It also may show some debits or charges you don't recognize, such as "monthly maintenance fee" or "service charge," which are bank fees for taking care of your account. If you have recently ordered new checks to be printed, the statement may not show to whom the amount was paid. The last balance shown should match the final or ending balance shown in the summary. This ending balance will almost always be different from the balance shown in your checkbook. We explain why in the "Balancing Procedures" to follow in this chapter.

**Reading Your Checkbook**

For this explanation, we must assume that all deposits made and checks written have been entered to the checkbook register, and that your final checkbook balance is different from the bank statement. If you haven't recorded the checks written to the register, you can complete your records when you receive the cancelled checks returned with your statement. Now you may proceed to balance your checkbook.

BALANCING PROCEDURES

The idea is to compare your checkbook register with the bank statement to be sure each entry is accurate and that the arithmetic is correct. In our illustration below we show first a sample "Check Register" followed by a simulated "Bank Statement."

1. Using the statement (shown on the following page), locate

PLEASE BE SURE TO **DEDUCT** ANY PER CHECK CHARGES OR SERVICE CHARGES THAT MAY APPLY TO YOUR ACCOUNT

| NUMBER | DATE | CHECKS ISSUED TO OR DESCRIPTION OF DEPOSIT | (−) AMOUNT OF CHECK | ✓ T | (−) CHECK FEE (IF ANY) | (+) AMOUNT OF DEPOSIT | BALANCE |
|---|---|---|---|---|---|---|---|
| | | | | | | | 478 96 |
| 29 | 9/3 | Safeway | 100 00 | ✓ | | | 100 00 |
| | | | | | | | 378 96 |
| 30 | 9/4 | Church | 20 00 | ✓ | | | 20 00 |
| | | | | | | | 358 96 |
| 31 | 5/6 | JC Penney Dress - wedding | 41 03 | | | | 41 03 |
| | | | | | | | 317 93 |
| dep | 5/6 | Social Security - May | | ✓ | | 594 28 | 594 28 |
| | | | | | | | 912 21 |
| 32 | 5/6 | Farmers Insurance Ford - premium | 145 10 | ✓ | | | 145 10 |
| | | | | | | | 767 11 |
| 33 | 5/10 | Sprint telephone | 85 42 | ✓ | | | 85 42 |
| | | | | | | | 681 69 |
| — | | | | | | | — |
| 34 | 5/15 | Amoco | 12 00 | | | | 12 00 |
| | | | | | | | 669 69 |
| 35 | 5/21 | Safeway | 100 00 | ✓ | | | 100 00 |
| | | | | | | | 569 69 |
| 36 | 5/21 | Fuller Brush | 11 43 | | | | 11 43 |
| | | | | | | | 558 26 |
| dep | 5/29 | Pay | | | | 689 22 | 689 22 |
| | | | | | | | 1247 48 |
| | 5/30 | Loan payment #47 | 20 00 | ✓ | | | 20 00 |
| | | | | | | | 1227 48 |
| | 5/30 | Service Charge May | 3 00 | ✓ | | | 3 00 |
| | | | | | | | 1224 48 |
| | 5/29 | Interest | | ✓ | | 5 61 | 5 61 |
| | | | | | | | 1230 09 |

REMEMBER TO RECORD AUTOMATIC PAYMENTS / DEPOSITS ON DATE AUTHORIZED.

the item "Service Charge. . . $3.00." Enter this to your checkbook as a debit and subtract it from your balance. Repeat this step for the automatically deducted "Loan Payment . . . $20.00." Be sure to enter $5.61 for interest earned on this account.

2. Proceed through the itemized descriptions showing every withdrawal or debit, then locate the matching entry in your check register. Verify that the amount shown on the statement entry is identical to what you've written in your register. Correct any

errors. Indicate each match with a small check mark in the space provided on the register.

3. Repeat the matching process for each deposit or credit.

4. Compare the statement ending balance to the balance shown in your checkbook. Usually they are different. On rare occasions, when the checking account has not been used for some time before the statement date, the checks you wrote and deposits you received will already have been processed, and the balances will match.

In our example below, notice that three checks have not yet cleared—numbers 31, 34 and 36. They were not shown on the statement, therefore on the statement it appears we haven't yet spent that money. Notice also that the "Salary" deposit in the register dated May 29 is not shown on the statement. It wasn't processed in time for this statement.

**BANK STATEMENT**

| Jane Doe | | Check Account No.      12345 | | |
| 1234 Any Street | | Social Security No.      123-45-6789 | | |
| Anytown, USA 00000 | | Statement Date May 30, 1987 | | |

| Date | Description | Withdrawals | Deposits | Balance |
| --- | --- | --- | --- | --- |
| | *Item* | *beginning balance 4/30/87* | | 478.96 |
| 5/03 | Check 029 | 100.00 | | 378.96 |
| 5/04 | Check 030 | 20.00 | | 358.96 |
| 5/06 | Check 032* | 145.10 | | 213.86 |
| 5/06 | Deposit | | 594.28 | 808.14 |
| 5/10 | Check 033 | 85.42 | | 722.72 |
| 5/18 | Loan Pymt | 20.00 | | 702.72 |
| 5/21 | Check 035* | 100.00 | | 602.72 |
| 5/29 | Interest | | 5.61 | 608.33 |
| 5/30 | Service Charge | 3.00 | | 605.33 |
| Ending Totals | | 473.52 | 599.89 | 605.33 |

(*indicates break in number sequence)

To balance our checkbook with the bank statement, use the space provided on the back of the bank statement. Subtract the total of outstanding checks from the statement ending balance, and add the deposits not credited. The total should equal the balance of your checkbook.

Our sample check register and simulated bank statement are balanced. However, if you have problems balancing your own checkbook, consider the following "if" scenarios. They may help you understand the difference between the bank statement balance and what is in your check register.

## WHAT IF THE BALANCING DOESN'T WORK?

- If your checkbook register shows a smaller balance than the bank statement, it is likely that you have written checks to be paid from your account which have not yet been processed by your bank, and cannot be found on this printed bank statement. To reconcile this example, on the reverse of the statement, note your register balance and add to it the total of all checks that have not been processed or cleared, no matter how long ago they were written. In this example we noticed that three checks had not cleared through the bank, even though the checks were written a few weeks earlier. Often club dues or gift checks take a long time to be processed because the recipient may not deposit the check for months.
- If your balance is greater than the bank statement, it is possible that you have made a recent deposit, probably on or since the date the statement was prepared. And although the deposit is shown in your register, it doesn't show on the bank statement. You should see this deposit on next month's statement. Meanwhile, you have to subtract any deposits not shown on the statement from your register balance using the form on the back of your statement. Notice that in our example the "Salary" deposit on May 29 is entered in our register, but not shown on the statement. To get the bank statement balance to agree with our checkbook, we subtracted the unprocessed checks to Amoco, Fuller Brush and J.C. Penney, totaling $64.46, from the bank statement balance of $605.33, as well as adding the recent deposit of $689.22.
- If your checkbook total still doesn't agree or "balance" with the bank statement, review the statement for service fees, check printing charges or automatic debits such as payments to the utility company, loan payments, insurance premiums, etc., that are periodically deducted. Enter these to the check register and subtract them to get your new balance.

• If the two totals still don't match or balance, look for arithmetic errors. Did you inadvertently subtract a deposit? If the difference between the two balances is say, $30, an easy way to discover the error is to look for a deposit of $15 that was subtracted, which doubles the error!

The "balancing" procedure is to reconcile the bank statement with your personal checkbook records. In summary, the ending balance shown on the statement, minus the total value of outstanding checks not processed as of the statement date, plus recent deposits not shown on the statement, should equal your checkbook balance. It is not confusing when you realize the bank statement lags behind your records. When entering checks to your register, be careful to record to whom each is paid and for what, and be accurate with the amount. Balance your checkbook each month. Getting behind only compounds the likelihood of an error, and the more entries to match, the greater the effort.

## Your Credit

When your husband was alive, you may have used bank and credit cards based on his earning ability and long-time credit rating. "Bank" cards are multi-use charge cards issued by financial institutions, such as Mastercard, VISA, American Express, Diners Club and others. "Credit" cards are usually issued by specific corporations for use in only their stores. Examples include AT&T, Sears, Roebuck and Co. and oil companies. Now that you are a widow you may be concerned about paying the monthly statements and continuing to use your husband's credit and bank cards. What should you do now that he's gone? Will the financial institutions or shops cancel or reduce your credit if they know you are a widow?

## Notifying Creditors of Your Husband's Death

There are no hard and fast rules about how your credit will be affected now that you're on your own. It may make sense to notify each of your husband's creditors of his death. If the accounts were insured, the outstanding balance will be paid. Furthermore, if your husband died in an accident involving travel, and his ticket was purchased using a major bank card, he might have been covered by a life insurance policy. He might not have been aware of the coverage. The creditors may require a copy of the death certificate.

Some companies will allow you to keep the credit card, but

will reduce the monthly maximum limit that can be charged. They are aware that a widow's monthly income usually drops and are concerned about her ability to pay her bills, specifically theirs! In most cases, the financial institution or department store will ask you to apply for credit based on your own sources of income. One major financial institution advertises that it will help a widow maintain credit that was established by her husband, yet other companies may cancel credit after they are notified of the husband's death.

Some women, through inaction, simply do nothing and continue paying the bills as though their husband were still alive. The risk is that if any accounts were insured, they lose those benefits. And while the widow continues to pay the bills, the good credit rating continues to apply to her late husband. He no longer needs it, but she may!

**Changing Account Billings to Your Name**

In small communities where the widow is known by the business community, there is probably little need to change account billings to her name. However, in large urban areas the telephone and utility companies, as well as businesses, will be unaware that there are any changes in who is responsible for paying your accounts. When Carol needed to begin telephone service for her college sons in a nearby town, she had to pay a large security deposit even though as a widow she had regularly paid her bills on time for years. Carol had neglected to change the billing name from her late husband's name to hers and had not been establishing any credit history for herself.

In some cases a phone call or letter will suffice. Offer to provide a copy of the death certificate if required. Often a photocopy will do. Don't be surprised if some creditors are indifferent about whose name is on the billing, so long as they receive timely payments. It only makes a difference to you—if you want a credit payment history in your own name!

**Establishing Credit in Your Own Name**

It is to your advantage to apply for credit in your own name. The credit rating companies and private corporations evaluate your ability to repay them based on all your sources of funds compared to your monthly living expenses. Although your monthly income may be down, monthly expenses should also decrease somewhat.

When you apply for credit or a loan, you will be expected to complete an application form detailing your employment history (if applicable), all your sources of income and any assets you own. Then you list all your obligations—mortgage or rent, loan payments, average utility bills, average monthly balance on other charge or credit cards, age and model of your cars (you may need a new one, which is another expensive commitment) and so forth.

To get an idea of what is required, call your bank and ask for a standard *Consumer Credit Application* form. Once you have completed the form, make photocopies and attach a copy to each creditor's specific application form. Be sure to update the information as changes occur.

Once you have received credit cards in your own name, you should try to make your payments on time. This is your opportunity to demonstrate your financial management skills. If possible, pay your entire balance each month, as the interest rates on the outstanding balance are high. When using your cards, make sure they are returned. A good strategy is to keep your wallet or purse awkwardly opened as a reminder until you put the card away. Ask for the carbons and rip them apart so your card number can't be copied. Carol had the misfortune to have one of her credit card numbers fraudulently used when someone copied the information from a carbon found in the trash!

Review your monthly statements carefully to make sure you recognize the charges. If not, call for an explanation.

Photocopy all your bank and credit cards for a permanent record of their numbers. Store the copy with your important papers. Major bank cards offer insurance covering up to specified limits if fraudently used. You may want to insure your cards against loss or theft. Most companies have twenty-four-hour, toll-free numbers for assistance if the cards are missing or you have billing questions.

These initial encounters with your new and probably confusing financial concerns may seem overwhelming. You needn't deal with your budget, your checkbook and your credit all at one time. If you have some cash to tide you over and someone to help you, wait a month or so before you begin worrying about managing finances. Then deal with one thing at a time—first comparing your income to expenses, then learning how to balance your checkbook, and last getting a credit rating and changing the billing names on accounts.

# Chapter 11

# *Your Auto and Home— Care and Maintenance*

Along with your emotional well-being, your finances and your health, you may now also have to care for your home and car. In many marriages the husband and wife divided the tasks according to their interests—auto and home maintenance for him, the housekeeping for her. Even though the widow may not do her own auto or home maintenance, she needs to be able to intelligently compare what she is getting with what she pays. In addition to keeping up with maintenance chores, she needs to understand her auto and home insurance. For example, do you know how to reduce auto insurance premiums or what to do in case of an accident? Do you know if your home or condominium is insured for "full replacement cost" or "actual cash value," and the difference between these kinds of insurance? This chapter describes different features of auto and home insurance coverage, and why you may want to review your existing policies.

**Auto Care and Maintenance**

There are two reasons you need to be concerned about auto care. First, *you can't afford to risk your personal safety with an auto breakdown because you failed to pay attention to the car's maintenance needs!* Second, even if you have family members or friends who will perform maintenance chores for you, you will probably have to pay for the repair parts and any professional service that is required.

Sometimes in the past, and to some extent even now, women have been taken advantage of and occasionally "ripped off" on auto care. This chapter provides you with some simple guidance and a checklist for taking care of your car and of any of your children who may drive. You can quickly learn the basics about the "what" and "how often" of car maintenance and repairs without mastering the theory of how and why every component of a car works the way it does. For a woman on her own we suggest three alternatives for auto care:

- The simplest is to let someone else, such as a family member or friend, take care of your car. That person can recommend what maintenance chores need to be done or can actually perform them. Some dealerships offer scheduled maintenance checkups for preferred customers. This method works well for the older woman.
- A second choice is to be your own mechanic. In that case, we don't attempt to tell you how to do repairs.
- The third choice is for you to understand what parts and functions of your car need to be monitored, and then to decide if you want to perform the simple tasks or take it to a service station or mechanic and let them do it. You still need to know how *frequently* to check your car's functioning systems. The list on page 119 describes frequent maintenance chores that are easy to learn and do.

**How Often and What to Do**

The following paragraphs describe in more detail how to do some record keeping, checking, maintenance and *what to be aware of* in your car's performance. This list is simplified and general. Refer to your owner's manual for scheduled routine maintenance. By consistently purchasing gasoline at one service station, you may become a preferred customer who can ask questions and request instructions.

Keep a small notebook in your glove box and and use it to record every time you fill the car with gas (optional), each time you change oil, have chassis lubrication, rotate or change tires, or have any maintenance or repairs done. Use the mileage as a guide or "tickler file" for the next time a particular maintenance function is

| TASK | FREQUENCY |
|---|---|
| Record keeping | As needed. In a small notebook, record gasoline purchases; oil changes; lubrication; mileage when tires are rotated, balanced, aligned or changed; list all repairs, including mileage at time of service. |
| Oil | Weekly. Check level. Should be full. Use full-service island at station and let attendant check level or check yourself.<br><br>Every 3,000 to 7,500 miles change oil and filter. |
| Coolant | Monthly. Check fluid level when motor is cool. Should be at "full when cold" mark. |
| Tires | Weekly. Visually inspect for wear.<br>Monthly. Check air pressure.<br>About twice a year. Rotate, balance and realign if necessary. |
| Lights and wipers | Weekly. Visually inspect for wear and cleanliness. |
| Brakes | Occasionally. Listen for squeaking or unusual noises when braking.<br><br>At 30,000 to 50,000 miles, reline or replace. |

required. The Textron Company has developed *At a Glance Auto Record* notebooks for sale in auto and office supply stores.[17]

Whether you purchase an auto record notebook or create your own, in one place note pertinent information such as (1) brand and weight of oil normally used in your car, (2) tire pressure and size, (3) month for annual inspection stickers if required in your state, (4) month for license registration renewal and (5) month(s) for auto insurance renewal. Some states issue citations for not having up-to-date inspection stickers, or proof of insurance and registration in case of an accident. An example for organizing your own notebook might include the following headings:

| DATE | ODOMETER | ITEM | AMOUNT |
|---|---|---|---|
| 4-17-87 | 28,964 | 16.8 gal. | $16.42 |
| 4-17-87 | " " | 1 qt. oil | 3.48 |
| 4-23-87 | 33,701 | mount, balance 2 tires | 10.00 |

**Self–Service Tasks**

- Gas—Pump your own to save money, or use the full service and ask the attendant to check fluid levels, tire pressure and the battery.
- Oil—Oil lubricates and cools the moving metal parts inside the car's engine. Check the level weekly or at each fill-up. If you don't know how, ask the service station attendant to check it or instruct you. If oil needs to be added, use the same weight and, if possible, the same brand as is already there. Most auto manufacturers recommend you change the oil and oil filter about every 3,000 to 7,500 miles. Look in your owner's manual for specific instructions for your car and driving conditions. A car can't be driven indefinitely without adding oil! In your small notebook record each time the oil is changed so you can plan ahead for the next required change.
- Tires—It used to be you could tell if your tires were low on air (they bulged a little at the sidewalls), but today's steel-belted radials are supposed to bulge and always look a little low.

Different brands and sizes of tires require different amounts of air. If you don't know how much, read the sidewall of your tire. In small print it will say something like "MAX LOAD 635 kg (1400 lbs) at 240 kps (35 PSI) MAX INFL." This means that the maximum safe air pressure is thirty-five pounds per square inch when your tires are cold, as shown by the "35 PSI" figure. Don't overinflate them! Properly inflated tires, in good condition, will assist with safe driving by reducing the risk of a flat tire. They will also last longer.

To check the tire pressure, go to a full-service station and ask the attendant to do it for you or show you how to check and inflate them yourself. You can buy a pressure gauge at an auto parts store. Keep tires inflated to the recommended pressure. (Rotate and balance them about every 5,000 miles, or as recommended by the tire manufacturer. Get the front end realigned about twice a year.)

Examine the tires' tread and sidewalls each time you inflate them. Cracks, bulges and uneven wear are dangerous. The tread should look about the same across the width of the tire. If the tread is worn unevenly the tires could be over- or underinflated or out of balance. Again, ask the attendant to help you understand this.

To check the "tread depth" you can use a tread gauge or simply insert a penny edgewise with Lincoln's head in an upside down position in the space between the tread ridges. Looking across the tread at the penny, if any of Lincoln's forehead is showing, you don't have enough tread. On a tire with sufficient tread, typically one-third to almost half the penny will disappear from view.

Tires rarely get the full mileage advertised! Poor balancing and improper alignment accelerate tire wear. If you have to make the purchase decision for new tires, first read the sidewall of the tire to see what size you need. The size reads something like "P195/75R14." Look in the sporting goods section of your newspaper for tire sale advertisements. Once you decide to buy the tires, you will have to pay for mounting the tires on wheel rims, getting them balanced and aligned, then put on the car.

• Coolant—This is the antifreeze-water mixture in the radiator that cools your engine in summer and keeps it from freezing in winter. In the newer cars you can look in the plastic overflow reservoir to see if the coolant level is up to the "full hot" or "full cold" mark. Add coolant to the overflow reservoir.

• Lights and wipers—Check to see if they all work and are clean. Keep the wiper fluid reservoir filled. If the rubber wiper blades are worn or cracked, replace them.

There are several other maintenance requirements for your car, such as getting tune-ups, cleaning battery connections, checking rubber belts for cracks and wear, and flushing the coolant system. The owner's manual that came with your car will outline the most common maintenance requirements. Otherwise you have to trust your mechanic or auto dealer's repair department. It is very helpful to talk with numerous "car buffs" who are proficient at doing their own repairs for ideas about problems your car may have.

**Emergency
Supplies**

A woman traveling on the road should always keep some emergency supplies in her trunk. These include an extra quart of oil, a flashlight that works, Phillip's head and flathead screwdrivers, pliers and an adjustable wrench. If you choose not to do this, at least get towing insurance or join an auto club for emergency help in case your car is disabled. Large auto parts stores sell emergency supply kits with battery cables for jump starts, an emergency triangle, flare, flat-tire inflators, etc.

At all times keep up-to-date proof of auto registration and insurance with you. Also include the auto insurance company's instructions about what to do in case of an accident. The whole idea is that now *you* are in charge and in control of your autos!

**Auto Insurance**

Almost daily you or your family members are likely to be driving a car, usually on your own. Do you know what your auto insurance covers? Do you know how to save money on your auto insurance? Do you know what to do in case of an accident? Do you know that in many states auto insurance is compulsory—you can't get or renew your operator's license without evidence of insurance? The following discussion of auto insurance covers elementary language, typical categories of coverage, reducing premium costs, and what to do in case of an accident. Our suggestions are general, since auto insurance requirements vary widely from state to state. Ask your insurance agent or broker for specific guidance.

There are six auto insurance elements to consider, depending on what state you live in. We define each element and discuss the necessity or benefit to having more or less coverage in each case. You can purchase insurance for "named" persons only or for your family as a whole. If you have teenagers and college students driving cars that you own, you may want to consider "family" insurance.

**Elements of
Coverage**

LIABILITY

Most insurance companies list liability as the most important element requiring coverage. If you are driving your car, have an accident and cause injury to another person or property, you could be sued and, if found guilty, financially responsible or "liable" for paying all the other person's legal and medical expenses. Without insurance, this could be an economic disaster.

Liability is covered in two separate ways—for injury to a person and for damage to property. There are maximum limits that will be paid for each bodily injury and each accident. Ask your agent to explain them. You may want to have the maximum liability coverage, which in some states pays up to $300,000 per person and $500,000 total for each accident. The property liability should be about $50,000 to cover today's more expensive cars. Years ago cars cost under $5,000, but now you may hit a limousine!

## NO-FAULT

No-fault means that if you have this coverage on your auto insurance (available in some states), your own insurance company may pay for the damage sustained in an accident when fault or blame is not determined. If you live in a no-fault state, your own liability insurance covers you no matter who is at fault for the accident. It also may pay something toward loss of income for a specified number of weeks. Coverages vary widely from state to state, so make sure you understand the limits of the policy before you buy.

## COLLISION

Collision insurance pays for damage to your car (when it collides with something) regardless of who is at fault. If you are not financing your car and the car is more than four years old, consider choosing a high deductible amount in order to save on the premiums.

A deductible is a set amount that is automatically subtracted from a loss amount before payment is made, and becomes a part of the loss absorbed by the policyholder. Here is how the "deductible" works: if you have a $50 deductible clause, you pay the first $50 of expense on the claim, then the insurance company pays the rest. A higher deductible clause in your insurance policy means a lower premium rate. For instance, a $100 deductible clause may cost about $20 less per year than a $50 deductible plan. A $200 deductible may save you a lot of money, assuming you have only a rare accident. Ask your agent to figure the differences for you.

## COMPREHENSIVE

Comprehensive coverage pays you for losses on your car—other than collision—including fire, theft, lightning, glass breakage, windstorm, hail, earthquake, explosion, flood, riot and vandalism. Usually a deductible applies. If your car is relatively new, you should have this coverage. Some authorities recommend dropping comprehensive insurance on cars more than four years old. If you have an expensive stereo or other visible electronic equipment in your car (no matter how old the car is), protect it with the comprehensive coverage. Homeowner's insurance rarely covers the loss of auto stereos and tape decks in your car.

## UNINSURED OR UNDERINSURED

Uninsured or underinsured coverage protects you in case you suffer bodily injury from a hit-and-run driver, or from an uninsured or underinsured driver whose insurance does not cover all your expenses. It also covers your family members riding in someone else's car, or if they are injured as pedestrians. It covers each person in your car, with a maximum limit for the entire accident. Some major auto insurance companies separate the coverage for uninsured and underinsured. In this case, coverage of $100,000 per person and $300,000 per accident isn't too high, considering the cost of medical care today.

## MEDICAL PAYMENTS

Medical payments coverage pays medical expenses for you or your passengers in an accident, no matter who was at fault. One major company calls this personal injury protection. It is different from liability, because you collect from your own insurance company without having to prove the other party was negligent. It also covers everyone riding in your car and your family members injured as pedestrians.

## OPTIONAL COVERAGE

Towing insurance is inexpensive and worthwhile coverage. If your car is disabled, you'll need to have it towed. Some companies include this with comprehensive insurance. You may have to pay cash or write a check to the tow truck, but your insurance company will reimburse you. There are additional optional coverages, such as accidental death and dismemberment, and your agent will be more than happy to present these to you. Just be sure that, as a vulnerable person, you don't buy more than you need! You can add options later.

Now that you are considering auto insurance, there are ways to save money and still have adequate coverage. First, shop around or work with an independent agent who represents several companies. Compare prices and methods of settling claims between two or three companies. Ask which factors will reduce your premiums; for example, some companies offer "good student discounts" for teenagers who have good grades, or a reduction in premiums for students who took driver's education.

**Reducing Auto Insurance Premiums**

If you are insuring a high-risk driver, such as a son under twenty-five years old or any person with a poor driving record, your agent may suggest insuring him or her, under a separate policy.

Ask about a reduction in premiums if you insure more than one car with the company. This is called a multiple car discount. Let your agent know if you haven't had any accidents, because you may be eligible for a good driver discount. You may be entitled to a discount if you are a non-smoker, non-drinker, senior citizen or belong to a car pool.

Consider increasing the deductible amounts you pay on comprehensive and collision coverage. If your car is more than four years old and depreciated, you may want to drop the collision coverage.

If you are paying your insurance premiums in monthly installments, consider making annual or semi-annual payments instead. There is often a service charge added to monthly payment plans. Most companies will allow twice-a-year premium payments without charging you extra.

In addition to buying auto insurance, you have to keep evidence of this insurance in the car or in your purse in case of an accident. We suggest keeping an envelope with the registration and insur-

**Keeping Track of Auto Insurance and Registration**

ance card in the glove box, or in your wallet if you are the only one who drives the car. In case you forget to pay the renewal premium on time, most companies extend coverage for a thirty-day grace period. During the grace period your insurance is still good, but after that your policy could be cancelled.

## What to Do in Case of an Accident

Immediately following an accident, drivers who are able to walk usually jump out to survey the damage and make accusations about whose fault it was. Others simply sit in their cars until the police arrive. In either case, if no one is injured and if you or your passengers are able to talk and are reasonably aware of what has happened, you will want to record your own version of the accident. *Don't admit any fault or accuse the other party.* Give your statement only to the police. If police are not involved, exchange information, not blame, with the other driver. Immediately report the accident to your insurance agent, no matter how minor it is. The other party may later decide he or she has injuries, and your failure to report the accident to your insurance company could void your insurance.

If no police are involved, as is sometimes the case during snow and ice storms in which minor "fender bender" accidents occur, you need to protect yourself by making your own observations and recordings. You don't know anything about the honesty of the other driver. If you get erroneous information, you may never be able to collect any damage award from the driver at fault. Following are examples of accident recording cards that you can prepare to have available in your glove box; five-by eight-inch index cards will serve well.

Even when the police make a report, you may want to make notes about the accident to have for referral when you telephone your agent. The police forms may not cover all the information needed by your agent. Remember, you are usually upset following an accident, and sometimes cannot remember later which issues are important. Be sure to complete information about the other car first and your car last.

Perhaps you will suffer nothing more serious than a cracked windshield, which, while it may not be critical, will have to be replaced at a later date through your comprehensive coverage. Use

## OTHER CAR—ACCIDENT NOTES (complete first)

Today's Date _____ Time of Accident _____ a.m. _____ p.m.

Car License No. _____ State _____

Accident Location (hwy no., intersection, mile marker) _____

_____

Weather/Driving Conditions (clear, rain, fog, ice, snow, sun) _____

Make _____ Model _____ Yr _____ Color _____

1. Registered Owner Name _____ Phone _____

Address _____ City _____ State ____ Zip _____

Injured _____ Y/N _____

2. Driver Name _____ Driver License No. _____ State _____

Address _____ City _____ State ____ Zip _____

Injured _____ Y/N _____

3. Auto Insurance Co._____

Policy No. _____

Agent _____ Phone _____

Address _____ City _____ State ____ Zip _____

4. Other Passenger Name _____ Phone _____

Address _____ City _____ State ____ Zip _____

Injured _____ Y/N _____

5. Witness Name _____ Phone _____

Address _____ City _____ State ____ Zip _____

(enter accident notes and sketches on reverse)

## ACCIDENT NOTES—MY CAR (complete last)

Today's Date _____ Time of Accident _____ a.m. _____ p.m.

1. Accident Location (hwy no., intersection, mile marker)_____

Weather/Driving Conditions(clear, rain, fog, ice, snow, sun) _____

2. My Car Make _____ Model _____ Yr _____

My Auto License No. _____

3. Driver Name _____ Phone _____

Driver License No. _____ State _____

Address _____ City _____ State _____ Zip _____

Injured _____ Y/N _____

4. Passenger Name _____ Phone _____

Address _____ City _____ State _____ Zip _____

Injured _____ Y/N _____

5. Garage Location (if towed)_____

6. Towing Company _____ Phone _____

Receipt for Amount _____ Y/N _____

7. Witness Name _____ Phone _____

Address _____ City _____ State _____ Zip _____

Notify In Case of Accident _____

Phone _____

Health Insurance/Doctor _____ Phone _____

(Enter accident notes and sketches on reverse. Notify your agent immediately) the card "Accident Notes: My Car" (page 128) to record all the information for submitting your claim to your insurance company.

In exchanging information with the other driver about his or her car, be sure to make your own observations, and always ask to read his or her operator's license and auto insurance card yourself. Jot the numbers down. Don't take their word for it. Look on the back of the driver's license for a change of address.

Most widows stay in their homes for several years, if they can afford it. At some point you will probably need home repairs or mainte- nance. Do you know how to find reliable, expert repair help? Do you know what kinds of damage or loss are covered by your homeowner's insurance? In this section we suggest how to locate good repair persons and how to review your home and property insurance.

**Home Maintenance**

We assume that your late husband ordinarily took care of most of the repairs and general upkeep of your home—or at least he knew whom to call on for help. And we assume that now you may not always have someone at hand who has the time and skills to willingly perform routine maintenance. Now that this home is your responsibility, you should be aware of the following general areas of concern:

- Appliances,
- Heating and air conditioning systems,
- Plumbing,
- Electrical and gas systems,
- Water and sewer,
- Outside plants and lawn,
- Condition of the exterior finish of the house and
- Roof, gutters and chimney.

Because homes vary so widely, we will direct you to some helpful references and techniques that have worked well for us. You can call your local public service utility company to ask if they make repairs to major appliances, as well as heating, air condition- ing and gas systems. When you call anyone for repairs, they will need to know what type or brand and model of system you have. Ask a neighbor or friend to show you how to find the model numbers. Record them in a "master notebook" for home maintenance. Keep this notebook in one place, along with the instruction manuals for appliances, tools and equipment, and receipts for repairs you have recently had completed. Use these receipts to refer to later; they will help in deciding whether to use the same repair service again.

To get advice about the lawn, shrubs and trees, try calling your local county extension agent listed in the government blue pages in the phone directory, or call a local garden shop. Neighbors with attractive landscaping are usually happy to share their experiences and references with you.

In our experience, two reference books have been especially helpful—the *Reader's Digest Complete Do-It-Yourself Manual*[18] and the *Fix-It-Yourself Manual*.[19] Learning about maintenance chores may not be exciting, but at least you get to visit with your neighbors and friends and learn something new. Most important you will gain control of another part of your life.

## Homeowner's Insurance

Your home is usually your most valuable asset, and the need for insurance protection is obvious. What if there is a fire, theft, vandalism or someone just trips and falls on your property, claiming it's your fault. Nowadays, with everyone "lawsuit-minded" and with burglaries on the rise, you can't afford to be without home insurance. If your late husband arranged your present insurance, you now need to understand what is insured and, more important, what is excluded!

As Stephen Mink reminds us in *Insuring Your Home*, "Legislators are forever making laws that affect the insurance industry. . . . Policies are revised, updated, and changed without the knowledge of consumers. . . . Then when notification of such a change is made, the policyholder may put the new policy in a drawer somewhere assuming that it is the same as the old one, when it is in fact different."[20]

You need to consider how much insurance is enough—yet not too much—for your circumstances. Widows may feel especially insecure and vulnerable. Don't let an agent or broker talk you into changes until you understand clearly how much more it will cost and what you are getting for what you are paying! A good agent will appreciate your concerns.

In the following section we briefly discuss costs of home-owner's insurance, describe general types of insurance coverage and review how to read and understand a policy.

As with other kinds of insurance, homeowner's insurance costs and coverages differ tremendously. Talk with friends and neighbors about their insurance companies, how satisfied they are and what kind of results they have had when claims were submitted. You want a company that handles claims in a timely manner, and an agent or broker who takes time to answer questions or discuss policy changes. An *agent* usually represents a particular insurance company and sells insurance for that company. A *broker*, on the other hand, represents the buyer and will obtain insurance for you from any one of several insurance companies.

**Costs and Shopping for Homeowner's Insurance**

Your insurance costs may be lower if you qualify as a "preferred risk." For example, if you live in a well-maintained neighborhood, relatively close to fire protection, and your former insurance claim history is good, you are preferred because you seem to be a lower risk for a future claim. Installing smoke detectors and burglar alarm systems should reduce your premiums. Another cost-reducing strategy is to increase the deductible amounts for certain coverages.

TYPE OF COVERAGE

Every state has different insurance regulations, and each insurance company may offer different types of insurance. The coverage types that are reviewed below are general categories. Ask your insurance agent or broker for specific guidance for your area. We discuss two types of insurance coverage, including four standard policies.

*Named peril* insurance coverage protects property from specific or named perils listed in the policy. Examples include windstorm, hail, lightning, theft, vandalism, aircraft, riots and fire.

- The *basic* policy, under named peril coverage, offers the lowest cost and most limited coverage. Your dwelling and personal property are insured for losses due to only "named perils" as specified in the policy.
- The *broad* policy covers additional named perils, such as

ice and snow damage, falling objects and sometimes steam or water damage, electrical equipment failure and collapse.

*All risk* coverage protects your dwelling and other structures on your land against all risks not specifically excluded in the policy.
  • The *comprehensive* all risk policy insures losses for the dwelling, structures and personal property *except for* damage from specified exclusions such as flood, sewer backups, tidal waves, earthquakes, war and other extreme instances. It is usually the most expensive coverage.
  • The *special form* policy features a combination of the comprehensive coverage for the dwelling and other structures on the land, but is limited to "broad form" coverage for personal property.

LEVEL OF COVERAGE

Besides the standard policy features, you must decide on the level of coverage, either "full replacement cost" or "actual cash value," for buildings and personal property. These terms describe methods of valuing your property for insurance purposes, that is, the amount the policy will pay for insured property that is damaged by a covered peril.
  *Full replacement cost* pays for the full cost of repair or replacement of the damaged property, without deducting for depreciation. When a claim is approved, a cash settlement may not be taken in lieu of the replacement or actual repairs made.
  *Actual cash value* generally pays for the actual cost of replacing your lost property (house), minus its physical depreciation. *Most policies cover actual cash value, unless full replacement cost is specified.* Although this insurance can be 20 to 30 percent cheaper than full replacement cost insurance, the depreciated value on older property could be considerably less than today's cost of repairing the damages. For personal property, actual cash value is also based on replacement costs less depreciation.

**Inventorying Your Property**

When you initially purchase homeowner's insurance or update your existing policy, a complete inventory will help you get the appropriate amount of insurance and will be invaluable in case of a loss. When Carol's sister-in-law suffered a disastrous home fire, she couldn't recall all of their possessions, and her insurance claim was not as complete as it could have been. Carol recommends an inventory strategy of taking photographs of all your personal property. Open all cupboards, closets and bureau drawers. Photograph each room, including all the furniture and wall hangings, tools, sporting goods and collectibles. Then store the photos in a safe place *away* from your home, perhaps in your safe deposit box.

Most widows have an existing homeowner's insurance policy that covers loss and damage to the dwelling and to personal property, loss of use of the dwelling, and liability and medical payments for personal injuries. The policy describes what is included, states limits of coverage, lists deductible amounts and, more important, describes what is excluded.

**Reading Your Policy— What It Means**

- The premium notice lists who is insured, the location of the property, the effective dates and who pays the premiums. Additionally, it shows amounts of coverages, limits, options and endorsements (also called floaters). It should state if the level of coverage is full replacement cost.
- Within the policy, coverage A includes the residential premises and may include certain other structures, materials and supplies.
- Coverage B may refer to other buildings or personal property, depending on your insurance company. For discussion, coverage B refers to personal property. Personal property generally includes clothing and furniture. Coverage on these "contents" is typically limited to no more than 50 percent of the value of the dwelling coverage. If you want additional coverage, you must get a "floater" or separate policy.

Coverage B always has limits on furs, jewelry, coins and cash, etc. Ordinarily these items are limited to only a few hundred dollars per group per claim. If you have furs or jewelry worth thousands of dollars, you may want a separate floater policy.
- Coverage C describes how you will be compensated if you can't use your residence because it was damaged.
- Liability coverages are for paying claims for injuries sustained by other people on your property. Virtually all homeowner's policies include liability insurance, generally

up to $100,000. However, if you are affluent or have extensive assets, someone may be inclined to sue you. If you have a pet that could injure someone, you should consider increasing your liability insurance either through your homeowner's policy or by a separate Umbrella Liability Policy. Ask your agent about qualifying for an umbrella policy and additional costs associated with it.

## Condominium Owners and Renters

If you rent your home or own a condominium or if you are going to sell your present house and rent or buy a condominium, you should consider insurance to cover your personal property and the interior fixtures and furnishings of your apartment. As a condominium or townhouse owner you are responsible for the interior fixtures and furnishings and personal liability as well as your personal belongings. A renter is responsible for personal property and liability. Condominium (homeowner) associations usually insure only the common areas.

## Keeping or Selling Your Home

Widows are typically advised to stay put in their homes for the first year at least. It is assumed that during this stressful and emotional time a person could make a hasty and unwise decision. In Carol's work with a townhome construction firm, she met Ethel, a widow of only three months with a large beautiful home in a nearby state. Ethel was determined to sell her home filled with memories and buy a small townhome in a city where she knew no one. Few women are emotionally prepared to make a major move so early in their widowhood.

Charlotte was widowed while living on the East Coast, and within the first month had to move her family back to Denver, where she owned a home that was temporarily rented. She was so distressed to return to that home full of memories, that for a year she refused to finish unpacking or hang pictures on the wall. She thought she wanted to move some place new and begin new memories. Now, after four years of staying put, she and her children feel happy that they stayed in their old neighborhood.

Staying put may not work for everyone. You simply may not be able to afford the upkeep or monthly mortgage payments now that your husband is gone. The house may be entirely too large and costly to operate or too remote for a woman alone. Whatever the reason, should you decide you have to sell your home and move, we offer some pointers to help you select and work with a real estate agent. We also include a few tips to help you make your home more attractive to a potential buyer.

**Working with a Real Estate Agency**

Selling your home through a real estate agency brings expert skills and market visibility to your property. A real estate agent is trained to list your home for sale at a price likely to be attractive to the market in your area. Furthermore, an agent can point out features that make your home desirable and unique, as well as point out deficiencies that you may want to correct. There are three steps to selling your home that you are required to initiate. First, you must decide whether you want to work with a real estate agent, and if so, choose an agent. Then you must get the property ready to sell. Finally, you must price your home so it will sell.

Some persons choose to sell their home privately to reduce the selling price because no sales commission is required. There are some risks and disadvantages to this method. First, the seller has to understand real estate sales and contracts. Second, showing your own home to prospective buyers may not be personally safe. Employing an agent places professional expertise and a buffer between you and strangers.

**Choosing an Agency and an Agent**

To find a real estate agency first ask your neighbors and friends for recommendations. Next try the yellow pages phone directory. Contact several firms and ask them for names and phone numbers of previous clients, preferably in your neighborhood, to call as references.

Both real estate "brokers" and real estate "salespersons" (agents) are licensed by the state, but agents must be supervised by brokers. A Realtor is a real estate broker who is a member of the National Association of Realtors, a professional group. Not every broker is a Realtor. The term *real estate agent* is used loosely to refer to any licensed real estate person.

The professional skills to look for in an agent begin with

personal rapport. Do you feel at ease with this person? Do you trust him or her to put forth a determined, professional effort to sell your home? If you have any misgivings whatsoever, interview another agent before you sign any listing agreements. The agent you finally contract with will be your "listing agent" and will be responsible for advertising or "listing" your home. In small communities, the advertising may be placed in newspapers or simply with a small sign in your front yard. Most people also want the agent to list their home on the Multiple Listing Service (MLS), a broker information network showing homes for sale.

**Interview Questions**

• When screening potential agents, ask each to perform a market analysis of your house to estimate the selling price.
• Ask about the marketing plan, that is, how your house will be advertised and for how long.
• Will there be open house days (days when the agent sits in your home waiting for interested persons to drive by and drop in, and when you will have to be absent)?
• Will the prospective buyer's agents be allowed to show the house?
• Why did he or she price the house at that amount? How much experience does he or she have?
• What should you do to get the house ready to sell?
• Is he or she experienced in financing? Discuss what kinds of financing you will allow. Make sure you understand what alternate financing terms mean for you, the seller, and the differences between them. You may hear about "carrying the loan with a "balloon" or a "wrap around." Ask your agent to clearly explain what these mean. Do not agree to anything you do not understand.

**The Listing Contract**    The American Association of Retired Persons describes two commonly used types of listing contracts:

"You will be asked to discuss and sign a "listing contract" or agreement with your broker. This contract includes
the terms of sale for your house (such as the asking price),
your brokerage arrangements (such as what the broker will
do for you and how much you will pay the broker)and the ex-

piration date of the contract.

Generally, if you want your home placed on the MLS, there are two basic kinds of contracts you may enter into with a broker.

In an exclusive *right-to-sell contract,* you agree to pay your broker a commission no matter who finds the buyer—even if you find the buyer independently of a broker. This contract is preferred by most brokers.

If you know specfic people who may be interested in buying your home, you may want to include a special "reserve clause" in this type of contract. This reserve clause would allow you to sell your property to any specifically-named person and would require you to owe either no commission or a reduced commissioned.

In an exclusive right-to-sell contract, your broker usually benefits regardless of who finds the buyer. However, you still may be able to negotiate a contract that is more favorable to you. For example, you may try to negotiate a lower commission, more extensive advertising, or other special terms of services in return for your agreement to sign an exclusive right-to-sell contract. You should be sure to have the negotiated terms written into the contract.

In an *exclusive agency contract,* you agree to pay your broker a commission if that broker, or any broker, finds the buyer. However, if you locate the buyer yourself, without a broker's help, you owe no commission, or, perhaps a reduced commission. Although there are some restrictions on who may use the MLS and what types of listings will be accepted, you should be able to have your home placed on the MLS under an exclusive agency contract.

Because an exclusive agency contract does not guarantee a broker a commission if the house is sold, some brokers may agree to your terms without cutting back on service."[21]

Some people have found that listing their home for sale with a friend or relative acting as agent is not often successful. The agents tend to put their friends or relatives last, after their other clients.

Beware of an agent who "buys your listing" by suggesting a higher selling price than other agents. This agent knows full well

**Be Wary of . . .**

you will have to come down to a fair market price to sell the house. This is just a ploy to get your listing.

**Timing the Sale of Your Home**

If you have a choice, try to determine the best time of year to sell, such as during school summer vacation when families are relocating for the next term and your lawn may look its best. Read your newspapers to determine the selling price for homes of similar size and age in your neighborhood.

**Preparing Your Home for Sale**

First impressions are important. The appearance and neatness of the front and outside of your home indicate the pride and upkeep of the owner. Keep the lawn and shrubs trimmed, and toys and sporting equipment such as bicycles put away. Repair broken fences and screen doors. Sand and paint cat or dog scratches around the doors. Keep trash containers covered or out of sight. Park extra vehicles off the driveway, down the street. Some experts say the garage is a big selling feature. Clean it out and stow or organize tools in cupboards or on hooks.

Inside, keep the house immaculate. Simmer a pot of water with cinnamon and cloves to make the home smell pleasant. No cabbage dinners before buyers are scheduled for a visit. Most agents suggest that any new paint inside or out is recovered in the selling price. Be prepared to have to be away while your house is being shown. Prospective buyers like to feel free to comment with praises or criticism.

**Alternatives to Selling**

Some widows who think they can't afford to keep their homes without their husband's income are able to restructure their loans by refinancing them. This works only if the mortgage interest rates have come down at least two whole percentage points since you initially took out your mortgage. Ask a real estate agency or an attorney for specific guidance for your situation.

Another choice is to sell the "remainder interest" in your home to another person, which allows you to continue living in the home for the rest of your life, with the property passing to the new owner after your death. This is also called a "life estate." If you want to consider this choice, ask your attorney for assistance.

As of this writing, if you are fifty-five years of age or older and sell or exchange your house at a profit, up to $125,000 of the profit may be excluded from taxes, just this one time in your life. Under certain conditions, this tax exclusion benefit also applies to condominiums and townhomes. There are several rules and qualifying factors that apply to this exclusion. The life estate or remainder interest mentioned above do not qualify. Ask your attorney or tax accountant for specific advice.

**Tax-Free Residence Sale**

Selling your home can be an emotional experience. If possible, wait a year or two after you are widowed. You need time to settle your husband's estate and get your life somewhat back together before you make a major step such as changing homes.

Auto and homeowner responsibilities can seem enormous. Insurance considerations are initially burdensome, but once they are in place, need be reviewed only once or twice a year. If you choose, property maintenance can be delegated to a handyman and auto care can be performed by your favorite service station. You needn't personally assume all your late husband's responsibilities. Armed with the basics in this chapter, you are now informed about when and how your property can be protected with preventive maintenance.

**Notes**

# Chapter 12

# *Single Parenting*

*The hardest of all is learning to be a well of affection, and not a fountain, to show them that we love them, not when we feel like it, but when they do.*
> —Nan Fairbrother (1913–1971), English writer and landscape architect

Chances are, never having planned on becoming a single parent, you are not prepared to be one. Yet suddenly you are the only parent for your children. The responsibilities may seem overwhelming. How can you possibly be both father and mother? Who will take the boys fishing? Can you find quality day care, let alone afford it? In this chapter we focus on the problems of the widow caring for very young children, parenting school-age children, and coping with teenagers. We include discussions about family structure and rules, children and their grieving, and suggest ideas for keeping in touch with their father's family.

## Getting Back to Being a Family

At first you may not be aware that you are now a "single-parent family." The associations and stigmas attached to this label are not always easy to face. Susan, the stereotypical housewife and mother, was dutifully attending a school Parent Teacher's Association meeting, when the principal related the story of a boy who had been in some kind of trouble. He finished with, "Of course, he's from a single-parent family." Several heads, including

Susan's, nodded in agreement. But then, stunned, she realized *she* was now the head of a single-parent family! In that instant Susan resolved to work on disproving that negative image and to pour her energy into assuring her children that they were still part of a complete family.

The first step in unifying your family is to show your children your love frequently. Tell each child openly that you love her or him. Each day give hugs, a pat on the back, a touch on the arm—some gesture of affection. Your children need the reassurance that you still love them and will not leave them. Share your grief with them. One woman told us that her father had died when she was six years old. Her mother would lock herself in the bathroom to grieve and cry, leaving the girl sitting outside the door, alone and fearful. The child is now a woman, thirty years older, and still feels bitter that she was left to face a lonely, diminished world, devoid of her mother's love and attention at that crucial time.

**A Memory Scrapbook**

Early in your single parenthood, if your children are old enough, you may want to offer each child some favorite possessions of their father's to keep: clothing, mementos from his desk at work, sporting equipment or perhaps even tools. Items that may seem unimportant to you may have special meaning for your children. Before giving away or selling your husband's things, give the children a chance to decide what belongings they want to have. If your children are too young to understand, you should decide what to save for them. Make a photograph album with snapshots of him and the kids; or a scrapbook including some of Dad's childhood souvenirs, such as school report cards or Father's Day cards the children may have crayoned for him when they were younger. With something tangible like this at hand, the child can browse through the pages and reminisce whenever he or she feels the inclination.

**A Family Routine**

No matter what ages your children are, getting back to a family routine will provide them with structure and stability, a sense of something they can count on. One widow has said, "If it weren't for the children and the dog, I wouldn't want to get up in the mornings." For the first few weeks, possibly months, most widows experience a loss of appetite and have a difficult time preparing meals. They tend to heat frozen dinners or not eat at all. But Charlotte's and Carol's children let them know that the evening meal was important to them. With the stresses of being a widow, you need to keep up your health and strength with a balanced diet, and your children do too. Surprisingly, it helps to invite one or two of their friends to share dinner; it is hard to feel sad around cheerful young faces.

If grocery shopping and cooking are difficult, try meal planning a week at a time. Use a shopping list to help keep your cupboards well stocked. If your children are old enough, assign them responsibilities for helping with the meals. Let them know you are all working together as a team.

## Setting Family Rules

Now that you are the sole parent and disciplinarian, guidance and enforcement are up to you. Older children may feel that since Dad is gone, the rules don't matter any more, that you cannot or will not enforce them. If you have tended to be the more gentle parent, assuming the role of disciplinarian can be very difficult.

Mothers who work outside the home often feel especially harassed—trying to be "Supermom," doing everything for everyone. Clearly defined rules and shared responsibilities will help alleviate the pressure and restore some order to the home environment. One way to establish certain limits is to call a family council where everyone helps write the rules. Among the activities you may want to consider are: acceptable hours for television viewing, study times, frequency of schoolnight activities, curfews, having guests in your home, when meals will be served, and communicating where each of you is going and when you will return. In establishing the rules, you may want to suggest options for each one and take a family vote on which to adopt. Getting your children to participate lets each of you clarify your expectations and allows compromises rather than resistance. Making the rules is easy compared to enforcing them, especially compared to enforcing them consistently and with love.

An important rule for dealing with older children is for each one of you to *always* communicate where you are going, a phone number where you can be reached, and when you expect to return. If your return is delayed, you must call home and leave a message, no matter how late the hour may be. Keep a steno pad near the phone for messages, together with a list of the phone numbers of your children's close friends. List the names and numbers of your own friends and business associates so your children can reach you during the day. Peace of mind in knowing your offspring (or their mother) are safe is more important than uninterrupted sleep.

**Household Chores for Everyone**

Household chores can be dull for anyone. Now that you have additional family management responsibilities, you may need to delegate the daily, weekly or occasional chores. Make a list of the things to be done and pass it around for each child to indicate what he or she wants to do. If you draw up a fresh list each week no one needs to feel stuck with an undesirable chore forever! Even young children will feel more important about their position in the family if they are given some special duties—perhaps some simple task their father usually did. Make a list and let each child choose two or three new responsibilities. You will need to follow up frequently by giving positive comments or affectionate gestures for successfully completed chores.

Working mothers will probably have to readjust priorities about household "spotlessness" and yard maintenance. If your children are too young to take on outdoor responsibilities, consider hiring someone to cut your grass or shovel your walk. Older children are often too busy with their own extracurricular activities to take time voluntarily for housework or yard work. Try to establish a system that rewards prompt or timely completion of chores.

**Sharing Feelings**

Regularly, perhaps once a week, set aside a time for family sharing and talking about feelings. You are probably grieving as well as trying to be mother and father, and your family is going through a difficult emotional time. You may not be at your best or as perceptive as you could be with your children. Each of you needs a chance to air your opinions, even your frustration and anger. Let each person speak uninterrupted. You must be the arbitrator and not let the meeting end on a negative note. Help your children resolve their problems, or determine whether they need outside help. Make this a time the family draws together for mutual support. On a daily basis, make time to talk with and listen to your children.

Two pressing concerns for mothers of very young children are having an income to live on and finding qualified child care. A few fortunate, young widows may have adequate monthly income enabling them to continue their careers as full-time mothers, but the majority of young widows have to find a job to earn a living for themselves and their children. We offer job-hunting strategies in Chapter 16, "Volunteers, Careers and Getting a Job."

**Parenting Very Young Children**

Qualified day care is presently a national problem. With ever-growing numbers of women entering the work force, the demand for child care has increased exponentially. Determine what child-care resources are available in your community, then call your county social services office to find out what features you should look for in a high-quality day-care facility. If none are available, and you think you have the temperament for it, consider starting a day-care center yourself. Again, check with your county social services office for licensing requirements.

Even young widows may qualify for Social Security benefits for children under age eighteen, if your late husband's contributions to the Social Security system warranted it. See our guidance on how to apply in Chapter 9. You have nothing to lose.

Be sure you still have health insurance coverage for yourself and your children. Few people can afford present-day medical expenses without insurance. Since mid-1986, if your husband had health insurance coverage from his employer at the time of his death, you have the choice of continuing coverage for yourself and his dependents, providing you pay the premiums. Compare the costs to getting your own group plan. (See health insurance guidance in Chapter 9.)

School-age children usually have some notion of death and may understand what has happened to their father. The fact that they no longer have a father may make them feel different from their friends—only they don't want their friends to think they are

**Parenting School-Age Children**

different. In the book *How It Feels When a Parent Dies,* Jill Krementz recorded children's perceptions of death and how they felt about it.[22] The book is intended for children, but is also helpful for a parent who needs to understand what may happen with her child.

You may have to help your children tell their friends that their father has died. At the same time, reassure the friends that all of you are still a family and want to continue friendships and to do things together. Be positive. Children are often apprehensive when they hear someone they knew has died. They need to be reassured that your child (their friend) hasn't really changed as a result of the loss.

Notify your child's school principal and each teacher that a family death has occurred, and stipulate that you want to be informed of any changes in your child's behavior. Carol wrote a personal note to each of her children's teachers to let them know she was concerned about her children and that she would appreciate being notified of any problems they might notice. Your child may be unaware of any anxiety or distress he or she is feeling or be unable to verbalize it, but a teacher is often able to pick up on it. Grieving children often do not know how to describe their pain and may act it out by being physically violent to themselves or others, destroying property, lying, running away, withdrawing or being disobedient. If there are problems at school, discuss them with the teacher and ask for suggestions on how to deal with them. Offer your complete support.

## CHILDREN'S FEARS

You may not be the only one who is grieving, anguished and frightened about your husband's death. Your children may also be scared about what will happen to them now that their father has died. From toddlers to teens, children sense your anxiety and, depending on their ages, have their own fears about the future.

The first fears are usually about their own well-being—for example, "What will happen to me if you die, Mom?" Very young children may feel anxious about who will take care of them or who will feed them. Older children may have fears, yet assume that since they are older, they shouldn't burden you with what may seem to them to be ridiculous apprehensions. Common fears, which they may or may not verbalize, include the following:

"Will we still be a family, now that Daddy is gone?"

"What will happen to us now?"

"Will we have to move away from here—away from our school and our friends?"

"Will my friends still like me?"

"Who will take me to soccer practice?"

And from the older children:

"How will we have enough money to live?"

"Can I still go to college?"

"Do we have to sell our house?"

"If you die, too, who would I live with?"

These fears are as real and as important as the ones you have about being the only parent, having enough money to rear your children and taking care of your home and car. Even though your children may not ask these questions, be aware that they are confused and worried about themselves and their family. Try to address their sometimes unspoken concerns about your security as a family.

If you don't have the answer to any of these questions, simply reassure your children that you are doing your best to keep your family together and provide security for all of you. If they are old enough, ask for their opinions before making far-reaching decisions.

**Parenting Teenagers**

Nowadays older children may have an idea of what it is like to have only one parent, especially if their friends live in divorced families. But they probably never imagined that one of their own parents would die. The teen years may be the time when your children most need their father's advice about what to study in school and what kind of career to pursue. Be sure to notify their school principal, counselors or advisors, and teachers of the death of their father. High school students experience incredible pressure to compete and achieve. They need sustained family support, even though they appear physically mature and claim they want to be independent.

The teenager is experiencing a time in life when he or she needs to be gearing toward tomorrow and the long-term future. What is accomplished today means a better chance for success tomorrow. Yet your teenager has just seen the end of his or her father's tomorrows. The planning and hard work didn't guarantee the future. Your child may react in confusion or refuse to make commitments for any tomorrows. A grieving adolescent may try to use the death of a parent as an excuse to "cop out" or escape responsible behavior, claiming "It isn't fair that I lost my dad." Life isn't always fair for any of us.

The grieving, frustrated student may be unable to study. He or she may fail one or more courses in an otherwise normal school performance record. The student may skip classes, drop out of school, or begin using alcohol or drugs. Ask his teachers to notify you of observed changes in behavior or classroom performance. If counseling is recommended, don't wait. If you feel counseling is necessary, and your child's advisors have not suggested it, arrange a meeting with the school counselor to present your case. Offer to participate in the counseling yourself. It is constructive and gratifying to have support from others in dealing with your troubled adolescent.

On other occasions, teenagers may behave as adults trying to assume their father's place. Assure them that you can get help with special projects. Let them know that some way you'll continue to attend the ball games, and that you might get friends to go camping with you—to help carry the tent! Then stick to your promises.

**Keeping in Touch with Their Father's Family**

Although your children have lost their father, you may be able to help fill that void by strengthening your family ties to his parents and siblings. If, during your marriage, your family had a close relationship with the paternal grandparents, it will be easy to continue the association. If the former encounters were strained, you may feel inclined to retreat into the background, but, for your children's sake, try to maintain communications.

Encourage an exchange of letters, phone calls and visits. Remember holidays and special occasions with a card or gift. You may help start a genealogy project between your children and their paternal grandparents, while they are still around to share the stories. Children feel pride and a stronger sense of identity when they learn about their ancestors. Charlotte's son was delighted when they attended a family reunion three years after her husband's death, and many of the relatives complimented her son on how much he resembled his father. The grandfather's favorite Christmas present that year was a photo of each of his late son's children.

The single parent may not easily recognize when her children are bereaved. Immersed in her own daily struggle to be both mother and father, she may fail to notice grief behavior. Children haven't developed the analytical and verbal skills to clearly describe emotional pain. Instead, they may become withdrawn or act out their fear and anger with unacceptable behavior. Frequently, mothers aren't certain how to recognize grief behavior in their children or how well their children are handling the grieving process. To illustrate, one newly widowed mother, while attending a grief support group meeting, expressed her concern, "I wish I could be a little mouse in the corner to see how my children really feel and how they are dealing with their father's death." Every mother in the room nodded agreement.

**Dealing with Your Grieving Children**

To address the issue of children and grief, we raise issues, then suggest coping strategies. The widowed mother may have many concerns for her children. For example: "Is my child old enough to feel grief ?" "What can I do to provide emotional support and stability for my family?" "Is my child effectively working through the grieving process?" "How will I know if my children need help working through their grief?"

There are no rules about how old a child must be to experience grief. Generally speaking, all offspring from infancy to adulthood sense disorder or loss following the death of a parent, and they fear abandonment by you, their only parent. Universally, their greatest and most urgent need is for you to show increased love and affection and to reassure them that you, too, will not leave.

**At What Age Do Children Feel Grief?**

Some immediate steps you might take to help your grieving children are (a) getting the family back into familiar routines for meals and school, (b) allowing your children to return to all their normal activities, such as sports practices or spending time with

**Providing Emotional Support and Stability**

friends, and (c) increasing the frequency of your gestures of affection. Although you may feel desolate, your children require additional love and reassurance.

As the weeks and months proceed, continue to show affection and occasionally share your own grieving with them. One family of three teenagers recalled that they thought their mother hadn't loved their father, because they never saw her grieve for him. She had kept her tears hidden.

Children lack the informal support networks their mothers may have. Caring friends may frequently inquire how you are and offer consolation. Yet, to a child, they may offer only a pat on the head and a rhetorical question, "How's it going?" A lengthy response isn't expected. Suggest or encourage supportive family members or friends to spend extra time with your children. Younger children, especially little boys, miss their fathers and need to identify with a male father figure. Some communities offer Big Brother, Big Sister or Foster Grandparent programs, which bring children and adults together. Many school districts now sponsor support groups for children who have suffered a loss.

**Working Through the Grief**

There are no easily read signs that indicate whether your child is effectively working through his or her grief. It is difficult to differentiate whether grief or other normal stimuli are affecting the child's behavior. Generally, if your children continue normal behavior (the same as before the death of the father), or soon return to it, they are coping, although they may not be recovered. Children, as well as adults, can continue grieving for years. Don't expect your children's grieving to necessarily proceed any more quickly than yours.

Children sometimes need to feel close to the lost parent. One normal coping behavior is for the children to wear something of their father's that fits them and looks natural. Teenage girls especially like to wear their father's tee shirts for pajamas.

**Does My Child Need Professional Help?**

To help you decide if your children may need outside, professional counseling to work through their grief, we look at the typically normal grief behaviors shown in five age groups. Generally, your common sense will suggest that if your children change their normal behavior for extended periods of time, or with increasing frequency, then they may need professional help in resolving their grief.

For example, Linda's teenage son, Dan, was on the verge of dropping out of high school. He was cutting classes and not turning in assignments. He refused to follow through with any commitments to the future—even homework due tomorrow. A concerned teacher suggested Dan try Outward Bound, an out-of-doors environmental, emotional and physical experience designed to challenge young people and instill in them a sense of self-confidence and inner strength. It was an unqualified success. In the physically demanding environment, Dan freely expressed his grief to sympathetic strangers for the first time since his father's death a year earlier. Each day the group's three hiking teams would plan a separate route to reach a predetermined camp site, then race to see which team could arrive first. Dan led his team on two occasions. By setting goals and pushing himself, Dan learned he could have some control over his immediate future again. He learned his future depended on himself. Outward Bound provided an environment that this young man needed to work through part of his grief—the anger that his father had left him and could not be counted on. But the young man was learning to count on himself.

## INFANTS

In the infancy stage of child development, grief is felt only as tension or diminished nourishment and physical affection from the mother. The infant may become fretful and anxious. If you are unable to continue sustained nurturing, try to find someone to help. Don't let the child feel abandoned.

## TODDLERS

The toddler may be old enough to notice that Daddy is gone and to understand that mother is upset and not behaving normally. Like the infant, the toddler is quick to sense any lack of physical affection. Relatives, neighbors and friends who once were familiar may now seem like frightening strangers. The upset toddler likes to cling to mother, turning away from other willing arms. The child may regress to younger behaviors such as bed wetting, frequent crying, thumb sucking, forgotten toilet training and other gestures that express fear of abandonment. Spend an extra amount of time giving your full attention to the toddler, perhaps reading aloud or looking at pictures.

## PRESCHOOLERS

The young child may react with great sadness to the death of a parent. The child may fearfully worry, "Who will feed me?" If your child seems sulky and withdrawn, gently encourage him to express his sadness. Let him know by your cuddling and love that you will not abandon him and will take care of him. Don't be alarmed at "No" comments. Preschool children are normally assertive and occasionally resist anything that is suggested. They may feel an intense need for love and affection.

## CHILDREN IN SCHOOL

Children from six to eleven years are family oriented. The family is the center of their universe. They are able to feel anger, sadness and grief over the loss of a parent. Both sexes need a male role model. Little boys especially need adult male companionship. You may want to encourage male relatives, neighbors or friends to occasionally spend time with your child. However, sadly, in light of heightened awareness of child abuse, we suggest you exercise extreme caution in selecting any adult companions for your children.

## JUNIOR HIGH STUDENTS

The junior-high-age child or preteen may normally exhibit bizarre or challenging behavior, which means that he or she is trying to find an identity. The preadolescent may become easily exasperated with parents, flaunt authority, dress in outrageous fashions, or generally behave obnoxiously. Drugs and alcohol are easily available for experimentation. Some preteens will become grief stricken, some will show few outward signs of grief, and still others will become withdrawn. Discerning abnormal grieving in a preteen is almost impossible, yet Dr. Fitzhugh Dodson suggests that this age group more than any other may benefit from professional counseling.[23]

## ADOLESCENTS

The adolescent or teenager's response to the death of a parent depends on the degree of maturity already attained. The teenager is like two persons, both an older child and a young adult. A teen can feel all the adult phases of grief, including shock, denial, anger, guilt, acceptance and recovery. Adolescent responses to grief may vary from retreat and depression to feelings that run wild. A teen may feel that since the family "rule maker and enforcer" is gone, he or she can escape responsible behavior. A teen may try to use the father's death as an excuse for not meeting his or her obligations. If depression or escapism behavior persists, your teenager may need counseling to strengthen self-esteem.

At times the additional burdens of single parenthood are especially challenging. Your children need increasing reassurance that you can be depended on, that you will still be there. You may be the sole breadwinner and stabilizing influence for your family. To meet your children's needs, you must sustain yourself physically and emotionally. Ask for help when you sense that your personal strength and resources are low. An overstressed parent cannot effectively nurture and love grieving children.

As a single parent, you alone shoulder the responsibilities and you alone deserve all the credit for guiding your children toward adulthood. You and your husband shared the most precious gift of all: the gift of continued life through your children. Cherish, love and nurture them in tribute to your late husband.

**Notes**

# Chapter 13

## *Three Widows*

---

*What we have once enjoyed, we can never lose. All that we love deeply becomes a part of us.*
—Helen Keller (1880–1968), American author and lecturer

Most women have some warning or sense that they are about to become widows. Often their husband's health has been deteriorating, with frequent doctor visits and possibly hospital care as part of the daily routine. Some husbands have lingering terminal illnesses requiring long-term care. Their wives and families rearrange their lives to devote themselves to caring for their husbands and fathers, no matter how long it lasts. At the other extreme, there are the suddenly widowed women who lose their mates in accidents, totally unexpectedly. It is perhaps most difficult to be the widow of a suicide victim or the "non-widow" of a disappearance. In this chapter we present some of these special cases—and examine how these women survived and got their lives back together.

Bruce was barely fifty when he suffered what seemed to be a stroke. After extensive testing, a brain tumor was found; surgery confirmed it was malignant. He lived about a year and a half. His wife,

**Long-Term Illness**

Mary Ann, agreed to share her experiences and coping strategies with us because they seemed to work well in helping her husband deal with his illness, in helping the rest of the family to support him, and in helping her deal with her emotional needs.

We asked Mary Ann how she felt when it was finally all over. She admitted feeling intense grief and sadness that he was gone, yet also some relief that he was no longer suffering. She had been able to care for him at home until the last few days at which point he required hospitalization and constant pain-killing drugs. Many widows feel guilty that they can possibly feel any degree of relief. Yet one woman whose husband was terminally ill for three years explained that he had to die so she could live. She had put her life on hold just to care for him.

## Family Support

From the beginning, Mary Ann and her three young adult children were able to adjust their daily schedules to take turns being with Bruce. Mary Ann would stay at home while the children were at school. When they came home from school, she would run errands and at least get out of the house. On the weekends, she continued working part time as a licensed practical nurse. These arrangements allowed the children to help both parents and gave Mary Ann some respite from being the primary care-giver.

As Bruce's illness progressed, he needed increasing attention. Mary Ann continued to be the sustaining care-giver. She now feels that the greatest help over this strenuous period was getting regular respite—scheduled intervals of rest or relief. A friend came regularly one afternoon a week to stay with Bruce. Mary Ann was free to spend the time as she wished without feeling guilty about leaving her husband alone for even a few hours. She would return feeling renewed. Andrew Scharlach, a University of Southern California assistant professor, reports that in a survey of ninety-nine care-givers to those with chronic or long-term illness, 72 percent said their own health improved after receiving some respite. They caught up on sleep, caught up on chores, visited with friends, or got medical care for themselves.[24]

Later, after Bruce's death, Mary Ann said one of the best things they had done was to take Bruce to visit his relatives. They had encouraged the relatives to write, phone or visit Bruce as often as they could. Together with Bruce, the family made some special purchases for him—a computer and a new truck. Helping him in these ways helped them show how much they loved him. During Bruce's last few days in the hospital, his children would sit or lie on his bed and read to him. He couldn't talk to them, but he could sense their closeness and would open his eyes whenever they stopped reading.

To help Bruce adjust to his increasing limitations, both Mary Ann and his supervisor let Bruce decide when he could no longer work. For a time Mary Ann drove him to the office where he could read his mail, until, finally, one weekend the children helped Bruce clear his desk.

**Career and Financial Considerations**

When Bruce and Mary Ann realized he would not be able to return to work, they applied for disability benefits from his employer. They prepared a will. They also consulted with a financial planner, who had them locate all their important papers and record the pertinent information. As a result, after Bruce's death, Mary Ann knew where to find everything she needed.

It is important to establish a file—one you will have ready access to—listing the useful data from all your important papers (which may, themselves, be out of reach in a safe deposit box). You may want to use five- by eight-inch index cards to list this information—a separate card for each insurance policy, mortgage, other type of loan, bank account, stock market account, bond, birth and marriage certificate, passport, IRA account and property deed or title. A speedy way to record credit cards is to photocopy them. This information would also be helpful for your relatives or friends if you should become ill or die. A suggested format is shown here. File the cards alphabetically.

**SPECIAL PAPERS**

Name or Type of Document _____

Account Number _____  Date _____

Company Name _____

Address _____

Person to Contact _____  Telephone _____

Where Original Located _____

Where Copy Located _____

Other Information _____

**The
Disappearance
Death**

During late December 1985, an Eastern Airlines flight to La Paz, Bolivia, crashed in the Andes mountains.[25] There were no survivors among the twenty-nine passengers and crew. Because of the snow and ice, no bodies were recovered. Each of the passengers became a disappearance death. Charlotte's husband was lost in the Caribbean while scuba diving. No trace of him was ever found. Occasionally a man will walk out the door and apparently vanish into thin air. These circumstances are rare, but they can happen. If you are the widow of a disappearance and assumed death, perhaps what Charlotte experienced and learned will help spare you some pain and expense.

As indescribably painful as it is to be a widow, under any circumstances, that is only compounded when the loss of your husband has come about as a disappearance. Legally you're not a widow until you can prove your husband's death. In a sense you're a "non-widow." You can't have a funeral, only a memorial service. You become involved with investigations and inquiries. The confusion and uncertainty are overwhelming. Each case is unique, and there is no easy way to resolve the death. The process can take from several months to years.

Most people are familiar with the federal United States law that you must wait for seven years until the disappearance becomes a legitimate death. But if there is convincing evidence of an accident, and search and rescue efforts were made, you may be able to prove the death in less than seven years.

There are four major areas of concern for the assumed widow: understanding your lack of clear legal status, getting the best professional legal help you can afford, dealing with your finances and continuing responsibilities, and knowing what to expect after a determination of death is made.

**Limitations to Your
Legal Status**

As we mentioned, you are not legally a widow until your husband's disappearance is proven to be a death. You won't have a death certificate, so you won't be able to claim any life insurance proceeds or retirement or survivor annuity benefits. You are not eligible for any veterans' or Social Security benefits. You have no access to any accounts or property titled in his name only. His will cannot be probated. In Charlotte's case, she could not even publish a funeral notice in the newspaper because there was no death certificate, although she was allowed to publish a notice for a memorial service of the assumed death of her husband. On the other hand, banks and credit card companies legally cannot close your accounts.

Almost immediately the widow will want to get the best legal help she can afford. Charlotte asked friends and relatives to help her find a law firm that was highly qualified to handle a disappearance death. Because her husband died while vacationing in a foreign country, she had to retain attorneys in both countries. In each instance she asked what experience they had in resolving disappearance deaths. How were those past cases similar to hers? How long did each take? What were the results? What kind of payment schedules would be required? Could some of the payment be delayed until the case was resolved, no matter how long it took? (She had only her own earnings to pay the bills at that time.) How could she help, and what should she be doing next? **Legal Assistance**

Depending on your particular circumstances, you may choose to wait the seven years. Still, at that time you will have to appear in court to get a judge to make a determination, and you may need an attorney to help. In cases where there is no evidence of an accident or foul play, you almost certainly will have to wait the seven years. In Charlotte's case, there had been air and sea search efforts, and the police had delayed the family's departure for several days until an investigation could be completed in the foreign country. She can still remember her horror when the police considered the possibility of foul play while they questioned her and the children. When she finally did get home, she was determined to prove her husband's death as soon as she could. The children were in high school and would be through college before the seven years would be up. How could she afford that financial burden on one-third of their former income?

Because Charlotte's husband disappeared thousands of miles from home, she had to retain a local attorney in the foreign country to resolve the death according to their legal requirements. Once that was accomplished, she had to prove the death a second time in the United States. It took two and a half years, cost thousands of dollars, and finally required the help of her congressman!

In her home state of Colorado, Charlotte retained a highly qualified and very supportive attorney. The fact that the attorney was a woman was a coincidence, but perhaps that provided an extra bond of trust. The attorney and her firm were quite open and willing to work out a payment schedule.

The first stage of proving the disappearance to be a death required the foreign attorney to get together the police reports and schedule a court hearing with all involved parties except for Charlotte and her family, whose sworn, written statements had been accepted previously. The only sensitive aspect of this stage was being patient with another country's legal system. It took over a year to get the hearing completed and another year to get the translated, official court documents from Saint Maarten to Colorado. Because Charlotte was the only one of her legal team who had been in the foreign country and the only one who had personally met with the attorney there, her advice for dealing with the other country's legal procedures was carefully considered. She felt that being patient and somewhat formal would prevent her documents from being lost or suffering other mishaps. She also promptly paid any bills submitted by the Saint Maarten attorney.

Meanwhile, the Colorado attorneys took charge of three areas: informing the Saint Maarten attorney of what questions had to be answered to satisfy the Colorado court's requirements, patiently cooperating with him over the course of several months, and complying with Internal Revenue Service tax requirements. The tax situation was confusing because, since Charlotte's husband had disappeared, he could not file a regular tax return. The IRS had to treat this as a death, and tax returns were filed for three years, as for an estate.

The only major delay occurred when the Saint Maarten attorney seemed to forget the case and did not respond to Charlotte's requests for the final court documents to be sent to the United States. As a last resort, both Charlotte and her attorneys appealed to her congressman for help. They were completely successful, and a few months later the district court judge ruled a finding of death.

Until the court rules that your husband is dead, you have no legal status as a widow, and your finances are also without clear status. You will most likely be dependent upon your own earnings. Life insurance companies cannot pay a death benefit without a death certificate. Your husband's employer may not be able to pay out any survivor annuity without a death certificate. And most assuredly, the bills will continue to arrive.

First you must determine what sources of income you have. Then you must determine what expenses you will have. Contact your husband's employer about getting his final paychecks. Next, ask in writing and in person if the employer can put your husband in a "missing" status, so you can collect some amount of his pay. Some employers have contingency plans for this rare circumstance. For example, if Charlotte's husband had disappeared while on the job instead of while on vacation, his employer could have classified him as missing and continued to pay his salary for up to a year.

If you have problems paying your creditors, approach each of them with a letter explaining your circumstances. Most creditors would rather work with you, in expectation of being paid later, than not collect any money at all. On an insured new car loan, Charlotte was able to sign a letter that stated if her husband were ever found alive, she would repay the loan with interest. The credit union and insurance company trusted her claim and cleared the car loan.

## HIS LIFE INSURANCE

If you or your husband owned any life insurance policies on his life, you must continue to pay the premiums and keep the policies in effect. Keep careful records of the premium payments and, after death is determined, request your reimbursement.

## INCOME IN HIS NAME

After the disappearance, checks and other income will probably continue to arrive—payable to your husband. How do you handle them? We recommend asking your attorney for guidance. He or she will probably advise you to establish a separate "estate" account for this "income in respect of a decedent" (deceased).

These legal terms may sound intimidating, but this is a way of keeping track of your late husband's income that was earned before he disappeared, and that arrived after his assumed death. Keeping separate accounts is important for tax reasons. Your attorney will guide you in the tax considerations.

To deposit checks written to your husband only, simply write "For deposit only to account (enter account number)." If the bank requires an endorsement, first sign your husband's name as it appears on the check. Then just below his name sign "by (your name)." If necessary, show a photocopy of your temporary designation as the person in charge of your husband's affairs. In Colorado this person is called a "special representative" and is appointed by the probate court. Your attorney helps you apply for this appointment.

## WILLS—HIS AND YOURS

If your husband did not have a will, his estate will be distributed according to the state laws where he resided, after his death is proven. In the meantime, if you don't have a will, you may wish to have one written. See our explanation of the problems of dying without a will and the benefits of having one in Chapter 17, "Estate Planning."

However, if your husband had a will, it cannot be probated until his death is resolved. That is, his estate cannot yet be distributed as he wished. It is in limbo, as though he were still alive. What would happen if you were to die before your husband's death was proven and your present will leaves everything to him? Charlotte realized her children would be in dire straits if she kept her existing will, which left everything to her husband, who had disappeared and was not yet legally declared dead. To prepare for this possibility, Charlotte bought some term life insurance and wrote a new will, leaving her estate to the children.

**After the Determination of Death**

In a disappearance death, do go to court, if only to establish a legal record of what happened. The life insurance companies or other institutions and creditors may require complete explanations, in order to make their decisions about how to pay benefits and transfer titles to real property.

Get about a dozen copies of the certified finding-of-death document. This is not a death certificate, but it represents the same thing. Based on your attorney's guidance, either you or he can now submit claims for life insurance and other benefits. In some states, the law requires the insurance company to pay interest on the proceeds from the date of death to the date the proceeds are issued to the beneficiaries. Ask your attorney about this, and enclose verbatim wording or a photocopy of your state law. It informs the insurance company that you know what you are doing. Don't forget to ask for reimbursement of any premiums you paid after the date of death.

Once the life insurance proceeds are realized and annuity or other benefit payments have begun, your attorney and tax accountant can advise and guide you in filing the final estate-tax return.

After this long, complex series of events is over, there may be relief that at last your husband's death has been proven, enabling you to settle all the legal issues. However, you may also experience a feeling of letdown. Strangely enough, for Charlotte, while the intense and devoted effort to prove the death continued, there was a sense of importance to what she did. She had definite goals to meet. She felt she was the only one who could provide for her children by settling their father's death, that she needed to work toward financial and emotional security for all of them.

But when it was over, there was also confusion and a feeling of "What now?" It seemed the important work was finished. The only way to handle this empty feeling is to set new goals. Look for a new job, take a course in something you've always been interested in, volunteer to help other people. Above all, make every effort to get back that feeling of being needed by someone, someplace.

## The Suicide Death

Perhaps the most traumatic widow experience of all is that of a suicide. Unknown to you, your husband may have threatened this before, or even made an attempt that proved unsuccessful. Or perhaps he had been receiving counseling, and you were lulled into believing things would get better. You didn't get a chance for any last goodbyes; you didn't get to search for the missing person in the hope he was still alive. It was just suddenly, dramatically, over for him. And the agony is just beginning for you.

Like the rest of us, Carol had read about suicide in the newspapers, heard about it on the news, seen it dramatized in the movies, but it was certainly not the kind of tragedy that she thought would turn up in her own family. Then one crisp November day, she answered the door to confront a policeman who said officiously, "I have bad news for you. Your husband committed suicide today."

Carol's husband, Wayne, was fifty when he took his own life, leaving behind four wonderful, young sons. Carol experienced all of the feelings—shock, denial, guilt, the agonizing litany of thoughts like: "I wasn't a good enough wife" and "If only I had. . . ." The sons still grieve: "If only I had told Dad how much he meant to me. If he had known how much I loved him, he wouldn't have done this." Every surviving member of a suicide victim has these feelings at some time or another. Carol shares her personal story here in the hope that it will help other suicide widows and children realize that they aren't alone.

To some degree, the suicide widow is "different" from other widows, at least in her own mind. She has the normal symptoms of grief—but with a searing intensity. Compounding these painful emotions are also many of the same rejection and desertion neuroses felt by the divorcee. Plus, there is the shame and embarrassment that this has happened for all the world to see; often the general perception is that there must have been some terrible problem with their marriage. The widow's self-esteem hits rock bottom. There are not many people with whom she can identify.

There are as many reasons why a person would choose to end his or her life as there are suicide deaths. What all of these people did have in common, though, was a deep emotional anguish for which they felt suicide was the only relief. They did not so much wish to die as to get rid of the terrible pain. What they will never know is that "Suicide doesn't end pain. It only lays it on the broken shoulders of the survivors."[26]

Many people have difficulty identifying with these feelings of despair and hopelessness. How could anyone feel this way? Carol got some insight into how her husband must have felt by talking with a woman who had attempted suicide herself. The woman described her own experience as being in a deep, dark tunnel of distress. Some of this was very painful for Carol to hear, but it helped her more than anything else to understand how a profoundly depressed person really feels. It also helped release some of the guilt that she had been carrying around. To talk with a person who can speak from his or her own experience on this subject can provide some very therapeutic revelations. A local mental health department or a suicide support group would be a good place to find people who would be willing to share their experiences with you.

The mother of a young suicide victim kept asking herself, "Why didn't I see the signs? If only I had, I could have saved his life." A man in her therapy group said to her, "Maybe you did. You don't know how many times he thought of suicide and you did step in. You may have saved his life many times, but not this one time." Later, after reading and talking with others, some suicide widows become aware of the danger signs that a suicidal person sends out, and then realize that their husbands indeed had some of or all of these symptoms. But that is only in hindsight. **Why Didn't I See?**

The "if only's" and the "should have's" weigh heavy on the widow's shoulders. "If only I had been more patient" or "I should have noticed the signs." In retrospect, these symptoms may seem very obvious, but, at the time, how could she have envisioned that this would happen? This person she knew so well, shared her life with, would never do such a thing. They made important decisions together, and now he has made this irrevocable one without her. She cannot be expected to take the blame for this, but often she does. A friend once said to Carol, "Have you always taken credit for what your husband did—his accomplishments as well as his failures? Well, then, why do you take credit for this now?"

It is very important for the suicide widow to work through the events leading up to the suicide and her emotions afterward. You should be selective as to whom you choose as your confessor. Your minister, rabbi, priest, a trained counselor or a trusted friend would be the logical choices.

You might try writing a letter to your husband to tell him how you feel. Apologize, get angry, say whatever you want, but get it out! Join a suicide support group. If there is no such group in your local area, you might start one with the help of your doctor, your religious leader, health center or anyone who can give you the names of other suicide survivors. These generally are informal meetings where you can talk and tell your story and listen to others who share some of the same emotions. It is not easy to reach out at this insecure, unstable time, but you cannot recover alone. It is a great comfort to have a friend who understands. You can find such a person if you are willing to open the doors and let others in.

At first, you and one or more of your children will, to some degree, target yourselves for some of the blame. This can be very destructive for a family. You need to talk, hug, talk, touch and talk some more. Become a good listener, not only with your ears, but also with your eyes. Body language often reveals more than words themselves. Let your children and other family members know that you want to talk, encourage them to talk openly about death, let them know that you are there for them whenever they are ready to open up. At various times, say to them individually, "I love you, and you are very important to me."

"As soon as a suicide occurs, the surviving group has lost an inalienable right to live an unstigmatized life," says Dr. Edwin Shneidman.[27] People need an answer, and if you can't give them one that they can accept, they will make one up. Yet, you can't find an answer for yourself, so how can you be expected to explain it to others? You have to work very hard at holding up your head to let the world know that you have nothing to be ashamed of. Your feelings of self-worth are very low at this time, so you need to surround yourself with people who love and support you unconditionally.

**Observing Special Occasions**

At first you will dread the approach of anniversaries, birthdays, holidays, other special days—and, of course, the date of the suicide itself. As the first anniversary of Carol's husband's death approached, she became very nervous. During that time of anticipation, she decided to spend the whole week thanking her friends for being her friends. She felt she had always taken them and their friendship for granted, but she now felt so grateful for their love and support that she wanted to let them know how she felt. This was a rewarding experience, and she received many hugs and other expressions of affection, which she needed at this time.

After one woman had been widowed for a year, she observed the anniversary of her husband's death with a memorable grave-side ceremony to dedicate the headstone. A short religious service was held, and afterward family and friends were invited to her home for a meal. She found it gratifying to have family and friends gather around on this day to support her and help her look constructively toward the future. It was also a good way to say "thank you" to these caring people.

**Is Suicide a Sin?**

One evening one of Carol's children came to her very distressed about his father's soul, saying, "It's a sin to commit suicide." Suicide, or self-inflicted death, is mentioned many times in the Old Testament, but is neither condemned nor condoned. It has been only since the fourth century A.D., when Saint Augustine declared it a grievous sin, that the Catholic Church (and later some Protestant denominations as well) has taken a harsh attitude toward suicide.

No one can give us an answer as to the disposition of the soul of a suicide victim. Carol explained to her son that she believes in a compassionate, forgiving God who surely is a loving caretaker of the soul of this good man. She added that we are judged by the way we have lived our whole lives, not by the last few seconds of it. John Hewett says in his book *After Suicide*: "You need to rid yourself of the superstition that all suicides go to hell. This often results from a rigid logic which teaches that forgiveness occurs only after repentance. I believe the wealth of the Biblical evidence shows that God's grace and mercy are unmerited, given freely. We don't earn his love, we receive it! Already, in the midst of this tragedy, God is working to create goodness out of the ashes of your despair."[28]

You are a survivor! You will never "get over this," but by working through it, by expressing your feelings, by facing the facts and dealing with them honestly and realistically, you will learn to live with it or despite it. Your life will be forever changed, but this can be a positive change if you let it. You will become more sensitive toward the feelings and sufferings of others. You will become more appreciative of life, your family and your friends. "Direct your energy to learning, growing, and finding a new and richer meaning in the lives of others and your own. Refuse to let that death be for nothing."[29]

## Notes

# Chapter 14

# *Taking Care of Yourself—*
# *Getting Out and About*

*The day will happen whether or not you get up.*
—John Ciardi (1906–1986), American poet and critic

During the first few days and weeks of your widowhood, you are only dimly aware of yourself and the world around you. You are shrouded in feelings of disbelief and inertia. There is an awful emptiness and an unspoken hope that this is a bad dream. Somehow, numbly, you do what is expected, making decisions and holding up for the benefit of everyone else. Then, for a time, you occupy yourself sending thank-you notes and worrying about what you are supposed to do next. Hopefully your family and friends continue to call to inquire how you are.

It isn't long before others have returned to their normal lives—forcing you to confront your "not so-normal" life. Caring about yourself, your health and your surroundings may seem irrelevant. At first you may neglect your appearance, even to the point of not getting dressed some days. Your eating habits may vary from not wanting to eat anything to stuffing yourself with junk food.

You may avoid people by staying at home, certain you can never face a social occasion again since you are now a widow and alone. You may be unsure of ever making any future commitments for entertaining friends, taking a class for your own enjoyment or traveling. Everywhere you turn there are couples, and you're no longer one of them. These feelings are common and normal for widows. We have experienced them, too. We have also talked with several other widows about their feelings of aloneness, their pain and confusion, and how they began to live again. In this chapter we present some of their solutions.

**The First Months**

For the first few months, even years in some cases, the motivating factor that keeps a widow going is "doing things for him," or doing things the way he liked them done. The first winter after her husband's death, Carol said she would periodically exhaust herself shoveling the driveway free of snow, because that had been important to her husband. Another widow wrote in *Reader's Digest* that she felt good that she could mow the grass and coil up the hose the way her husband always liked it done. Before, he had always mowed the lawn.[30]

Very gradually, as you heal, you will begin to do things for yourself. Charlotte avoided using her husband's desk for over two years. Finally, one sunny day she mustered up the courage to go through his papers and rearrange the desk to suit her own needs. Some cheerful music on the radio helped. Barbara finally let her daughter rearrange the living room furniture, after having kept it just the way her late husband had liked it for three years after his death. Each of these stories points out that it takes time—a different time for each woman—to begin healing and to feel comfortable with taking care of herself. For herself!

**Your Appearance**

Carol wore a gray sweatshirt, jeans and house slippers for the first two months after her husband died. She stayed at home, except for going to church, and wore no make-up. A year later, after she had found a part-time job, her friends commented that she no longer looked so tired. (Nor did she wear a sweatshirt and jeans.) After the first year, Charlotte was surprised when her friends commented that she no longer looked "gray" and "strained." Instead, she seemed more relaxed and smiled more. She hadn't realized she had looked so wan and run-down.

The first clothes shopping excursions may be difficult, especially if your husband helped you select your clothes. If you helped purchase your husband's clothing, avoid the menswear section for a time. Don't go alone. Just sharing the shopping experience with a friend will help distract you. Ask your friend for a spontaneous comment about how you look in the clothes you try on. You might end up in a new color or style. Treat yourself to something special. It doesn't have to be expensive, and it can cheer you up. Kathy, who was widowed at twenty nine, wanted to find out who the real Kathy was. She bought an entirely different, "weird" wardrobe and tried that for a while. After a few months of experimentation, her self-confidence returned, and she went back to her former styles. For some women, a new hairdo, or just getting your hair "done," can do wonders for your self-image. Make yourself get dressed and put on your make-up every day. This will help you feel better prepared to deal with any problems that may arise.

**Sleeping**

At bedtime you are apt to feel especially lonely. It is an easy time to feel sorry for yourself. This is normal. After all, you are alone and there is no one to share your thoughts with; no one nearby to touch or to hear breathing. We, as working mothers, used the tactic of lecturing ourselves: "I'm tired, and I have to sleep so I can get up and go to work tomorrow! I miss him so much . . . but I can't take time to cry tonight." Surprisingly, sometimes it worked. The crying was postponed. On other occasions, the tears flowed freely.

After a few months, Carol found that it helped to rearrange the master bedroom and buy a new spread and curtains. Then it became more *her* room, not just a half-empty couple's room. If it appeals to you, move into the guest room and make it your own, then convert your former bedroom into a room for company. On the other hand, some widows find it comforting to sleep on his side of the bed and use his pillow, even to wear his pajamas. Do whatever gives you the most comfort or feels right at the time.

In her book *To Live Again*, Genevieve Davis Ginsburg suggests keeping a journal.[31] She advises that just writing down anything you wish, even rambling on, may help resolve your disquiet. She wrote her journal as letters to her departed husband and discussed things with him as though he were still with her. She missed him and wanted to share her feelings with him. Just writing her thoughts helped release the restlessness and allowed her to relax and sleep. You don't have to write every day, but the writing allows you to slow down and helps you identify your feelings—at least to yourself.

Many women find comfort in prayer or from reading the Bible or other spiritual and inspirational books. These can be a source of positive emotional reinforcement, and you may gain strength from the knowledge that you aren't alone.

**Your Health and Nutrition**

Although you may be grieving and lonely, this is a good time for you to focus on your own health. If your husband was ill and you devoted most of your time and energy to his care, this may be your first opportunity in a long time to consider taking care of your body. It is well known that stress, especially the death of a spouse, can decrease our resistance to disease. For a time widows are more susceptible to illness. And, as we grow older, we cannot take our health for granted. It seems that nowadays almost everyone is more health conscious—mindful of what is healthy to eat, exercising at a health club, taking aerobics classes, jogging or simply walking.

Make time for regular exercise in your weekly schedule. A daily walk with friends is an inexpensive way to exercise and socialize. If your community has a YMCA or YWCA, check to see what programs you might join, and, if you are an older woman, inquire about reduced-fee memberships for senior citizens. These family-oriented organizations offer exercise opportunities as well as a diversity of community interest classes. Before beginning any exercise program, it is a good idea to have a physical check-up by your physician, to determine whether you have any exercise limitations.

Perhaps for the first time in your life, you have no one to cook for, no one eating with you. Food has no appeal and little taste. Some widows eat almost nothing but frozen TV dinners, and lose weight. Others turn to "junk food"—whatever is in a package and doesn't have to be prepared—and gain weight. Habitually munching cookies, ice cream, potato chips, peanuts and the like can ruin your appetite for more nutritious fare. So can sipping soft drinks or alcohol. Sitting alone in the evenings, watching television and eating snacks is an easy habit to form.

In general, it is more important now than ever that you eat the appropriate foods, fruits, vegetables and meats. If you're physically debilitated, your emotional health will suffer. If you can't always eat well-balanced meals, take a multivitamin. And remember that, as we age, we need to get sufficient calcium to prevent osteoporosis.

If you don't eat wisely you can become run-down and be a sure target for illness. Breakfast is a relatively easy meal to get through alone. You can read the paper and sip your coffee or watch the morning news while you have toast and cereal. It might help to get an automatic timer and plug in the prepared coffee pot the night before, so when you awake it's to the aroma of freshly brewed coffee. Try to sit where you might be cheered or di-verted—watching the birds or the bustle of early morning street scenes.

Lunches are a perfect time to meet with friends. In some communities, women are afraid to be out after dark, especially alone. You can avoid this risk by making plans to eat out with friends at lunchtime. Or invite them to your place for lunch. Preparing a meal, no matter how modest, can be a very absorbing and creative activity for those who enjoy it. But if you look on cooking as more of a chore than a pleasure, don't fuss. Most friends want to be invited to enjoy your companionship, rather than to critique your cooking!

The evening meal can be difficult because it is usually the time for conversation and sharing. Eating alone is just plain dull—and lonely. For the first year of her widowhood, Charlotte didn't want to cook. Her life was no longer "normal" and she resisted trying to be normal. She and her children ate a record amount of pizza and take-out food. Finally, the second summer, both teenagers had jobs and came home starved. At last there was a reason to cook for someone, and on a regular basis! After school resumed that fall, her daughter suggested that they regularly exchange one meal a week with Carol's family. If someone had to eat and run, that was okay. The whole idea was that they had to plan for guests, and then got to enjoy their company. Dinner was prepared with special attention and served in the dining room. Everyone enjoyed the extra fuss, and it didn't seem like work but more like a party. If you don't know any other widows, go to a support group and meet some. Ask someone from your church for dinner. Two or three guests will enliven the conversation and will help you be concerned about someone besides yourself.

## Especially for the Elderly Widow

Some older widows are unable to care for themselves without help, but prefer to remain in their own homes. Few women can afford daily nursing care or a companion. Check with your county social services office to find out if your community offers Meals on Wheels, Home Health Care Aides, visiting nurses or Senior Companions.

Several states are beginning to offer day-care service for older persons. The person needing care can be dropped off in the morning and picked up at the end of the day, and then spend the night at home in her own bed. One such program at the Seniors' Resource Center in the Denver area provides care for physically handicapped adults of all ages and for the elderly who cannot spend the day alone. Another part of the program assists victims of Alzheimer's disease. Medicare covers the costs of $25 per day, if the family qualifies. Call your local hospitals to see if they sponsor a similar program.

## Activities for Your New Life

Widows who don't work outside the home may find it difficult to decide what to do with each entire day. It stretches before them for hours and hours, and then tomorrow is more of the same. The first step out of this trap is to get dressed each morning so that you look good and feel alert. Try to plan some activity that gets you out of the house every day. Have a destination already in mind, no matter how trivial—take some clothes to the cleaners, gas up the car, visit the library or go shopping. The point is to make opportunities to meet and speak to people.

Then, in time, make a real effort to look ahead—from a few days to six months—and write down some things you want to do or accomplish. Be realistic, but plan several things, including some that are repetitive, such as joining a card-playing group or taking golf or tennis lessons, and some that are one-shot affairs such as traveling to visit your sister. For each activity, outline what you must do to accomplish it. Set a time for achieving each step. Don't forget to consider your wish list. Maybe you have always wanted to learn to play the piano or speak a foreign language. Are there adult education classes available where you live? Can you be a volunteer for a community organization? To find out which organizations exist in your community, watch your local newspaper for a weekly or monthly listing of their upcoming meetings. Call them to see how you can help. Your skills will be needed and you will be involved with people.

You were needed by your husband, and now other people will need you. When others count on you, you have to get organized; you're important. You may discover talents or ideas you have never tapped before. Charlotte's widowed mother, for example, works as a volunteer assisting an elementary teacher with first-grade students. Not only is she needed but she is developing new skills.

It is self-defeating to sit at home alone and grieve. If you are physically unable to get out and be with people, try to communicate by telephone. Offer to act as the "phone tree" or contact person for your church or club. If professional people in your town need an answering service to take their calls, consider starting a business.

**Evenings, Weekends**

The first year of evenings, weekends and holidays is a series of survivals. Many widows, working or at home, say evenings are difficult. It is a time for sharing the events of the day. However, now that no one comes through the door except you, how do you cope? Consider changing your routine and doing something new to fill the early-evening hours, like taking a walk. To make the house more inviting and warm for your return, leave the radio playing and set a timer that automatically turns on a light at dusk. When you return, prepare yourself something to eat and set a place at the table. Watch television while you eat, to keep yourself company. Take up knitting or needlework. Read some books you've always planned to read but never had time for.

The weekends, too, will be much easier if you plan in advance what you are going to do. Try to include someone else in at least one activity. Consider daytime activities like shopping, gardening, going to museums or movies with a friend, taking someone to lunch or scouring garage sales. If you attend church, get involved with affiliated service or social groups. If you have friends or relatives who live away from you, arrange ahead of time to visit them for a weekend. Reciprocate with an invitation for them to visit you.

**Holidays and Special Occasions**

Dreading the approach of holidays and anniversaries seems to be worse than the arrival of the actual day itself. Charlotte expected the first anniversary of her husband's death to be a reliving of that experience. She anticipated a difficult and emotional day, but surprisingly it wasn't as bad as she had expected. She called his parents and her own parents just to talk about how she felt and to get and give some emotional support. Some special friends had sent flowers with a note that read, "Remembering with you. Our love and caring." Their expression of sharing softened the pain. Try to anticipate whether other family members may be feeling depressed or sad about the approaching anniversary of your husband's death, and consider making supportive phone calls or spending time together.

Just getting through each holiday the first time is challenging, to say the least. Several widows have said that they changed their traditional routine by inviting guests. Having to plan for company and consider their needs helps you keep busy and think about something besides how you feel. If you are the hostess, you are responsible for making a pleasant holiday for your guests. Sometimes it helps to go away to a different setting. Starting new customs gives you new memories for next year. Some families have switched the gift exchange from Christmas Eve to Christmas Day or the other way around. Charlotte and her children found it helped to go skiing on Christmas Day and not stay home as they had always done before. One widow, Frances, was able to treat herself, her adult children and grandchildren to a holiday at Disneyland. In any case, don't ignore the traditions you had before, but try to build on your happy memories. It does get a little easier each year.

For certain occasions, such as your wedding anniversary, indulging in your emotions is appropriate. Cry and look at your wedding pictures if you feel like it. You don't always have to be strong and push your feelings down. If this is the time and place for grieving, then go ahead. Charlotte confessed, "It helps me to go outside and look at the sky and talk to my late husband and tell him how much I miss him, especially on our anniversary." For your children's graduations or weddings of your children, all we can recommend is to wear dark glasses and keep *very* busy. These milestones of life seem even more difficult than anniversaries and memories.

For most of us, our social activities as a wife centered on couple and family relationships. We knew our role and what was expected of us. Our social life was relatively predictable and secure. Now life has changed.

**Getting Out and About**

You may have already noticed that since your husband's death, your married friends are busier than before. They don't call as often to invite you to dinner or for other events. If your social life centered around your husband's business associates, they may have forgotten you. You may not have even received a Christmas card from the office this year, whereas in years before there were gifts and parties. Many widows experience this abandoned feeling.

How do you begin to develop a new social life? Many women don't want to date yet, if ever. But their families or widow support groups can't provide all the social activity they need. It takes effort and time to meet new people and develop friendships. Each of us wants to be with stimulating people who are active and involved and positive about their future. *Being an interesting, stimulating person is the key factor to a widow's successful recovery!*

With energy and focus you *can* become an interesting person who is doing things and is excited about *your* future plans! Your enthusiasm will be contagious and other people will want to be with you.

## WHERE TO BEGIN

The biggest hurdle is getting started. Once you're involved in an activity, you have a new topic of conversation and you've met new people to share with your family and friends. You're on your way to becoming a more interesting person!

First, sit down and make a list of your dreams—the things you've always wanted to do but never did. Then organize the list according to:

*Things you can do alone;*

*Classes* you've wanted to take, including recreational and educational subjects such as tennis, golf, furniture refinishing, bridge, a foreign language, writing for publication, learning about antiques, etc.;

*Group activities* such as joining clubs for gardening or handicrafts, a square dancing or choral group, or one that discusses books or stock market issues;

*Volunteer skills* you would like to contribute (even if you don't yet have the skills) to a hospital, soup kitchen, church, foster grandparent program, teacher assistance program, day-care center; or, as Carol's seventy-year-old mother does, help build a community hiking trail;

*Excursions, travel and adventure,* such as taking museum tours or nature walks in your community, going for a hot-air balloon ride, rafting on a whitewater river (yes, there are trips for seniors and for beginners of any age), joining an environmental group such as Earth Watch, going camping with a group, calling several travel agents to inquire about trips for women or trips organized around a special theme such as archaeology, tennis, a dude ranch or conservation. Universities offer special travel packages for alumni—a way to meet some very interesting people.

The list of solo activities is for your personal satisfaction and education. You may want to read some of those classics you always planned to get to, but were too busy. Genealogy, needlework, practicing music lessons, redecorating or writing letters can be quite satisfying. Self-improvement activities such as aerobics, weight reduction, fashion and make-up sessions, or a health club membership can be pursued on your own—or enjoyed even more with a friend. (If you choose genealogical research, start with tape-recorded interviews of relatives. To locate records, you can write to the Archives of the Mormon Church in Salt Lake City, Utah. Other valuable sources for birth, marriage and death records include the Census Bureau, state office of vital statistics, churches, schools and hospitals.)

Now focus on classes, group activities and volunteer skills. In each of these categories rank each item in order of preference. These lists involve activities with other people. To become a more interesting, alive, aware woman, you have to get started somewhere. It is easier if you are gregarious and like to interact with others. But if you are somewhat shy, you can become a behind-the-scenes expert on a subject that interests you. Your library or a museum may welcome your guidance.

Next you have to determine what you can do, considering your personal circumstances and the activities that are available in your community. Read your local newspaper for notices about clubs and classes. (In some cases, club meeting schedules may be published only weekly or monthly.) Taking classes gets you into groups of people who share the same interests that you have—at least on one subject. Try to arrange a study group or work session outside of class, and volunteer to coordinate the effort. At the end of the course, invite your classmates for a farewell potluck. For volunteer activities, call the hospitals, library, museums and historical society, or call your county or city government to inquire about community service activities. You are needed. You just have to find out where.

The idea of travel or adventure outings may seem overwhelming if you have never traveled or have traveled only with your husband. Some brave women arrange to go as singles with travel groups. Others find it more fun to tour with a friend. Even though you may have known someone for years, or played bridge together regularly, you really don't know each other until you have traveled together. You might begin with one-day excursions or weekend trips, suggests Frances Weaver in her book, *The Girls with the Grandmother Faces*.[32] The expenses are kept at a minimum and the two of you have a chance to become better acquainted before venturing forth on longer journeys.

So as not to jeopardize your friendship, explicitly state the "ground rules" before you depart, with each of you describing your preferences for lodging, types of restaurants and food, activities you enjoy during the day and evening, and, most important, how the expenses will be handled. For example, you may assume you'll split the costs evenly, while your companion may not plan to pay for anything she (or he) didn't order. If you plan a car trip, decide who will drive and for how long, and describe the navigator's responsibilities.

Travel and adventure may seem like impossible dreams, but they can happen with careful planning. Charlotte's mother plans well in advance for about two trips a year. She doesn't worry about being single, but looks forward to making new friends in the travel group. To allow herself privacy, she selects single accommodations, but enjoys socializing during the day.

Travel for seniors sometimes has such added benefits as discounted prices on tickets from airlines, railroads and bus companies. Some travel agencies and seniors' organizations offer a variety of low-cost trips. One group offering travel specials is the American Association of Retired Persons (AARP), Membership Processing Center, Box 199, Long Beach, CA 90801. A $5.00 membership for persons age fifty and over entitles you to a year of *Modern Maturity* magazine; news bulletins; eligibility for group health, auto and homeowner's insurance; savings on pharmacy products; discounts on hotels, motels and auto rentals; and more.

The Elderhostel program for seniors over sixty offers outstanding opportunities for worldwide travel and educational courses in all fifty states, Canadian provinces and other countries. For a free catalog, write to Elderhostel, 80 Boylston Street., Suite 400, Boston, MA 02119.

## Entertaining Friends and Guests

For many women, this will be their first experience at hosting as a single person. For us, it was easy to begin by exchanging family dinners each week. We were widows about the same age and with children the same ages. From that beginning, we separately summoned up the courage to invite several people to brunch to celebrate a special occasion. It seemed easier to invite friends in the daytime, perhaps because our mood was brighter and perhaps because evening entertaining seemed more for couples. At any rate, once we had entertained guests at daytime occasions, it was much easier to consider the notion of a dinner party.

An easy way to begin entertaining by yourself, if it fits your budget, is to buy tickets for a cultural or special event and invite a friend. It is sometimes more relaxing to take someone out than to entertain at home. This is the time to consider the ballet or a lecture series, things your husband might not have cared for but you do. It's time for you! Look in your newspaper for community affairs or "free" activities, such as attending city-sponsored concerts or cultural festivals.

An idea for combining exercise and a social activity is to arrange a morning walk with a friend, then serve her herbal tea and nutritious fruit, cheese and biscuits. We know of one group of widows who, once a month, celebrates any birthdays in the group with a soup lunch and inexpensive (under $2) gifts for each celebrant.

When you're ready for at-home entertaining, we suggest starting with brunch or lunch. Daytime entertaining is more casual and less expensive as well as less couple-oriented than evening affairs. Some older persons (as young as forty) cannot see well enough to drive after dark and appreciate daytime invitations. For evening entertaining consider a small dinner party with close friends. Two or more couples and one or more single friends will keep the conversation going and your mood positive.

If you feel like mentioning your late husband, it is natural that you do so. Everyone will stay relaxed if you can keep the brief recollection happy or humorous, and keep your guests feeling at ease. It is healthy to occasionally refer to your late husband and share a positive experience, but move on to the present or future. While you are being the hostess, if you feel you might cry by mentioning your husband's name, then don't mention it. If someone else does, immediately get very busy; pour some more coffee or check on something that might be boiling over on the stove!

Charlotte has found it comfortable to occasionally describe an earlier pleasant experience she and her husband enjoyed—perhaps with the present guests—then relate it to the present occasion. For example, she has said, "Olin always chose the wine, and now I'm learning about wine. What do you think of this chablis I chose?" She put her guests at ease that she wouldn't break down and cry at the mention of his name, she shared a pleasant memory, and she steered the conversation to the present happy occasion.

## Dating

When a woman first becomes a widow, we believe she doesn't immediately feel "single." In fact, she probably considers herself a married widow until circumstances and casual remarks remind her that she is a single person, no longer half a couple. On one occasion, Carol was asked if she would like to go to the singles group at her church. Taken aback, she later exclaimed to a friend, "He might as well have pulled a chair out from under me! I'm not single! Why would I want to go to a singles group?" An instant later, she painfully remembered she was in fact single.

Accepting the label of "single" isn't easy. For some women, it is more comfortable to be remembered as someone's widow than to be thought of as single. Continuing to wear your wedding ring symbolizes your "still married" self-image. Charlotte recalls she didn't want to be referred to as a single person or want strangers to have any idea she was a widow. A year or so later, after some of her self-confidence in managing her life and feelings had returned, being known as a widow no longer seemed a problem. If thinking of yourself as "single" feels painful or frightening to you, we suggest you use the term "previously married."

Long ago someone courted you, fell in love with you and married you. Then, after years of being half a couple, you became a single woman. Now even though your social life is full, you might enjoy a man inviting you out. For many women, it's nice to once again touch a rough tweed jacket, to smell after-shave or just to share dinner with a man who doesn't belong to someone else! It would be a boost to feel desirable again, to know that someone would choose to spend time with you.

When or if you start dating is entirely up to you. For some it will be only a few months, for others it can be years, if ever. For new widows, just the thought of dating, even some day in the future, can be terrifying.  It is natural to be nervous about dating again after many years. The media would have you believe that every date leads to bed or indignation. Not so! More than one of our widower friends has confided that he, too, was nervous about dating. Where should he take the lady? Would she be comparing him to her late husband? Would he be tall enough, a good enough dancer, have a nice enough car? Would she be sad if he took her someplace where she was reminded of her late husband?

From ourselves the worries include: What should I wear? Should I have my coat on, or let him help me? Should I wait for him to open the car door? After being married for years and years and now taking care of yourself, you probably open your own doors. And it seems young men don't open doors for liberated young women. If your date is near your own age, then both of you will probably revert to the social mores that were in fashion when you were of a "dating age." If your date opened doors when he took a girl out in high school, then he probably will now.

Having heard stories about new widows being asked to date or offered sexual favors, Elaine feared that any single male friend might ask her out at the first casual encounter. She recalls that even when a man would walk toward her, she would turn away so she wouldn't have to speak to him. Years later, she realized her fears reflected an assumption that even casual conversation might lead to a date, and she couldn't bear the thought of being alone with a man. Happily for Elaine, her self-confidence in being a woman returned and, after her first dinner date, she began looking forward to going out again.

When you are ready to begin dating again, how do you meet someone with whom you would like to go out ? Do any of your friends know you would like to date? How do you explain to your children or other family members that you would like to date again? Are you presenting yourself as "married and unapproachable?" Do you still wear your wedding ring on your left hand?

Before we discuss these questions, remember that you are a widow, which is different from being divorced. Your family and friends usually feel empathy for you, understanding that you have had an unfortunate experience or suffered a tragedy. In conversations with you, acquaintances will be solicitous of your well-being. In your community you have a new, respected status. Although it may be unfair, divorced persons are often thought of as having failed in a relationship. You did not.

If your marriage was good (and we realize many were not), then you loved and cared for a man. You didn't leave your marriage in anger, filled with disgust for a former husband. If you can think of yourself as special because you contributed to a good marriage and enjoyed male company, you'll convey an image of a self-confident, positive person.

To meet men, take classes and join groups to which men might belong. Many men enjoy outdoor adventures like camping, river rafting, hiking, hot-air ballooning and sports of all kinds. Take up golfing or tennis. Read the sports section of the newspaper to begin educating yourself about what sport is in season and who is winning! Volunteer to assist with a campaign for a political candidate. Motivated, outgoing men seem drawn to political environments. Tell your friends you are ready to date, ask if they know anyone they think you'd like to meet. They may already have someone in mind for you!

**Children's
Resistance**

Don't be surprised if your children (young or adult) or other relatives are upset with the idea that you might want to date, that you could possibly have feelings for anyone besides your late husband. In progressing through your own grieving process, you may have kept silent about your thoughts of dating someday. Your family members' recovery from grieving may not be proceeding at the same rate as yours. If you haven't been hinting all along that someday you might again date, your announcement could be alarming.

Children of any age may exhibit concern when you begin to date. They feel anxious and vulnerable about the possibility of losing their only remaining parent. To young children, your three-hour absence may seem like forever. Fears and questions that they may have, but cannot analyze or verbalize, may include:

"If you go on a date, does that mean you'll go away with this man and leave me forever?"

"If you like this man, does that mean you will love me less?"

"Is he going to be my new daddy?"

"Will he be nice to me?"

And so on. Be prepared for questions or behavior that suggest contrariness, such as crying when you are leaving for the evening, or outright jealousy and anger. You must explain to your children that you like to be with people your own age, just as they like spending time with a friend. Reassure your children that your love for them won't be less, that you can have new friends and like many people.

Older sons may feel especially threatened by your dating. They may have notions that if you cannot be with their father, you shouldn't be with anyone. Both sons and daughters need to be reassured that no one else will ever take their father's place. He will always remain their father. You must repeatedly help them understand that you won't forget their father, that he was an important part of your life and that your love for him won't go away. Your children also need to understand that you can care for more than one person and that your capacity for love can expand and grow. Reassure your children that you won't stop loving them. Shortly after her husband died, Charlotte advised her children that someday she would hope to enjoy a rich, full life again with someone as wonderful as their father had been.

You may feel like you're sixteen again. What will you talk about? First, don't worry whether he knows that you are a widow. If mutual friends introduced you, they have already told him and complimented you to him. If you met him on your own, and he inquires, you can simply say, "I was widowed some time ago. How about you?" If he's interested in more details, he'll ask. Your answers can be matter-of-fact, without sadness or long explanations.

Otherwise, steer the conversation to things you're doing now and describe your future plans. As we've mentioned before, everyone enjoys being with a person who is positive about life and seems to have enthusiasm about what she's doing. A friend, Linda, told about her first date with a recently divorced man, who poured out his pain and frustration, assuming she would listen with a sympathetic ear. She had expected a lively, entertaining evening, but finally asked to go home. Your positive attitude can be infectious, and even though you've been through (and may still be going through) a difficult time, you seem to enjoy life again. Charlotte was able to briefly explain that she had celebrated life with her husband, and that some day she expected to experience that again. Not one date seemed threatened or disconcerted by that statement. Rather, each date sensed that she enjoyed male company and that she embraced life!

Because of what Charlotte had read and seen on television, she was apprehensive that her dates would expect her to be sexually liberated, which wasn't her style at all. After a few dates she was able to work her values into the conversation, for example, "I grew up in the forties and fifties when one made a definite commitment to one person, and I don't understand a casual attitude about sex." It worked! She never experienced any pressure for a relationship she didn't want. Dating doesn't require intimacy; it can simply be a social occasion to enjoy the company of a man and to once again be part of a twosome.

For many women, an intimate relationship is something they have put out of their minds since their mate died. The first period of time (several months or years) while you are grieving and struggling to cope with everything else, there is little thought of intimacy. You don't allow yourself to miss that part of your marriage—it's too painful and it seems disloyal. But the time may come when you notice couples holding hands or a wife retrieving something from her husband's jacket pocket, and you realize you miss the physical closeness, the touching. Jean confided, "What I miss most is having someone to care for me, listen to me and treat me as a special individual. I can find people to love—the children and grandchildren. But I would like someone to love me!" Fortunately, she has found someone to love her, and Jean feels joyously alive again at seventy-five! Her special man is a young eighty-two.

You're a mature woman now, and if you want a physical relationship with a man, that's your private business. When you choose to make a commitment to someone else is up to you. The time schedule varies with each individual. Just be sure you're comfortable with your decision and that you're not reacting to pressure from friends. Maintain your self-confidence as an interesting person. Your late husband loved the woman in you and you are still a woman worthy of respect and love!

If your new relationship develops to the point where you want to spend several days with your special friend, you might get away for a short holiday and a complete change of scene. It can free you from memories or chance encounters requiring introductions and explanations. We know of one widow, in her late sixties, who periodically spends time with her special friend in another state, then returns to her own home when she chooses.

If you have children living at home, you might ask a friend to stay with your children so the two of you could go away together. Or arrange to let the children visit friends or relatives for a brief holiday. This avoids the confusion of the children trying to understand another man in Daddy's bedroom or in Daddy's chair at breakfast. They, too, are trying to cope with these bewildering changes in their lives.

## REMARRIAGE

If you someday decide to remarry, you have our best wishes. We recommend you consider a prenuptial agreement—a legal document that specifies what property and assets are yours, what are his, what will be yours together, and what will happen to those assets when the marriage terminates. The idea is that each of you can protect your assets, in case you should divorce or when one of you dies. This is especially important if either or both of you have children.

Adult children and other relatives may worry that some man will make you lose your senses and turn everything over to him, that you might even name him the sole beneficiary in your will. This fear is very real and also legitimate: many widows have been victimized. Our feeling is that if you want to let a man into your life and your home, just keep him away from your assets! If you want to buy him gifts or take him on trips, that's up to you. But don't add his signature to your bank accounts or your credit cards! If this relationship becomes a marriage, you may want to consider a prenuptial agreement that protects both your assets and his.

There are more complex possibilities if, after this new marriage, you should die first and he later remarries. The difficult aspect of the prenuptial process is that it forces both of you to deal with what will happen to the assets when the marriage ends by death or divorce. You're happy about beginning a new, permanent commitment, while this process requires you to acknowledge the end of a marriage that hasn't yet begun. It's emotionally distressing. You should, however, prepare this document with the assistance of your attorneys several weeks before the wedding.

If you decide now is not the time for you to remarry, but you choose to live with the man you love, our attorneys suggest a "Living-Together Agreement." This document could protect your property in the event the relationship ends and one of you moves out. We know of one young widow whose former live-in companion is now suing her for what he believes should be his share of some property she inherited while they were living together.

Taking care of yourself includes more than your financial security, personal health and appearance. Caring for yourself involves your emotional well-being—feeling that you are beginning to live again. Becoming involved with other people by being a volunteer, getting a job or expanding your knowledge may help you to become a more interesting person. Your skills may be sorely needed; you have to offer them to find out. Lean on your experiences to give you strength and compassion. Because of what you've been through, you now have a greater capacity to love and appreciate life. Look ahead and share your new hope with those you love.

**Notes**

# Chapter 15

# *Changing Relationships with Family and Friends*

People change and forget to tell each other.
  —Lillian Hellman (1907–1984), American dramatist
  and writer

"I would never have made it without my family and friends!" Does this thankful refrain sound familiar? Fortunately, for nearly every widow, family and friends immediately gather round to console, to comfort, to offer help. Their frequent attentions divert us for the time being and keep at bay the bouts of loneliness that inevitably follow. The first few weeks are apt to be busy ones, marked by many gratifying moments, filled as they are with caring gestures of all kinds: condolences, flowers, food, visits. In this chapter, we focus on the questions of how and why our relationships with family and friends often begin to change once the funeral is over.

**Initial Attention and Perceived Avoidance**

Chances are, in the first days of widowhood, your home will be filled with visitors, and you will rarely, if ever, be left alone. You and your family are the center of attention. Friends reassure you that they will do anything to help, just call them. However, in a few short weeks, the visits and phone calls begin to dwindle. Although your relatives and neighbors still feel grief and concern for you, they have their own lives to live. You can't expect them to take control of your situation and make the pain go away for the long term. At the same time you are expected to begin getting on with your own life, even if only in small ways. But having become accustomed to so much devoted attention, you may feel somewhat bereft, and even resentful, at this point.

This lack of attention due to people being busy with their own lives might be called "benign neglect." Friends have good intentions and want to help, but unless they are directly responsible for your care and well-being, they frequently step back, assuming that you will be capable of functioning once again as you did before. But often they are unaware of how long the grieving process takes to run its course, and can't be blamed for what may seem to be a lack of concern. They really haven't a very clear idea of the desolation and loneliness you may still be feeling.

Before becoming a widow, Carol found herself in a classic example of benign neglect. A few years earlier, feeling awkward and uncomfortable, she had avoided a friend who had lost a close family member. Carol had occasion to drive by the bereaved friend's home frequently, but each time had an excuse for not stopping to visit. The first was, "There are too many other people there. I'll return another day." The next excuse was, "No one is home and they probably don't want company anyway." One excuse followed another until finally Carol decided it was too late to drop in for a visit. All along she had been afraid she wouldn't know what to do or say. After Carol became a widow, she understood that it is never too late to take time to visit the bereaved. She then visited her friend and explained why she had stayed away, why she hadn't called. Happily, Carol renewed the friendship with her long-postponed visit.

Well-meaning friends, neighbors, business associates and even some family members may seem to avoid you. People who have not experienced the death of a close family member, such as a child or spouse, don't know how intense the bereavement pain can be. Generally, most friends can handle attending the funeral and expressing sentiments to the widow during the formal grieving rituals. However, as the weeks pass, these caring friends can feel uncomfortable about making an informal visit. They aren't sure what to say and are concerned they might upset you. So they simply avoid you. Some friendships grow deeper and more meaningful through your grief process, while others become weaker or diminish altogether.

Many people are uncomfortable confronting any aspect of death and are unable to greet a newly bereaved person, feeling awkward and at a loss for words. Carol was saddened that a few friends failed to acknowledge her husband's death. When she met any of these friends by chance, she would make the initial greeting, trying to put them at ease in an effort to get through this "first encounter after the death" experience painlessly.

If you feel your friends are avoiding you socially, consider your mental attitude. Are you mournful? Do you seem depressed and sad? Does your conversation focus on what you used to have, and what you cannot do now that you are alone? Are you generally complaining about how people treat you? If you can answer "yes" to any of these questions, chances are you are not pleasant company. Do you enjoy being with someone who complains about how bad everything is for her?

Every person has his or her own concerns and prefers to avoid taking on anyone else's problems. No one expects you to be happy or energetic all the time. Unless your friends are trained psychologists or therapists, they are neither prepared nor qualified to resolve your pain. To be good company, try to be positive and talk about any plans you may have for your future. If you have mastered some new skill you didn't have as a wife, share it. If you are taking a class, if you have read some interesting books, if you have met some new friends, share your excitement. Other people enjoy being with a confident, cheerful person. When your friends sense that you are healing, even in a small way, they find it easier to maintain the friendship.

## Grief Felt by Your Husband's Friends

Have you ever considered that, besides yourself and your husband's family members, his friends may also continue to grieve for him? It is easy to immerse yourself in your own grieving and forget that your husband is sorely missed by many people. Think carefully about friends and family members who miss his companionship and his guidance. If they have reason to feel a special loss, try to offer some comfort with a fond recollection and a reminder of how much their friendship meant to your husband.

Out-of-town friends may be slower to grieve—or to show their grief—than you or those who see you frequently. Because they live away from you, they have fewer reminders of your widowhood, and their grieving may be somewhat circumscribed until they see you, or receive your letters and calls. When Charlotte visited out-of-town friends after a year and a half of widowhood, she had begun to recover, and described her excitement at having a first date again after twenty-three years. Surprisingly, her friends didn't share her enthusiasm. Instead they seemed to prefer to talk about the couple they had known—Charlotte and her late husband. These special friends had not had any opportunity to tell her how much they missed their friend. They weren't ready to accept the notion of her developing new relationships. To spare yourself a similar situation, on the first occasion with long-time friends of you and your husband, give them a chance to tell you how they feel. You may be the consoler rather than the consoled.

## WHEN FRIENDS HAVEN'T HEARD

Although your husband's death changed your life forever, not all your acquaintances will have heard the news. If at Christmas, or on some other occasion, you receive a card or have a chance encounter with friends who seem oblivious to your circumstances, it is possible that they haven't heard of your husband's death. Carol's son Jeff was competing in a high-school track meet when he was greeted by a stranger. The man introduced himself and asked if Jeff was indeed the son of his college friend. The friend then asked, "How is he?" Painfully, Jeff had to explain that his father had died. Not only did the son have to announce his father's death, but he also had to console his father's friend.

You will continue to receive phone calls for your husband years after his death. These are usually sales calls generated from old lists or selected from the listing in the telephone directory. To screen the call, respond with, "May I tell him why you're calling?" Although you may want to blurt "He died," you might be doing a disservice to an acquaintance. In most cases, a question will momentarily divert the caller and give you an opportunity to determine if this is an unaware friend or a sales call. Then you can decide how you want to proceed.

## AS FRIENDS DRIFT AWAY

Sadly, more often than not, married friends of you and your husband will drift away. We live in a couple-oriented society, and you are no longer a couple. Wives of friends with troubled marriages may consider you a threat to their marriage. Certain longtime friends will continue to include you in their social gatherings, though some may feel they need to invite another single person whenever you are included. If the other guest is a widow, you may feel you are part of a minority group; if the other guest is an eligible male, you may feel put upon, or simply not ready to be paired off.

Inevitably, widows undergo waning friendships with couples. This makes it all the more important to develop new relationships with both women and men. To fill your social calendar, consider volunteering, taking classes, joining clubs and traveling. In Chapter 14 we suggest how to get out and about, meet people and find interesting things to do.

Wives of deceased retirees have already experienced the withdrawal from "the office staff" and business affairs. But new widows of men who were still working at the time of their death may expect that, after the fact, the social gestures and "commitments" go on as usual. Don't be surprised, however, if you are not invited to the company picnic, or if you don't receive a Christmas card. Even if your husband was the owner or chief executive officer, you may not receive notices of important meetings. If you wish to remain in touch with your late husband's business associates, you will have to take the initiative. Susan called a business friend of her late husband's, and gently reminded him that she had enjoyed knowing her husband's associates and missed their continued friendships. She attended the next office party, only to find that she no longer had much in common with the office crowd. Her life was changing and she was recovering.

**Communicating with Business Associates**

Be patient and understanding of your own parents' efforts to help you. They may try to absorb your pain and protect you. They will be grieving for you and for themselves as well. They have lost a son-in-law, someone for whom they may have felt a very close

**Changing Family Relationships**

bond, a great deal of love. Parents worry about their children, no matter how old the children are. They behave defensively when their children are threatened. If your father seems overprotective, remember that you continue to be his little girl. If your mother is a widow, she has a very good idea of what you're going through and can be a source of comfort and guidance. If she has difficulty controlling her emotions, understand that she may be feeling unresolved grief from her own widow experience.

As you recover and gain coping skills, your relatives will sense your newfound strengths. In some families, a strong widow is turned to as a wise and caring person. If you become financially astute, other family members will want your advice about money. You have been through a challenging trial. And, as other women in your family become widowed, your counsel will be sought at many levels.

Adult children of a widow are often competitive in their efforts to please Mother. Sometimes they feel that since their father is gone, they are totally responsible for your care. They may urge you to move in with them, assuming you are lonely or unable to care for yourself. But carefully consider the ramifications of living with your adult children. They will probably have a very different lifestyle than you and your husband had. You may even be thought of as a live-in baby-sitter or housekeeper. The more dependent you become, the more control you relinquish.

Your husband's family has lost a son and brother. Their continued communication with you will depend on what kind of relationship you had with them as a married wife. In some cases, the husband's family will soon "distance" itself from you and your children. "Distancing" is a word that describes the withdrawal and cooling in the relationship between a widow and her husband's relatives. Soon after the funeral they may forget special occasions they formerly shared with you. Even phone calls and letters could be infrequent or stop. Perhaps you won't be informed of family news.

Almost immediately Marilyn sensed that her husband's family might forget her and her children. They were grieving for their son and brother, and that seemed to reduce the emotional support that they could give to Marilyn and her children. Marilyn was concerned that her children would lose the sustained closeness to their grandmother, aunts, uncles and cousins. She redoubled her efforts to keep the communications open between her family and her husband's family, writing letters, making phone calls and driving 2,000 miles for a visit. She told her husband's family how important their continued, loving relationship was to her sons. Today, as a result, Marilyn and her children remain in close touch with that side of their family.

Karen, a second-time widow, experienced an extreme case of "distancing" in which her late husband's family totally ignored his four children from a previous marriage. Karen was a young widow with one child when she married Dan, a widower with four children. They had ten beautiful years together with the five offspring. Karen had adopted his four children. After his death in an auto accident, Dan's children never again heard from their paternal grandparents or aunts and uncles, despite Karen's continued overtures encouraging a family relationship. Yet, inexplicably, many years later, an attorney notified them that the widowed grandmother had left her entire estate to these estranged grandchildren.

If you were close to your husband's family, try to continue the relationship, especially for your children. Remember holidays, birthdays and special occasions with cards or phone calls. If possible, send your children to visit their paternal grandparents. Share your life by sending letters and photos.

As a widow, your relationships with family and friends will change. Some long-time friends will become closer, while others will drift away. Your relatives may become closer, leaning on your newly gained strength. Your husband's family may need your patience and understanding in working through their own grief. In every case, try to let your family and friends know how much their continued emotional support means to you. It seems appropriate to recall a Girl Scout campfire song that goes, "Make new friends, but keep the old. One is silver and the other is gold."

**Notes**

# Chapter 16

# *Volunteer Opportunities, Careers and Getting a Job*

Sooner or later most widows consider the prospect of working either in a paid position or as a volunteer. Here we use the term *work* in a broad sense to include meaningful activity for pay or for other rewards such as the satisfaction of helping others, either individually (teaching English to an Asian refugee, for example) or in groups (perhaps developing a new way to raise funds for an organization).

Some widows maintain that the work routine provides focus and structure to their days and gives them a sense of purpose. Many women claim that work is the primary factor that saved their sanity during an otherwise grief-filled time; having to interact with other people and concentrate on getting the job done meant they had little time to reflect on their personal problems. A more compelling reason to find work is if the loss of your husband's income has left you in dire straits, making you the sole family breadwinner. Of course there are many other reasons for working, among them: getting out of the house on a regular basis, companionship, learning new skills, sharpening old skills, having something to talk over with your friends and family, providing extra income for special purchases.

In this chapter we discuss how to find volunteer positions for the widow who is alone and wants to become involved with people and with her community. Next, we consider goals and alternatives for the widow who must now re enter the job market or who already has a career but needs a promotion to earn more income. For the widow who has never worked outside the home but who must now consider earning a living or supplementing her survivor income, we talk about how to begin looking for a job. Finally, we suggest alternative choices for earning income, other than getting a job.

Within a few weeks after she was widowed, Carol became alarmed about her family's financial security. In her grief and confusion, she hurried to follow the advice of concerned friends by immediately applying for jobs and taking a government skills test. Carol had not taken any exams or been interviewed for twenty years. Midway through her second interview, she excused herself with the statement, "I don't know what I'm doing here, but I know I don't want to be here." She cried all the way home, understanding she wasn't yet ready to begin working. Our message is, if you can afford to wait a few months, first take time to organize your personal affairs, get some control of your emotions, then begin your job search.

## Volunteer Opportunities

Almost all of us have, at some point, volunteered our time and talent for a club, our children's school, a charitable organization or a political campaign. Perhaps you have helped with the PTA, been a scout leader, served as a hospital aide, worked for the United Fund or for your church. Volunteers are the backbone of most nonprofit organizations in this country.

There are opportunities and needs for your skills all around you. To find out which organizations employ volunteers, ask your friends for recommendations, ask your hospital how you can help, talk to your librarian, get in touch with any museums or historical societies in your community, and call your county or local Chamber of Commerce to inquire about community service activities. Read your local newspapers for notices about volunteer organizations. You can volunteer to be a library aide, train to be a nurse's aide, lead tours of your home town, become a docent at an art or history museum, assist teachers or serve on a town board. With some looking around, you will find a volunteer position that is compatible with your interests, your personality, your time strictures and your goals. Your sense of personal loss will be diminished by the knowledge that a needy person or a worthy cause is receiving much-needed help.

If you are interested in working with a particular national organization, check your local phone directory. If no listing is available, and you are interested in starting a local chapter, you may want to contact one of the following national headquarters:.

The League of Women Voters of the United States
1730 M Street, NW
Washington, DC 20036 (202) 429-1965

Volunteers of America
3813 North Causeway Boulevard
Metairie, LA 70002 (504) 836-5225

American Red Cross
2025 E Street, NW
Washington, DC 20006 (202) 737-8300

You might start a volunteer program for a cause you are particularly interested in. Here are examples of how two women went about doing just that. One widow decided that her grandchildren would never know about the town the family had lived in for generations. To launch her program, she first joined the local historical society, did a lot of research and eventually wrote the town history. The woman made numerous friends in the course of this undertaking and the book sold well. She is now thinking about writing a county history.

Another woman had long been interested in birds and flowers. After her husband died she began to take long walks near her home studying the local landscapes. She shared her observations with friends and neighbors. Before long they asked if they could walk with her to learn about the spring and fall bird migrations. She now leads nature walks around her town and teaches beginning classes on birding and flower identification.

Even though you may be financially secure and not need additional money, you must be active in your daily life. Although your husband is gone, life is not over for you. Volunteering allows many opportunities to make friends, offer your talents, become involved with people and help others in a constructive way.

**Careers**

If you were formerly employed but stopped at some point, perhaps to rear your family, you may need to consider re-employment now that your husband is deceased. If you were working when your husband died, you may need a promotion to increase your income. Typically, widows receive a greatly reduced survivor's portion of their husband's pension or retirement pay. Still others lose his monthly salary entirely, or his share of the business could be distributed to his partners.

There are a few rules of thumb about looking for a better position. First, don't leave your present situation to job hunt. The old saying, "A bird in the hand is worth two in the bush," is particularly apropos when you are considering leaving one job for another. Being employed is also an advantage because employers prefer already working people over unemployed job seekers. If you need time off between jobs, try to take it after securing, but before starting, the new job. In your present position, don't advertise that you are considering leaving; this could lead to your dismissal.

If you have never worked at a paying job outside the home and you need to go to work, it is difficult but possible to find paid employment. First we discuss the obstacles—not to discourage you but to advise you how to deal with them. Then we talk about taking a hard look at yourself and your experience as a way of perceiving some of the advantages you may have. Then we show you how to assess your strengths and skills, and how to prepare a résumé.

Age can be a major obstacle to getting a job. If you are over thirty-five, the opportunities are limited and become more so the older you get. Experience is the other hurdle. Every employer hopes to hire someone who already has the skills for the job or who can be trained in a relatively short time and at as low a cost as possible. Rather than considering your age as a problem, offer your years of living experience as an advantage: you are more stable, and unlikely to need maternity leave or to relocate in the near future; and you have had years of experience dealing with people's problems, setting priorities, organizing family activities, co-ordinating schedules and managing on a limited budget.

To begin your job search, you need to decide what you want to do and determine what skills you have that are needed in the job marketplace. Consider whether you want to work full or part time. Are you able to work evenings or weekends, or travel on the job? To help you decide exactly what you want to do, try answering the following questions.

**What Do You Want to Do?**

*What kinds of people would I enjoy working with?* Are you stimulated by professional types like scientists, engineers, lawyers, teachers, sales and marketing executives? Or rather by the needs of children, young adults, senior citizens, patients requiring care? Another way to group types of people is by industry, such as construction, stock market, advertising, retail merchandising, banking and so on.

*What types of work have I enjoyed previously?* Did I like working as part of a team, or independently? Did I enjoy interacting with people, or did I prefer less gregarious activities, such as writing or organizing reports and accounts? Some persons work better with books and computer terminals, while others are more stimulated by people contact, as in sales or the health care professions.

*What types of jobs did I dislike?* If, for example, you disliked repetitive, routine tasks that resulted in a high level of boredom, or if dealing with customers or patients made you feel apprehensive, try to avoid that kind of occupation in the future.

*What skills do I have?* Ordinarily we think of our skills as those for which we received training or formal education, such as typing, word processing, carpentry, music, teaching, nursing, etc. But you have other skills that you may not be aware of that are valued in the business world. You have acquired many of them just in the course of daily living, being part of a family and learning to deal with a wide spectrum of human problems—arranging schedules, managing money, directing children's growth and development.

The following list may help you generate your own ideas about other skills you may have. If it isn't practical to include all your skills on a résumé or on the job application, try to work them into the conversation when you are interviewed. The skills you mention should be appropriate for the job you are trying to get.

Ability to:
- Define and analyze problems,
- Plan and organize work,

- Work independently without immediate supervision,
- Coordinate the work of several others,
- Work under pressure,
- Meet tight deadlines,
- Check long technical records,
- Edit for grammar, punctuation, spelling,
- Order supplies, foreseeing what may be needed,
- Explain new procedures,
- Do detail work repeatedly,
- Remember procedures and directions well.

You may have skills from being a volunteer at your children's school, your church or clubs. You may be good at organizing events, fund raising, public speaking, writing articles for publication or motivating other people.

*What personality traits do I possess that would benefit a business?* Traits to consider include:

- Reliability,
- Initiative,
- Adaptability,
- Judgment,
- Creativity,
- Cooperativeness,
- Perseverance.

*What are my interests and hobbies?* Your interests and hobbies may guide you toward a specific job. For example, if you are an antiques buff, you could work as an appraiser for an insurance company or start your own antiques business. If you are especially good with house plants, consider starting a house plant supply and tending service for local businesses.

*What educational or technical training do I have?* For women with little work experience, training and education are perhaps the primary factors that come to mind when they begin job hunting. Do you need to update your training?

If you need help assessing your abilities, local colleges usually have testing and placement centers where you can evaluate your skills. Typical classes teach job readiness, résumé writing, assertiveness and self-esteem. You may need to take vocational or technical classes to bring your training up to date.

Two national sources for career counseling are:

Displaced Homemakers Network
1010 Vermont Avenue, NW, Suite 817
Washington, DC 20005
(202) 628-6767

Catalyst
250 Park Avenue South
New York, NY 10003
(212) 777-8900

Once you have considered what you do or do not want to do, and have listed your skills and traits, you are ready to find out where the jobs are.

When you know what you want to do and are confident you can do the job, how do you find a position? The following job-hunting techniques will require time and effort on your part, but, with persistence, they should pay off in the end.

**Where Are the Jobs?**

*Networking.* Informally, you can let all your friends and associates know you are looking for employment; tell your dentist, attorney, minister—anyone who may know of an opportunity. The advantage is, these friends and professionals know you. Determine who can best help you locate a job, contact them, follow their advice and keep them informed of your progress. Ask if you can use them as a reference when you apply for a job.

Your best chance of finding a first job is through someone who knows you. If you are a woman who has never worked outside the home and has no formal career history, your attitude and enthusiasm are your two greatest advantages. People who know your personality and character traits, or who have observed your volunteer efforts, are more likely to take a chance on you in the business world. Networking is your best avenue for a job.

*Unpaid Work.* Sometimes you can work into a paid position by first working as an unpaid intern or by "shadowing" a professional and learning through observation. The prospective employer is spared the training expense, and you get the opportunity to demonstrate your abilities.

*Temporary Agencies.* Working with a temporary agency can provide contacts for a later permanent position. You will get a variety of jobs, gain experience and develop new skills and confidence.

*Newspaper Ads.* Reading the newspaper ads gives you an idea of what is available in your community. Answer the ads that appear interesting to you, giving enough details to get an interview. Never elaborate on what you *cannot* do, whether in a written application or in an interview. That can result in your application being disqualified or screened out before the interview.

*Employment Agencies.* If you choose to use an employment agency, your best bet is one that collects the placement fee from the employer. Many employment agencies test your skills and aptitudes. You may have to pay a testing fee. Some agencies charge you a fee if you are placed in an acceptable job. Avoid agencies that charge an up-front placement fee even if you are not placed in a job. If you can qualify as a high-level executive, it may be worth your while to get in touch with an executive search firm or a "headhunter" agency.

## Writing a Résumé

Whether you are applying for a promotion, re-entering the job market or looking for a first-time job, you need to write a résumé. This abbreviated account of your skills, work history and personal background is intended to pique the interest of a prospective employer. It may be the only information an employer has about you. The information in your résumé will be compared to that of other applicants.

In a résumé you are expected to toot your own horn, but include only information directly applicable to the jobs you are seeking; for example, your prowess at college volleyball is not pertinent to an office job. Résumés are written in three styles— chronological, functional or a combination of the two. If you have never worked or have little work history, we recommend the functional style, which emphasizes your skills. We include two sample résumés, one functional and the other chronological. Study both types and try writing your résumé each way to see which seems the most impressive to you.

In writing your résumé, keep these guidelines in mind:

- Type or print the résumé to fit on one page of good-quality paper. Avoid typographical errors, erasures and corrections. Try to avoid running over to a second page; it might get lost, plus busy employers with hundreds of applications won't take the time to read two pages.

• Include your name, address and telephone numbers at the top of the page. If you are often away from those numbers, list the number of a friend who will take messages or attach a phone message recorder to your phone.

• Describe each skill or work experience with clear and concise language. Some résumés begin each phrase with an "action" verb, such as "organized," "planned," "directed," "scheduled," "coordinated" or "reported."

• Include volunteer experience if it is applicable to the job.

• List other qualifications that may apply to the job, such as education, honors, community activities, fluency in foreign languages or equipment skills.

• List three references or, if space is short, state "Available upon request."

• Ask a business friend or career counselor to critique your résumé.

On the following sample résumé, notice that Jane Doe has never worked in an office environment. Her skills have been learned as a family manager, PTA president, volunteer student-exchange coordinator, and hostess to welcome new residents to her community. Her résumé is functionally oriented, that is, she focuses on what she can do, using verbs that describe her actions or functions: e.g., "directed," "coordinated," "planned," "managed," "presented," "counseled." Jane Doe has had experience speaking in public, organizing and motivating people, and resolving problems. These skills are readily usable in the business world. When you write your first résumé, include your people-managing experiences. Working with people can be learned only by doing, whether it is in an office situation, at home or in the community at large.

You may want to omit mention of a specific career objective if you are using the résumé to apply for several types of positions (and if you do not have access to a word processor). You can always state your career objective in the cover letter that accompanies your résumé, and tailor it to fit the position for which you are applying. The objective should directly relate to the position you are seeking.

The second sample résumé is chronological and better suited to a person who has a work history. Her experience is from her office work, rather than through the volunteer route.

## SAMPLE RESUME—FUNCTIONAL

(typical style used by non-career person)

Jane Doe
1234 Main Street
Anytown, USA 00000
(800) 555-0000

| | |
|---|---|
| Career Objective | Position in office administration with potential for office manager. |
| Career-Related Experience | 1985–Present  Area coordinator for International High School Student Exchange Program. Screen, interview and assist with host family selections. Counsel families or students with problems, host students on as-needed basis. Present speeches to community organizations to promote program. Coordinate advertising for program at area high schools. |
| | 1963–Present Home administrator and family manager. Direct children's activities, coordinate schedules, plan and manage financial affairs. |
| | 1986–1987    President, High School Parent Teacher's Association. Directed support staff, successfully chaired fund raising for Junior-Senior Prom, recruited 22 merchants as associated members. |
| | 1984–1986    Welcome Wagon Hostess. Solicited merchant support, independently canvassed real estate agencies and business newspapers to track newcomers, arranged appointments to welcome new area residents. |
| Education | 1987          Assertiveness Workshop, Womanschool Program. |
| | 1978          PTA President Training Workshop. |
| | 1959–1962   Attended State University with a major in Physical Education. |
| Interests | 1984–Present Homeowners Association Board Member. |
| | 1982–1986   Meals on Wheels food service to Seniors. |
| | 1983          Newcomers Club President. |
| | Camping, Church, Girl Scouts. |
| References | Available upon request. |

## SAMPLE RESUME—CHRONOLOGICAL

(typical style used by persons with work history)

Jane Doe
1234 Main Street
Anytown, USA 00000
(800) 555-0000

| | | |
|---|---|---|
| Career Objective | | Personnel Manager. |
| Career Experiences | 1983–Present | Public Service Company of Colorado. Training officer in charge of Upward Mobility Career Option. Plan curriculum and create selection criteria for instructors, track student career progress, develop training policy revisions. |
| | 1981–1983 | Public Service Company of Colorado. Staff Personnel Analyst. Reviewed and ranked job applications, conducted interviews, analyzed and wrote position descriptions for summer-hire students. |
| | 1980–1981 | Sport and Health Club Assistant Aerobics Instructor. Scheduled weekly aerobics classes, filled in as lead aerobics instructor as needed, instructed new members in using Nautilus exercise equipment. Summer and part-time position. |
| Education | 1981–Present | Continuing education courses for personnel and training officers. See attached schedule. |
| | 1980 | Bachelor of Science, Political Science, State University. |
| Interests and Activities | | Member, American Assn. Personnel Administrators. Treasurer, Green Acres Townhome Association. Skiing, guitar, French. |
| References | | Available upon request. |

Always include a cover letter with your résumé. It identifies who you are and the position for which you are applying. If possible, address the letter to an individual by name, not title only. Call the company and ask for the appropriate person's name. The cover letter should be brief and cover three points: the position you are applying for, why you are qualified, and your interest in the firm and the position. Include phone numbers where you can be reached.

**Submitting Your Résumé**

## SAMPLE COVER LETTER

March 4, 1988

Name or Personnel Department
Address of Firm

Dear Sir or Madam:

    I am writing to apply for the position of _____ as advertised in
_____ on _____ .
(Or you could write: "I am writing to apply for the position of _____
as mentioned to me by _____ .)

    My qualifications are especially appropriate for this position because
_____
_____ .

    Enclosed is a copy of my résumé. If my qualifications are of interest to you, I am available for a personal interview at your convenience.

Sincerely yours,
*your signature*
your typewritten name

Enclosure

---

**The Application Form**

Many firms prefer an application form to a résumé. These forms usually resemble the standard blank application forms that can be purchased in an office supply store. Like a résumé, they specify personal data like name, address and phone numbers and usually include a chronological job history. List your most recent experience beginning with the present date, then proceeding in reverse order showing your previous jobs; your oldest job experience will be last.

    If you are unemployed at the present date, state the fact or consider a creative alternative, perhaps something like the following:

From____ to Present.     Position Title: Career Homemaker.
Job Duties: Manage family finances, direct children's activities, maintain home environment, coach soccer team for B-division girls. For community service, serve as homeowner association secretary and member of county parks and open space planning. Direct church choir.

You may want to purchase a standard application form and complete it at home. Make photocopies. If a standard application form is not acceptable, you will already have the information organized to complete the company form when you appear in person to apply for a position. Attach a copy of your résumé.

**The Interview**

The purpose of the résumé and application is to get you an interview. It is hoped that the prospective employer will want to know more about you. Are you someone who would be able to do the job and fit in the company? In the interview the employer gets more information about you from your responses, your appearance and your attitude.

Arrive ahead of the scheduled interview time. (Finding an unfamiliar address and office may take more time than you anticipate.) Freshen up and check your appearance in the restroom. Don't let yourself be rushed, breathless and late; you will appear disorganized.

Your personal appearance indicates how attentive you are to detail. A neat, clean person has taken the time to pay attention to clothing, hair, nails, shoes. Wear tailored, subdued clothing—a business suit for an office position. No strappy evening sandals, bright nail polish, clanky jewelry or scuffed shoes. Scents or perfumes should be light or not worn at all.

Do your homework about the business beforehand. At the library you will find information about major companies in the Dun & Bradstreet reports or in *Moody's Industrial Manual.* If it is a small, local business, call your Chamber of Commerce for information about it.

Be prepared for interview questions. Some of the common ones are:

- Why have you applied for this position?
- Why should you be hired for this position?
- What do you expect to gain from our company?

- What are your greatest strengths and weaknesses?
- What are your short- and long-term career goals?
- Tell us about yourself.
- Why are you leaving your present job?
- How do you handle pressure?
- What questions do you have for us?

When you are being interviewed, don't say anything negative about a former employer or your current employer. The reason you leave an employer is for a "better growth opportunity," or "to learn new skills," or "to assume greater responsibilities and accept new challenges." Be positive about why you are seeking new employment.

Once you have been offered a position, but before you make an irrevocable commitment, you should be sure you understand the work hours, salary, overtime and weekend work requirements; whether travel is involved; what benefits are provided, such as health, dental or life insurance; and any retirement plan. If you don't clearly understand the job responsibilities that were described in the interview, ask the interviewer to review them.

Your general demeanor or "body language" also makes an impression. Sit attentively forward in your chair; don't slouch. Make and keep eye contact during the interview. Save your smoking for outside. Unless asked, avoid discussing your personal problems (especially grieving), lest you seem unable to devote your attention and energy to the job. At the conclusion, thank them for the interview and follow it up the next day with a brief thank-you note.

## Alternatives to "Nine-to-Five" Work

If you are not able to leave your home for the workplace on a regular basis, try to come up with a money-making activity that can be undertaken in your own environment: free-lance typing or word processing, telemarketing (selling things by telephone contact), catering, making handicrafts for sale through local shops, consultation work, teaching music lessons or a foreign language.

Another possibility is to provide a day-care home for children of working mothers. Most communities have licensing requirements, so call your local social services office for guidance in starting a day-care center.

"Bed and breakfast" homes offer lodging and breakfast for the traveling public. The benefits include meeting new people and generating income. In some towns, renting two or fewer bedrooms constitutes a "host home" and does not require licensing. For guidance about how to start , order the book *How to Open a Bed and Breakfast Home*, by Jan Starkus, Travelers' Information Exchange, 356 Boylston Street, Boston, MA 02116. To advertise, register with a reservation service.

Another idea is to rent a room in your home to students or to relatives of hospital patients. Call your city or county planning and zoning board to determine if there are any restrictions about renting rooms in your neighborhood. Register with the housing office of the college or hospital.

"Foster Grandparents," sponsored by the Volunteers of America, pays a small hourly fee, car fare and lunch to grandparents who spend time with infants and children in hospitals or other institutions. To see if you qualify for this low-income senior program, write the Volunteers of America (address shown earlier in this chapter.)

An alternative to increasing your income is to decrease your housing costs by sharing a home. Project Share is a nationwide housing program designed to match people offering homes with people seeking affordable housing. Contact the Gray Panthers, a senior citizens' advocacy organization, at 6342 Greene Street, Philadelphia, PA 19144, (215) 438-0276. If your income is quite limited and you have few assets, you may qualify for Supplemental Security Income. Call the Social Security Administration in your area to find out how to apply for benefits.

Whether you plan to enter the work force or to serve others as a volunteer, you are beginning another phase in your new role as an independent woman. Sitting at home alone, grieving for what you had and what you lost, will turn you even more inward and cause you to lose touch with the world outside. Getting involved with people—helping them or interacting with them in other ways—forces you to look ahead and outward. You have warmth, caring and skills to share with the world around you.

## Notes

# Chapter 17

# *Taking Care of Those You Love— Estate Planning*

By now, in looking to your future, you are aware of how important it is to plan ahead—to arrange what will happen with your estate for your heirs. In this context the term *estate* refers to personal and real property. An estate is the whole of one's possessions. You are in charge of managing your estate assets—for yourself and for the ones you love. You may decide that you need life insurance and a will to direct who gets what benefits and to take advantage of tax savings. In making a will you are starting an estate plan, which requires that you review what you own and how you want it distributed when you die. Without an estate plan or will your state laws determine the distribution for you, which often involves onerous legal costs.

A note is in order to clarify the difference between "estate settlement" and "estate planning." Estate settlement is the process of distributing a deceased person's property (personal belongings and real property) according to the terms and conditions of the will, if one existed, or according to the state laws where the deceased lived, if he or she died without a will. The process occurs *after death*. Estate planning, on the other hand, occurs *during life*. People who have reason to plan for the well-being of heirs or who wish to arrange for charitable contributions often develop an estate plan to manage present assets for themselves and to determine how the assets will be distributed after death.

**Your Estate**

In this chapter we discuss planning your estate, understanding a will and trusts, and deciding whether you need life insurance. For some people, making a will becomes the first step in estate planning. For example, the first time Charlotte and her husband created their wills, the attorneys advised them to list who owned what property, to consider whether to transfer title to any property in order to distribute the asset values between husband and wife, to name who the children's guardians would be, and to estimate the value of any assets each might inherit. The will became a simplified estate plan that suited their assets at the time. Once she became a widow, Charlotte reviewed and changed her estate plan to provide security for her almost-adult children and to minimize the taxes they might have to pay when she dies.

If you know with certainty that the total value of your estate is less than $600,000 (or the amount specified by current law), including life insurance, then estate planning is not required in order to save taxes. But, for an estate of any size, no matter how modest, a will that stipulates how your assets should be distributed will simplify your heirs' responsibilities in settling your estate. If you die intestate (without a will), your dollars may be absorbed by the legal costs of estate settlement and your state laws will decide who receives your possessions.

**What Is an Estate Plan?**

An estate plan is an expression of your own desires and objectives for the ownership, management and preservation of your property during your lifetime and your desires for its disposition upon your death.[33] During your lifetime it can benefit you by giving you tax advantages and a feeling of security. In establishing an estate plan, you must decide whether you should buy life insurance and place property in a trust. Your estate plan could save your heirs substantial sums in tax bills and administrative fees. In some circumstances, there are benefits to giving gifts during your lifetime as opposed to giving them by will.

**Who Creates an Estate Plan and How?**

You initiate an estate plan with your attorney and may later solicit the advice of a tax accountant, an insurance advisor, a trust officer or a certified financial counselor. You begin with a review and an analysis of ownership of all your property, your life insurance policies (or any you plan to purchase), business interests, your will and any benefits you might inherit. You must consider the ever-present taxes for every aspect of your estate.

As a result of the estate plan, and on the advice of your attorney, you may decide to update your will, change the amount of life insurance you own or change the title to some of your properties. The estate plan will be a custom-designed and confidential document between you and your attorney.

If you are a farm or ranch widow you may wish to plan for continuing the family farm business with one of your children or another family member. There are a number of arrangements that permit a farm or ranch owner to gradually relinquish the burden of business, yet protect your investment and assure yourself a good income. Your lawyer can work out a plan that is best for you. If it seems feasible, consult with your attorney and ask about the following possibilities. You might:

- Form a *partnership* that will divide income on a formula based on the relative value of contributions of land, equipment and labor.
- *Incorporate* the farm business (if permitted in your state), gradually giving ownership to your successor by gifts of stock, yet assuring an income for yourself. You can also work out option arrangements so that, after your death, operating family members will be able to retain control, while off-farm heirs also will be treated fairly.
- Consider an *installment sale contract* with a family member. This can minimize capital gains and often reduce taxes in your estate. It can assure you a steady income, yet permit your successor to acquire the business gradually.
- Arrange a *long-term lease* with the successor operator.

**Things to Consider in an Estate Plan**

Always consult your attorney or trust officer for specific legal or tax advice about your estate plan. *In estate planning, all you are doing is determining the value of your possessions and deciding how you want them distributed in the event of your death.*

The complicating factor is current tax law. The way your property is owned, either by yourself or with someone else, and how much you direct to any one individual, will make a difference in the amount of taxes due.

To begin the plan, you need the following:

• A list of personal information, including (a) your name and address, (b) marital history of your late husband and your own marital history and plans, (c) complete name, address and birth date of each intended beneficiary, (d) location of assets, (e) your power of attorney. For every piece of property having a title, you need the information about how the property is owned—that is, by yourself or with someone else;

• Income tax returns for the past three years; these indicate your tax bracket and show different types of assets;

• A copy of your current will (unless this is the first time you have made a will as well as an estate plan);

• Life insurance policies on your own life;

• A statement of your net worth based on your assets and liabilities. To determine your net worth, you first have to locate and describe your assets, which is all that you own having monetary value, including money anyone else owes you. Next, determine the value of your liabilities, which is everything you owe. The difference between assets and liabilities is your net worth. If you were the personal representative in charge of settling your husband's estate, you are probably familiar with the concept of net worth determination. Remember, however, this time you are describing *your* estate, not his, and yours will be different.

You may encounter numerous requirements for a personal "Asset and Liability" statement, so we include sample forms in this chapter that are similar to those in Chapter 7. But first, there are some explanatory comments. Most people recognize the asset headings shown on the worksheet; the problem is how to determine the value of each item. If you have already completed the estate settlement, you have many of these valuations at your fingertips. But your assets may be different, because they will reflect assets in your own name, as well as those you inherited from your late husband.

You can easily determine the newest cash balance in your checking, savings and money market accounts by reviewing your last statement. If you need recent values for stocks and bonds, ask your broker for assistance. Closely held business interests and real estate valuations done for the estate settlement may apply, if you were the beneficiary; otherwise, ask your attorney or trust department for assistance. If you work full time, include your own employee benefit and retirement plans.

In addition to listing each asset, you must state how title is held for each and what they cost when they were purchased. For example, whose signatures are allowed on each checking account? Is the real estate solely in your name, in joint tenancy with someone else, as tenants in common, or as community property? The same question applies to all personal property, such as autos, furniture, art, boats, etc. We discuss these terms next in this chapter to clarify the difference. Ask your attorney for help if you don't understand.

"Joint tenancy," the most familiar form of plural ownership, exists when two persons own a given asset like a bank account or their common residence. The intent is that when one dies the ownership of the property will pass *automatically* to the surviving owner. Joint tenancy is fairly common between husband and wife. Some persons mistakenly think that owning assets in joint tenancy will avoid all concerns and costs associated with probate. However, joint tenancy with other family members may cause problems. If you, for example, should decide to include one or more of your children as co-owners of your home, then you would need their approval if you ever wanted to sell the house. What if you were tired of the cold and snow and wanted to sell your home and move south, but your joint tenants felt the "family home" should be kept for sentimental value? If you could not get the joint tenants to agree to the sale, you would stay in the cold, snowy climate.

"Tenancy by the entirety" is another kind of spousal joint ownership in some states that allows the entire property to go to the surviving spouse. But unlike joint tenancy, neither spouse may dispose of the property without the other's approval.

"Tenancy in common" allows joint ownership with each owner having an undivided interest in the property and provides that each owner may sell or otherwise transfer his or her own portion. If any owner dies, his or her property passes to the heirs or beneficiaries named in the will. The survivors do not automatically take title. An example of tenancy in common is income or business property between family members other than spouses.

"Community property" co-ownership is recognized in only a few states. Half of what is acquired or earned during a marriage is held to be equally owned by husband and wife. When one

**ESTATE PLANNING ASSETS WORKSHEET**

*Cash* (bank, credit union, savings & loan, checking, money market, CDs, Christmas club, etc.)

| Financial Institution Name/Phone | Type of Account | Account No. | Ownership Sole (his name) Joint (other names) | Amount |
|---|---|---|---|---|
| _____ | _____ | _____ | _____ | $ _____ |
| _____ | _____ | _____ | _____ | $ _____ |
| _____ | _____ | _____ | _____ | $ _____ |
| _____ | _____ | _____ | _____ | $ _____ |
| | | | Total Value | $ _____ |

*Life Insurance*

| Company Name/Phone | Policy No. | Beneficiary(ies) | Cash Value* | Face Amount |
|---|---|---|---|---|
| _____ | _____ | _____ | _____ | $ _____ |
| _____ | _____ | _____ | _____ | $ _____ |
| *(accumulated dividends, credit for unused premiums, etc.) | | | Total Value | $ _____ |

*Real Estate*

| Description Location | Date | Purchase Price | Ownership Sole/Joint | Cost Basis | Appraised Value |
|---|---|---|---|---|---|
| _____ | _____ | _____ | _____ | $ _____ | $ _____ |
| _____ | _____ | _____ | _____ | $ _____ | $ _____ |
| _____ | _____ | _____ | _____ | $ _____ | $ _____ |
| _____ | _____ | _____ | _____ | $ _____ | $ _____ |
| | | | | Total Value | $ _____ |

*Securities—Stocks, Bonds, Mutual Funds, Unit Trust, Government Securities*

| Inst./Broker Name/Phone | Account No. | Ownership Sole/Joint | Cost Basis | Value at Death or Alternate Date |
|---|---|---|---|---|
| | | | $ | $ |
| | | | $ | $ |
| | | | $ | $ |
| | | | $ | $ |
| | | | Total Value | $ |

*Pensions, Annuities, Retirement Plans, Profit Sharing, IRAs, KEOGHs*

| Description & Location (firm name) | Account No. | Value of Survivor Benefits (if any) |
|---|---|---|
| | | $ |
| | | $ |
| | | $ |
| | Total Value | $ |

*Business Interests (corporations, partnerships, sole proprietorships)*

| Firm Name/Address/Phone | Type of Business | Cost Basis | Appraised Value |
|---|---|---|---|
| | | $ | $ |
| | | $ | $ |
| | | $ | $ |
| | | Total Value | $ |

*Debts Owed to You (notes, mortgages, royalties, patents, etc.)*

| Name of Person/ Firm Owing | Address/Phone | Ownership Sole/Joint | Date Due | Amount |
|---|---|---|---|---|
| | | | | $ |
| | | | | $ |
| | | | | $ |
| | | | Total Value | $ |

*Personal Property (collections such as coins, guns, stamps, vehicles, art, furniture, etc.)*

| Description | Location | Estimated Current Value |
|---|---|---|
| | | $ |
| | | $ |
| | | $ |
| | | $ |
| | Total Value | $ |
| | TOTAL OF ALL ASSETS | $ |

## ESTATE PLANNING LIABILITIES WORKSHEET

*Mortgages, Liens, Property Taxes*

| Description of Property | To Whom Owed | Date Owed | Amount |
|---|---|---|---|
| | | | $ |
| | | | $ |
| | | | $ |
| | | | $ |
| | | Total Value | $ |

*Loans (auto, personal, insurance, average monthly bills, etc.)*

| Description | To Whom Owed–Address/Phone | Amount |
|---|---|---|
| | | $ |
| | | $ |
| | | $ |
| | | $ |
| | Total Value | $ |

| | |
|---|---|
| TOTAL VALUE ALL LIABILITIES | $ |

## NET WORTH WORKSHEET

| | | |
|---|---|---|
| | Total Value Assets | $ |
| (less) | Total Value Liabilities | $ |
| | Net Worth | $ |

spouse dies, that property is subject to disposition by the will according to specific state laws.

Liabilities (in estate planning) are debts that you owe, payments due on contracts you have signed, and unpaid taxes on property you own.

To compute your net worth, make the best estimate you can of what your value would be if you could sell all your assets and pay off all your bills right this minute. What is left over is your "net worth." Ascertaining your net worth is a time-consuming effort. It changes from year to year and requires regular updating.

## Your Will

It is never too early to consider how your property should be distributed to the people you care about. If you have a home, a car, collectibles, jewelry, antiques or items with sentimental value, do you want your state laws deciding who gets what and how much? If you have children who are minors—under age twenty-one in most states—and you die without a will, the state will decide who their guardian will be. It might not be the person or family you would choose! With a valid will, you can save your heirs substantial sums in taxes and legal fees. And you can choose who gets what.

First we'll review the benefits of a will. In the Glossary we list the most common elements or clauses of a will and define commonly used terminology. We mention considerations for establishing a trust and scheduling periodic reviews to change your will to fit your ever-changing estate.

## Benefits of a Will and Problems of Dying Without a Will

If you die "testate"—that is, with a will—you protect your family's present and future financial needs, name a guardian for your underage children, and avoid delays and added expenses that dying "intestate"—without a will—might involve. You decide who will be the personal representative who makes sure your wishes are carried out. And most important, you can minimize potentially huge tax bills!

You may already be sadly aware of what happens when someone dies without a will. Your state laws will settle the estate for you (causing additional legal expenses). These laws are inflexible and impersonal, often leaving out distant relatives, friends or charities. The intestacy laws dictate to whom and in what amounts your property (except for jointly owned property) will be distributed.[34] It could cost your heirs more to settle the estate without a will than it could cost to have one written! The state will also appoint the executor of your estate and name guardians for your children. (For example, if you were the stepmother of your late husband's children, the state could appoint their natural mother as their guardian.) There are three essential things to remember about a will. First, the will is revocable during life, meaning you can change it as often as you like. Second, it doesn't take effect until after death. Third, it applies to the conditions that exist at death. For example, if when you made your will you owned some stocks that you planned would go to a certain family member upon your death, but you sold them before you died, then the stocks are no longer available for distribution.

**Assistance in Writing a Will**

We recommend working with an attorney to write your will. The do-it-yourself approach can leave you at great risk; for example, crucial elements might contradict each other or simply be left out. An attorney who specializes in wills and trusts should have a thorough knowledge of tax-saving strategies to suit your needs.

To save yourself time and money, have the following information available for your first appointment:
- List of assets, with titles and abstract descriptions for real property, and names of those to whom you wish them distributed,
- Guardians' names and addresses, and their relationship to you,
- Designated executor's name and address.

**Understanding the Will**

Many people avoid executing or writing a will because they are afraid of something they don't understand. Writing a will won't hasten your death! Writing a will saves problems, time and money for your heirs. The term *will* comes from "last will and testament." The dictionary defines it as the legal document that contains the declaration of how a person wishes his estate to be disposed of after death. The will is composed of articles or clauses, each with a specific purpose.

A few clauses are as simple as your own name, legal residence and signature; the others make common sense if you look beyond the legal jargon and are not intimidated by those long pages. Remember to review and rewrite your will as your life circumstances change. Amending your will with a codicil (supplement) is risky because of potentially conflicting terminology.

## Trusts

In estate planning and will making, another way of transferring ownership of property is through trusts. With the dozens of important decisions you have had to make, it is understandable that you might want to avoid establishing something as complex as a trust, but these under-used devices can be flexible plans for providing economic security not only for yourself but also for the people you love. It is even more important for the widow to consider how a trust can provide tax savings and asset-preservation benefits for her dependents; the estate tax consequences are vastly different when the second spouse dies! (We are assuming that within your immediate family your husband was the first spouse to die and that you will presumably be the second spouse to die. The tax laws allow certain deductions and exclusions when an estate is passed between spouses; however, the tax rules are different when an estate is distributed to heirs such as children or grandchildren. Your attorney can provide specific tax advice with respect to your circumstances.)

Before you begin drawing up a trust, or start educating yourself on the subject of trusts, consider the size of your estate and determine your net worth from the asset and liability worksheets. If your total estate is worth less than $600,000 today, you probably don't need to establish a trust for tax purposes. Nonetheless, if you need help managing your property or money, to preserve its value or to manage it for your underage children, then by all means consider a trust.

## What Is a Trust?

A trust is a written, legal document in which you entrust another individual or an institution to responsibly manage your property (assets) for another person (such as a son or daughter) or for an institution (such as a charity). There are many kinds of trusts, each for specific purposes. In this book we discuss only personal trusts established by individuals for the benefit of other individuals. For you the widow, the main considerations of a trust are to reduce taxes for your heirs and to provide for children who are minors or elderly dependents.

Should you wish to establish a trust, consult an attorney who specializes in estates, trusts and wills. A basic understanding of trusts and the benefits you might receive will help you decide whether you want to establish one. Trust management is regulated by state laws, and federal law prescribes how and when taxes are paid on the income from the trust. The two main reasons to establish a trust are for tax advantages and to take care of people through sound asset management.

## TRUST TERMINOLOGY

You, the creator of the trust, are called the "grantor" or "settlor." The manager (there can be more than one) is named the "trustee," and the recipients of the benefits of the trust are the "beneficiaries." Often property placed in a trust is cash to be invested. But it also can be land, buildings, stocks, bonds, life insurance proceeds, savings or money market accounts—just about any asset you wish, providing the trustee is willing to receive and manage it. Frequently, the grantor puts existing investments into the trust, directing the trustee to guard them and make changes only according to the instructions in the trust. Learning the terminology will save you time and money in being educated by your attorney!

## PURPOSES OF TRUSTS

Often trusts are set up to manage assets for minors until they reach a legal age or the age specified in the trust. Another common use is to provide care for an older person who may become incompetent to manage assets. You can even establish a trust for yourself. Persons with extensive holdings may choose to have a trustee manage their properties because they are busy with other affairs. Perhaps your late husband established a "life estate" trust for you, in which the income from the trust assets is payable to you, and after your death the principal of the trust passes to your heirs without being included in your taxable estate. In this life estate trust, your bank may have been named trustee because your husband didn't want to burden you with managing the assets.

TYPES OF PERSONAL TRUSTS

One commonly used personal trust is the "living" or "*inter vivos*" trust, which is in effect while you are still alive. Living trusts may be "revocable," that is, the grantor who created the trust may alter, amend or revoke the trust. If you set up a revocable living trust and later change your mind (returning the trust assets to your ownership and control), then the value of the assets in the trust become part of your taxable estate, upon which death taxes may be levied.

The value to estate planning in using wills and trusts is that it can help the widow manage her assets, eliminate the need for guardianships and save death taxes. Professional trustees such as attorneys, banks and trust organizations charge a minimum annual fee for managing a trust. If your assets are very small, consider the size of the annual management fee compared to the income generated by the trust.

**Life Insurance**

As we have discussed, it is important that you take steps *now* to provide for those you love after you are gone. For many people, the first solution that comes to mind is life insurance. However, if you have cash or any other liquid asset that your heirs might use to pay your last debts, and if your family's longer-term financial security is provided for otherwise, you may not need life insurance. For example, Charlotte currently has life insurance to provide for her college-age children, should something happen to her. But when they are educated and on their own, to lower annual premium costs, she may reduce her life insurance coverage to pay only funeral, administrative and tax expenses.

Now that you may be the "breadwinner" or primary source of income to support not only yourself but your dependents, you should consider what would happen to your children or aging parents if the unthinkable happened—an accident or a terminal illness resulting in your own death. You have just been through a major unexpected event—your husband's death—and you know how important it is that insurance is or will be available. If there was no insurance, you have even more reason to read this chapter—to protect the people you love.

Why should you consider life insurance? What kind? How much? If you have children or aging relatives who are financially dependent on you, you owe it to them to provide some protection against their losing your paycheck. If you die, who will pay your medical and burial expenses, legal fees and estate taxes? Who will provide a livelihood and education for your children? These questions are not meant to alarm you but to remind you of your responsibilities.

**Types of Life Insurance**

Do not be confused by life insurance choices. There are currently two popular, basic kinds of life insurance—term and universal. Persons over age fifty may be familiar with the older, and still sold kind, "whole life insurance." Other types are but variations on these three.

*Term life insurance* is coverage for a specific term of one or more years (until you reach a certain age, often sixty-five). After that point the insurance coverage ceases. This is the least-expensive type of insurance you can buy. Some term insurance policies are renewable without an annual medical examination for one or more additional terms even if your health deteriorates. However, the premiums usually increase each year or term for the same amount of insurance coverage. Be sure to ask if your term policy can be converted to whole life insurance if you choose and at what price.

*Universal life insurance* offers lower premium rates similar to term insurance, builds a cash value similar to whole life, and allows choices of variable premiums, variable amounts of insurance and different premium due dates. Premiums paid toward the policy accumulate a cash value and earn a variable interest rate. Universal life is flexible and allows you to change your insurance to meet your changing life circumstances.

*Whole life (straight life, ordinary life, or permanent) insurance* provides death protection at any age, or as the policy reads, providing you pay the premiums to keep it in force. Generally you pay the same premiums from year to year. The premium is used partly to buy pure insurance; the remainder goes into reserves and builds "cash value." The cash value is somewhat like a savings account, and you can borrow money from it, sometimes at very low interest rates. Because it has cash value, this type of insurance is more expensive. Whole life insurance has problems because a non-expert can't always tell a good from a bad policy. You sometimes pay a huge penalty if you drop the policy after a few years, and the interest earned by the cash value savings is at a low rate. *Single premium whole life* is a variation on whole life insurance in which a lump sum single premium is paid, earning interest at a variable rate.

## Choosing and Working with an Agent

A life insurance agent usually represents only one company, while a life insurance broker can sell policies from many insurance companies. In every state these people are required to be licensed to sell insurance. Ask your friends about their agent or broker and how helpful he or she has been. The initials CLU—Chartered Life Underwriter—following an agent's name indicate that the agent has spent considerable time studying life insurance and family financial services. Membership in the NALU, the National Association of Life Underwriters, indicates that the agent subscribes to both the professional and ethical standards of the industry. To learn more about individual insurance companies, go to your library and look up their ratings in *Best's Insurance Reports* by A.M. Best Company.

An agent should be willing to explain various policies and other related matters. Make certain that he or she intends to review your coverage from time to time. Life insurance is not static coverage. As your dependents' needs decrease, your insurance needs may decrease.

## Deciding How Much Insurance to Buy

Deciding how much life insurance you may need requires a little common-sense thinking as well as your making a list of what your survivors might need money for if you died. As a rule of thumb, some experts suggest from two to five times your yearly take-home pay. For example, if you take home $20,000 a year, you might need up to $100,000 in life insurance. However, you should consider several other factors in making your decision. You do not want to buy any more life insurance than you need.

To decide how much insurance to provide, first estimate cash needs to settle your estate, and monthly income and long-term needs for any dependents. A worksheet list is provided below for your estimates. (These "what if" exercises are guesses at best.)

This should give you a rough estimate of how much insurance you may need. For example, in 1984 Charlotte estimated $10,000 per older teenager per year for college and living expenses, with an additional $10,000 for burial and legal fees. As the children mature, she will reduce the amount of insurance.

**Understanding the Policy**

Once you have purchased a life insurance policy, you usually have a ten day "free look" which entitles you to change your mind. If you decide not to follow through, don't be intimidated by the agent's protestations. (Widows can be particularly vulnerable to life insurance sales pitches.) The company must refund your premium. When you buy life insurance (or any other kind), read every word of the policy. There are four major players in any life insurance contract: (1) the insured (probably yourself); (2) the beneficiary (person who gets the money from the insurance company when it pays off); (3) the owner of the policy (this can be you or someone else), who is responsible for paying the premiums to keep the policy in effect; and (4) the company issuing the contract.

A life insurance policy is a legal contract between the owner and the insurance company. As long as the premium payments are made, the insurance company promises to pay "proceeds" (money) to the beneficiary when the insured dies. You make this kind of contract to protect the people you care about and who are dependent on you.

**Reading a Life Insurance Policy**

To understand your life insurance policy, ask your agent to go over it with you. Every policy can be divided into three parts: (1) The first page outlines the basic features of the contract. It tells what kind of insurance you have, when benefits or proceeds are payable (at death), when premiums are payable and when dividends (if any) are payable. It also describes the amount of death benefit (same as face amount of the policy). (2) The details spell out the basic agreement. (3) The application contains the information you give to the company about yourself, which then becomes part of the policy.

## LIFE INSURANCE ESTIMATOR

*Estate Settlement Needs*

| | |
|---|---|
| Medical Costs (beyond health insurance) | $ _____ |
| Funeral Costs ($4,000–$10,000 is typical) | $ _____ |
| Legal Fees (to settle your estate; estimate $150 per hour for ten hours minimum) | $ _____ |
| Estate Taxes (ask your attorney—this is complex) | $ _____ |
| Other Debts (immediate bills that are due) | $ _____ |
| Sub-Total Estate Settlement | $ _____ |

*Monthly Cash Needs*

Mortgage/Rent (include property taxes).    $ _____

> Also consider here that you may have an extra-term life insurance policy to cover this mortgage. You can buy a "decreasing term" life insurance policy, which pays less money each year, and get just enough to cover the remaining mortgage on your home.

| | |
|---|---|
| Utilities (heat, electricity, water, phone) | $ _____ |
| Food | $ _____ |
| Clothing | $ _____ |
| Installment Payments (auto, other loans, charge accounts) Check to see if they are insured against your death. | $ _____ |
| Medical/Dental (Now that you are a widow, do you have to make monthly health insurance payments, and will your survivors have to make monthly payments?) | $ _____ |
| Education (away-from-home expenses, tuition) | $ _____ |
| Entertainment | $ _____ |
| Child Care/Housekeeping (Will your survivors need to hire child care or nursing care that you presently provide?) | $ _____ |
| Home/Auto Maintenance | $ _____ |
| Sub-Total Monthly | $ _____ |

*Long-Term and Occasional Cash Needs*

| | |
|---|---|
| Insurance– Auto | $ _____ |
| House | $ _____ |
| Life | $ _____ |
| Health/Disability | $ _____ |
| Taxes | $ _____ |
| Vacations | $ _____ |
| Other Lump Sums | $ _____ |
| Sub-Total Long-Term | $ _____ |

*Summary Cash Needs Estimated for Life Insurance Coverage*

| | |
|---|---|
| Total Immediate Needs | $ _____ |
| Monthly Needs x 12 Months x Number of Years Needed | $ _____ |
| Long-Term Needs | $ _____ |
| TOTAL ESTIMATED CASH NEEDS | $ _____ |

In addition to deciding whether you should buy life insurance, **Special** and how much, you need to consider who the beneficiaries are (for **Considerations** tax reasons) and whether they can handle large sums of money. This consideration is called the "settlement option." Ask both your agent and your attorney for advice about how to arrange the death proceeds payout. Should it be paid in one large sum over a specified period of time? Or should it be left with the insurance company to invest while the company pays your beneficiaries the interest? Be aware that some states require the insurance company to pay interest on the proceeds from the date of death until the check is written and sent to the beneficiary.

When you buy term insurance, the better policies allow conversion to whole life within a specified period (preferably to age sixty-five). A whole life policy should be convertible to a limited-payment or endowment plan without company approval, subject only to your paying the difference in cash values. An endowment plan is like a "retirement income insurance" that you can purchase for yourself.

Ask for a "waiver of premium" agreement, just in case you become disabled and can't work to earn the premiums.

Look for a "grace period," which allows you to make a late premium payment without losing your policy. Ask how long the grace period is.

Estate planning won't seem so overwhelming if you consider it in three phases: estimating the value of your estate, deciding whether you want your estate distributed to your heirs by will or by state law, and determining if you can reduce the tax burden for your heirs by establishing any trusts. Reviewing the basic terminology and working with professionals will help you put together a sound estate plan.

## Notes

# Chapter 18

# Taking Care of Your Money— Finance and Investments

Along with tending to their emotional well-being and personal recovery, many widows face immediate concerns of money, finance and investments. Years ago women were not expected to understand or care much about money—that is, in the broader sense of managing money for the family future. Traditionally, women have handled enough money to manage the home, while husbands initiated major purchases. She prepared dinner while he studied the financial pages. Today few women have the desire to become full-time financial experts, but they want to understand what is being done with their money, and on occasion make decisions about how their money is invested or review the recommendations made by their financial advisors.

If you are responsible for your own finances, you need to learn how to preserve your money and how to get it to earn more money. You should become acquainted with the basic principles of money management and investment in order to protect the estate you have inherited and/or to earn additional income. If you have as little as $50 to invest in a U.S. government savings bond, or an estate to oversee that is valued at as much as several hundred thousand dollars, you can try to increase what money you have so you have more to spend for special purchases or emergencies, or, more important, *to provide yourself with financial security for the remainder of your life.*

After you develop an understanding of what "investing" means, you need to decide whether you are in a position to be taking any chances with your money. Then you must decide whether you will make your own investment decisions or whether you will employ professionals to manage your financial affairs. The term *investing*, as used in this book, refers to any choice or decision you make about where to place your money to assure safety of principal (your originally invested dollars) and an adequate return. In his classic book, *The Intelligent Investor*, Benjamin Graham describes investments that do not meet these two criteria as "speculation."[35] It follows that hiding your money under the mattress or keeping your money in a checking account are not investments because they do not keep your principal safe and do not substantially increase the value of your savings. The mattress risks are obvious. Leaving your money in a checking account, which may not earn interest and which invites spending, runs the risk of eventually depleting your resources.

## Spending or "Misering"

The shock of widowhood can be so great, at least for the first few months, that it stops some women in their tracks, making it impossible for them to even think of planning for their future. They may vacillate between spending sprees and fear of poverty. They may be overwhelmed by "all that money" (the life insurance proceeds); it may seem, for a while, that they have a fortune. Eleanor, age thirty-five when she was widowed, received $125,000 from Rich's life insurance policies. She had a young son, and began her spending spree with a new car and some improvements to their home. Within a year she had only $70,000 left and the rest of their lives to plan. It had gone so quickly and easily!

At the other extreme, Gwen's widowed and well-fixed mother-in-law is so afraid to spend any money, she no longer continues the generous Christmas checks her husband used to give to their grandchildren. She has no will and refuses to consider one. This lady doesn't want to ever be a financial burden to her children, but doesn't understand that her inaction will eventually benefit only Uncle Sam!

Applying for and getting the life insurance proceeds and other assets from your late husband's estate is easy compared to deciding what to do with them. Immediate notions of wealth and comfort can suddenly be replaced by worries about future poverty and how to manage these assets to preserve their value. Consider the following situations with respect to your own circumstances:

**Why Take Care of Your Money?**

- Most widows face a reduced monthly income. Whether the husband was still employed or was receiving retirement checks at the time of his death, the surviving spouse may receive a significantly reduced monthly benefit. In some cases, the husband waived any survivor payments, leaving the widow without that monthly income. She may need Social Security or veterans' benefits. She will certainly need to hold on to her assets until she has a clear notion of what it will cost her to pay monthly bills and provide for her long-term financial future.

- Does $100,000 in life insurance proceeds seem like a fortune to you? Perhaps you and your husband lived modestly, yet were unable to accumulate more than a few thousand dollars. Before you go on a spending spree, consider how much it will cost you to live each year and how long you hope to live. If your living expenses are only $10,000 a year and the cost of living goes up each year, the life insurance will last less than ten years, without any big purchases like a new car. You may choose instead to take chances with the proceeds in order to try to earn additional returns for your future beyond the next ten years or to pay for a major purchase.

- Are you supporting yourself by working full time and also managing to save a little money each month? Do you understand how to compare investment choices so that you can decide where is the best place to keep your savings for maximum safety or greatest return?

- Did you inherit a stock and bond portfolio? Are you prepared to decide whether to hold the issues for a time, and do you know when to sell them? If you sell them, what do you intend to do with the proceeds? Spend them now on luxuries such as furs or jewelry, or reinvest them to earn perhaps a little more money for your future? If some of the stocks or bonds pay dividends or interest, you might be pleasantly surprised at how much they could augment your income.

The process of investing money concerns and confuses most people. Newspapers and magazines regularly feature "how-to-invest" articles. There are dozens of strategies suggested and investment choices advertised. Don't be misled by advertisements that imply that their interest rates are higher than anyone else's. The catch is that their rates may be higher, but for only a short time—a month or so; then they drop below the average return offered by other investment opportunities. For example, a recent bank newspaper ad touted that its new High Interest Passbook Account paid "X" percent interest on balances of $2,500 or more. What they didn't advertise was that this seemingly super rate was effective for only the first month, then the rate dropped by 2 percent!

**How This Chapter Is Organized**

This chapter is arranged in four parts. Three are termed "phases"; the fourth describes other investment alternatives. You may manage your resources according to the guidance in each phase, without proceeding to the next phase until you are ready. For example, if you have little interest in thinking about your money or are not yet ready to make important financial decisions, but you want to earn some return on your money, you can follow the plan suggested in the first phase. You need not move forward until you are somewhat recovered. In theory, you can stop after any phase without ever moving on to the next, managing your finances by simply continuing the procedures you are already following. However, the less you choose to mind your financial affairs the more you may have to depend on someone else to make decisions for you. *Ultimately, you are responsible for your own money!*

Phase I describes a "holding pattern" style for money management. You can place life insurance proceeds or other lump sums into secure, almost risk-free accounts, letting your money earn interest while you deal with other pressing matters. A few women, who might be described as "passive investors," use this holding pattern as their only money management strategy. Benjamin Graham has characterized the passive investor as one who places his or her chief emphasis on avoiding serious mistakes and who aims to be free from effort, annoyance and the need to make frequent investment decisions.[36]

Phase II guides you in learning how to determine whether you have resources to invest in financial vehicles such as stocks, bonds, mutual funds or other products; helps you determine what level of risk you can afford to take with your investment dollars; and explains how to define your investment objectives. Basic investment terms are discussed.

Phase III offers you guidance in working with professional financial advisors, discusses generic titles for these professionals, how you may select one, and what they may expect from you. If you want to understand what is being done with your money or make financial decisions, you need a basic understanding of what equity ownership means, and what are some of the differences between stocks and bonds. Phase III also helps you start taking more responsibility for your own financial affairs. You are not expected to become a financial expert, yet you may want to develop analytical skills to evaluate your financial advisors' recommendations and to take a more active role in making financial decisions.

The final section of this chapter suggests how you might continue studying investment choices and methods. In addition, we review some of the more speculative investment choices that you might see advertised and that are confusing to the beginning investor.

During the first months of your widowhood, it may be unwise to make major financial decisions unless it is absolutely necessary. Your ability to concentrate may be diminished. You may not understand or remember your choices about which investments to make or even whether you should be buying or selling anything. Take time to work through your initial bereavement. If you received a lump sum of money and you cannot decide what to do with it, follow the procedures in Phase I, placing your funds for the time being in a federally insured, interest-bearing account or money market fund. Wait until you feel comfortable thinking about money before you make far-reaching financial commitments.

At first most widows aren't ready to make money decisions, or they prefer not to have to keep a close eye on their financial affairs while they are deciding how to pay the monthly expenses and cope **Phase I— A Holding Pattern** with their house or car or family. In this case, consider the "holding pattern" strategy to preserve your principal and to earn a return on your investments until you decide what you are going to do next.

The selections presented in this phase are relatively secure and easy to access; some may earn a lower return than more risky investments. These low-risk investments may guarantee your principal or return, but they do not necessarily protect your money from the effects of inflation. Each of the choices shown below can, if necessary, be converted to cash within a year or less. They are not listed in any order of preference.

*Insured Savings Account*—You can deposit your money in an insured savings account in a bank, credit union or savings and loan association as the most basic form of investment. Make certain your accounts are federally insured by either the Federal Deposit Insurance Corporation (FDIC) or the Federal Savings and Loan Insurance Corporation (FSLIC). At this time, up to $100,000 can be insured for each depositor in any one bank. (Note that there are other insurance companies that will insure your accounts. But, you may be at greater risk, because the insurors other than FDIC or FSLIC may or may not be as dependable in paying depositors' claims.)

*Series EE U.S. Savings Bonds*—Savings bonds can be purchased at your bank, in denominations as low as $50. Check with your bank about when they mature, the interest rate they earn and when they can be redeemed (cashed in).

*Insured Certificates of Deposit (CDs)*—As the term suggests, the financial institution certifies that you have deposited a specific amount of money with them for a specific time at a specified rate of return. Banks or savings and loan institutions offer CDs for varying periods of time and at a guaranteed return (some as short as a few months or as long as ten years). At the time of this writing, CDs are being offered for as low as $500 in some banks, depending on the time to maturity. Make sure your CD is federally insured. If you cash it in before maturity, you may incur a penalty charge that reduces your return. Some institutions presently offer "no-penalty" CDs, which earn a lower interest rate.

*U.S. Treasuries*—The Treasury bill or "T-bill" is a short-term government-guaranteed obligation that can be bought through Federal Reserve banks and branches, the Bureau of the Public Debt, commercial banks and securities dealers. The minimum denomination is $10,000, increasing in increments of $5,000. An originally issued T-bill matures in three, six or twelve months. Many people consider the T-bill as virtually safe for preservation of their principal.

Treasury note and bond obligations are also guaranteed by the U.S. government. Treasury "notes," which mature in two to ten years, can be purchased for $5,000 each. Treasury "bonds," maturing in ten to thirty years, can be bought in denominations of $1,000 each.

Treasury obligations that you own can be sold before maturity on the "secondary market" to other buyers. But, depending on the interest rates offered by other investment opportunities compared to the interest rate being earned on your obligation, you could lose some of your principal.

*Money Market Mutual Funds*—One of the safer categories of mutual funds invests your money (along with others') in a mixed portfolio of money market securities. The most secure choice (offering safety for your principal) is the short-term government securities fund. Two others include the short-term tax-exempt and the taxable money market security funds. You can invest in a mutual fund by simply responding to advertisements in financial publications. Later in this chapter we offer guidance about how to determine which of the more than 1,500 mutual funds might best suit your needs.

Even though you may initially invest in secure vehicles, at some time in the future you will have to consider "what next?" Certificates of deposit, savings bonds and Treasuries mature on a specified date and stop earning interest; you then must decide what next to do with this money. Some people simply repeat their decisions and reinvest in the same vehicles. To help you decide if you want to consider other choices, continue on to Phase II to learn about basic investment attributes and how to assess your financial needs.

In the best of circumstances, a couple prepares for the possibility of widowhood long before it happens. A few fortunate widows already have established a rapport with their financial advisors. These women are relieved of an enormous number of problems at the time they are least able to make decisions. They have someone

**For Passive Investors**

to whom they can direct their questions regarding a wide range of financial concerns. Unfortunately, however, most women are left on their own to plan for their financial security.

Although the holding pattern idea may work for a time, some women are simply not interested in making investment decisions, now or ever. If you choose to be a passive investor, then you may want to employ professional financial guidance. In Chapter 6 we described what to look for in a good financial planner, stockbroker, banker, trust officer and accountant. In addition to these experts, you may also want to work with a "professional portfolio manager" or "asset manager," sometimes available in large bond or trust departments. One type of asset manager for large accounts is the "registered investment advisor," that is, a person who advises others concerning securities and who must be registered with the Securities and Exchange Commission (SEC). Registered investment advisors typically earn their fees as a percentage of the value of the accounts they manage. Sometimes they accept only accounts exceeding a stated minimum.

Smaller banks may not have trust departments, but they usually have access to trust department expertise available from their network of correspondent banks. Expect to pay an annual management fee based on the amount of your assets. Some managers and financial institutions accept only accounts that exceed a stated minimum value.

There is more to hiring professional money managers than simply turning your assets over to a trust department or professional portfolio manager and forgetting about them. The experts you choose need to know your "investment objectives" for both the short and the long term. That is, do you need to count on a certain percentage of fixed return from your investments? Do you need to count on dividends and interest to help you pay monthly expenses? Do you need occasional, large lump sums perhaps for your grandchildren or children's education? Can you afford to leave some of your assets invested or "tied up" for years? What portion of your assets must be relatively liquid or easily converted to cash? And so on.

To determine your need for monthly income, review the guidance on budgeting in Chapter 10. To help you decide how to determine your financial objectives, read Chapter 17 on estate planning and consider the issues described in Phase II. Although the advisors you employ may have an excellent track record in making investment decisions, you should review the status of your portfolio (collection of investments) from time to time to determine how well things are going.

Before working closely with professional financial advisors you need to understand the basics of investment terminology, decide what factors to weigh when you make investment decisions, and understand how to relate your personal circumstances to your investment decisions. Phase II does not include investment strategies, but describes the common attributes of many investment opportunities and guides you in evaluating your financial situation. Leave your resources invested in a holding pattern while you consider your next step.

**Phase II—
A Personal
Assessment**

The purpose of investing is to let your money earn more money. One way of earning money is to loan your money to a person, a corporation or a government agency. At some future date the "debt" or loan is to be repaid along with "interest," or the fee paid for using your money. In the financial world, loans issued by government agencies and corporations are called "debt securities."

**General Attributes
of Investment
Opportunities**

Another way to earn money by investing is to purchase "equity" or part ownership in a company. An investor can purchase part ownership of major corporations or private ventures. Equity owners are sometimes called shareholders or equity shareholders. A simple analogy would be if you bought part ownership of your brother's grocery store. You would share in the good fortunes and bad times, with the possibility for gain or loss when you decide you want to sell your part ownership.

In both types of investments, the originally invested dollars can be referred to as "principal" or sometimes "capital." In almost every case the investor wants to preserve or increase his or her capital. The typical investor also expects to earn a "return," or payment for the use of his or her money.

INCOME

Most investors are familiar with the idea of an investment earning a return in the form of "income" that is paid as interest or as dividends at regular intervals. (Note that the term *income* in finance is sometimes used differently than the everyday reference to income as annual salary or monthly cash.) Interest is the rent that is paid for the use of money. Dividends are the share of profit that can be distributed to the equity shareholders. Interest income is ordinarily earned at a rate that is expressed as percent per year. Your concern with the interest rate is with the amount and the frequency of "compounding." You want an investment vehicle that frequently compounds or adds the earned interest to your original investment. This process of grouping the interest with the original investment increases the overall value of your account, allowing both the original investment plus all earned interest to date to accumulate, and together they begin earning additional future interest. The more frequent the compounding, the greater the accumulation.

Another feature of interest rates is that some are fixed and known, while others vary. It may be important to you to know that you can count on a fixed interest rate that is guaranteed over a period of time. If you have $10,000 to invest, for instance, and you need to earn $500 on that investment in one year, you should look for a 5-percent fixed rate. Bonds and CDs usually earn fixed rates. Variable interest rates, on the other hand, fluctuate according to Treasury bill yields or money market rates. Bank money market deposit accounts, negotiable order of withdrawal (NOW) accounts and insurance retirement products are typical of variable interest rate investments.

As stated above, dividends represent a share of the company profit, which may or may not be distributed to the shareholders. When comparing investments, look for dividend growth and whether dividends have consistently been paid.

Another way to compare returns between different investments is to calculate the "yield"—the amount of dividends or interest earned over a period of time divided by the purchase price. For example, if you paid $30 a share for common stock, and the dividend paid to you in one year was $1.50 per share, then your yield would be $1.50 divided by $30, or 5 percent.

In addition to "ordinary income" realized from dividends and interest, another type of gain may be realized from an investment: the value of your purchase may appreciate in value between the time you buy it and the time you sell it, providing you with a "capital gain." Conversely, any depreciation in the value of your investment between the buy and sell times would result in a "capital loss." Through 1986 it was important to be able to differentiate between ordinary income and capital gains, because they were taxed differently. The tax regulations continue to change and even today you may still need to be able to differentiate capital gains from ordinary income for income tax requirements. Because the tax laws are complex (and confusing), be sure to consult carefully with your tax accountant or attorney as well as with your professional financial advisors.

## MATURITY

Every investment is either a loan or purchase made by you for a period of time. The longer someone else uses your money, the higher the fee you should be paid, since you are giving up the opportunity to spend your money now. Maturity refers to the period of time from when you purchase a debt investment until it must be repaid or the ownership can be sold. The time to maturity on most home mortgage loans is between fifteen and thirty years, after which the loan must be paid off. Some investment choices, such as bonds, have specific maturity dates. That means the borrower must pay you back, or redeem the bond, not later than the maturity date. Certificates of deposit can have maturity dates as short as a few months or as long as ten years. Depending on your personal financial needs, you may want to have some investments with short maturities and others with long maturities. Stocks and money market accounts have no maturity dates. You can liquidate them (convert them to cash by selling them) when you choose.

## SAFETY OF PRINCIPAL VERSUS RETURN

With many investments there is some risk that the value of your principal can go down as well as up. The greater the chance that you will lose your money, the higher the reward or return the borrowers should offer to pay you to entice you to loan them money or invest in their venture. Safety of principal can be thought of as the opposite of risk. Retired people, widows and other conservative investors are usually concerned about preserving their capital (keeping their principal safe). Unlike younger people with years ahead in which to live and work, they have less opportunity to recover any loss of principal from a higher risk investment.

## DIVERSIFICATION

"'Diversification' is one of those important-sounding six-syllable terms, like 'multiple vitamin,' that everybody can define but very few people really understand. . . . When you diversify, you simply give variety to the subject at hand. When it comes to investing, diversification means distributing your money among several different investments in order to spread out your risk." [37] Diversifying may not necessarily make you more money, but by owning assets that perform differently under differing economic conditions, you can hedge your chances of an overall loss. For example, if you distribute your investment dollars among stocks and bonds and CDs, you won't be as seriously affected by a decline in the stock market as someone who has all her money invested in stocks.

A similar way of diversifying between different types of investments is called "asset allocation." Professional financial advisors may advise allocating your assets among (1) *cash equivalents*, (2) *stocks* and (3) *bonds*. In a "balanced portfolio," for example, one investor might allocate capital as follows: 15 percent in cash or cash equivalents, 60 percent in stocks and 25 percent in bonds. Another investor with a preference for income might allocate his or her assets as 20 percent in cash equivalents, 30 percent in stocks and 50 percent in bonds. Your advisor can recommend asset allocations based on the predicted general economic and political environment, or, more important, according to your personal situation and objectives.

A second level of diversification is between different stocks or different bonds. For example, if you want to invest $50,000 in common stocks, it should be distributed between several issues rather than only one company's stock. You may want to diversify your stock purchases among industries, such as investing some in auto manufacturing firms, some in computer companies and some

in utility companies. That way your success isn't riding on the performance of only one industry. Bond purchases are often diversified according to maturity, with one or more bonds coming due
each year.

Another level of diversification is within an industry. For
example, within the automobile industry an investor might purchase stock in more than one blue-chip or highly rated company
such as Ford or General Motors. A "blue-chip" company, explains
Sylvia Porter, is one that has a long history of good earnings performance in recessions as well as in booms, a long history of cash
dividend payments in good times and bad, recognition as an established leader in an established industry, and a clear prospect for
continued earnings growth and dividend payments in the years
ahead.[38]

Diversification reduces your chances of spectacular gains as
well as spectacular losses. If you have diversified your investments
between money market accounts and bonds, and then stock prices
start to soar, you won't make as much as the stock owner. Prudent
investors spread their risk of loss by placing their money into
different investments—retaining some as cash and investing some
in bonds and some in equity securities. Diversification means you
are not putting all your eggs in one basket.

## LIQUIDITY

Investments generally require that your money be unavailable for
you to spend for a period of time ranging from a few months in
a savings account to several years in real estate. Liquidity refers to
the ability to convert the asset or invested capital to cash. Many
investors keep some of their funds available as cash or cash
equivalents—investments that can be quickly converted to cash.
Some non-cash assets such as stocks are readily liquid (that is, they
can be easily sold for cash), whereas bonds may be less liquid
because you cannot convert the bonds to cash for the full face
value until the maturity date is reached. Real estate is considered
illiquid because you cannot convert it to cash until a willing buyer
is ready to meet your price. Your checking account, money market
account and savings account are liquid assets and are referred to
as cash equivalents. Stocks and mutual fund shares are relatively
liquid, depending on their market value. Some investments such

as annuities, retirement accounts and certificates of deposit can be liquidated before their due date, but only by paying a penalty such as an early withdrawal fee, which could reduce the interest you have earned.

## TAX-FREE/TAXABLE INCOME

Investors paying high income taxes are usually concerned about whether the return earned on their investment is taxable or tax-free. The interest earned on bonds issued by the federal government is exempt from state and local taxes. The interest earned on municipal bonds issued by state or municipal government entities (also called munis) is exempt from federal taxes and may be exempt from state taxes (if the issuer of the bonds and the owner reside in the same state). Tax-exempt or tax-free bond funds often offer a lower interest rate than taxable bonds, but their yield may exceed the after-tax equivalent yield earned on taxable bonds.

## TAX-DEFERRED INCOME

Interest that is earned on individual retirement accounts (IRAs) and some annuities is not taxed until you withdraw the principal. You invest the money during your higher income years. Then when you reach a specified age and can begin withdrawing the retirement funds, you may be in a lower income tax bracket, resulting in a lower income tax liability. And you get the added benefit of compounding: each year's earnings are retained and reinvested, allowing new earnings to accumulate on the total amount (the original investment plus earnings).

**Determining Your Investment Objectives**

To help decide whether you wish to invest beyond the secure choices described in Phase I, it is important to evaluate your personal circumstances. To help you decide whether you have extra money to invest, or should consider investments other than those listed in Phase I, you should:

1. *Determine your current financial status.* For investment purposes, we assume that you have a positive net worth—that is, you have more assets than liabilities. We explain how to determine your net worth in Chapter 17, "Taking Care of Those You Love—Estate Planning."

Make a list of what assets you own that are already invested. These assets may already appear on the worksheets you prepared to ascertain your net worth or on lists prepared for your attorney to assist in settling your husband's estate (discussed in Chapter 7) plus your own investments. The list may include amounts in checking and savings accounts, common stocks, bonds, CDs, money market accounts, IRAs, real estate, life insurance proceeds and other lump sums you have received. If, in addition, you receive large amounts of money from other sources, that money can be invested for your future needs.

Investment dollars are not usually part of your monthly or quarterly cash flow, but come instead from other sources that you want to preserve and increase. These assets can include survivor annuity payments, life insurance benefits, retirement or Social Security income, or inherited securities or stocks.

*2. Next, consider your age and how long your nest egg or resources have to last.* Consider how much money you have to invest and how many years you will need to depend on the income earned or on the lump sum itself. For example, a young widow with few assets needs to increase the value of her assets to provide financial security for her later years. She may feel she can afford to take risks with her investments, because she has the opportunity to recoup losses. An older widow, on the other hand, is more likely to be concerned with keeping her assets stable and secure. She may have almost no chance of recovering any losses, so she invests in safe financial vehicles. To further illustrate this point we next look at women in three age groups. We assume that each group has different monthly income needs, and requires a different level of security for the original investment.

YOUNG WOMEN: If you are a young widow with small children, you need to provide financial security not only for your children's well-being but also for your own. You may never remarry, and if you are in your twenties, statistics indicate that you are likely to live another fifty years. We assume you are probably working full time to earn the daily living. For your later years, it would be wise to take advantage of any retirement plan offered through your employer. If you received any lump sums after your husband's death, you may want to invest them for your later years as well as for your children's education. Some young couples do not have life insurance. If you did not receive any benefits, perhaps the only source of investment funds you have is the equity in your home. You may be able to take moderate risks with your investments because you feel you are young enough to recover your losses.

MID-YEARS WOMEN: If you are a mid-years widow whose children are almost adult but still dependent upon you, your living expenses are about as high as they will ever be (considering tuition, cars, stereos and food). If both you and your husband worked, and he earned at least twice as much as you, then you have lost two-thirds of your monthly income. You may need to count on monthly interest income from your investments, but you also need to preserve a nest egg for your old age. If you are middle-aged, you may need to maintain your present income as well as supplement your retirement income. Your investment choices will probably be aimed toward safe, secure financial vehicles. You do not want to risk losing your original investment.

OLDER WOMEN: By the age of sixty, more than 48 percent of American women have been widowed. If you are sixty-five or older, and your late husband was retired, then you will probably experience the least change in monthly income. You have most likely adjusted to living on a retirement income. Investment considerations for your age group may focus on keeping the resources secure to maintain income for the remainder of your life.

In each situation, you must consider not only your responsibility to others but, primarily, your responsibility to yourself. If you are overly generous to others now, you may be destitute in the long run. You shouldn't be selfish, but you must be prudent. Is it sensible to give those you love everything now, only to need their support later?

3. *Determine your investment goals.* The first question you should hear from a well-qualified financial expert is, "What are your investment objectives or financial goals?" Related questions may include:

Why do you want to increase the value of your present assets?

Do you have short-term financial needs for travel, education or a move? This will affect funds to keep in liquid assets.

Are you planning for a retirement income?

Do you need a hedge against inflation, that is, do you need to earn enough extra income to offset the decrease in buying power?

Are you able to accept a greater risk for possibly a higher gain? In most (but not all) cases, the more risk or chance of losing your principal, the greater potential there is for reward. Conservative investors typically spread their risk between secure investments, such as Treasuries, blue-chip stocks, highest-rated bonds and federally insured money market accounts. If you have a moderate tolerance for risk, you may want to invest some money in growth stocks that may appreciate in value.

Do you need to earn a high income now to supplement your other monthly cash, or can you wait to receive your gain? (In this instance "income" refers to dividends or interest payments; it does not refer to a monthly salary or retirement check.) If so, you may want to consider *fixed income securities,* which specify exactly how much interest will be earned and when it will be paid. The interest payment doesn't fluctuate.

What maturities do you require, or, how long can you leave your money invested while you wait for your return? You can allocate your investment dollars, investing some for short periods of time while leaving other funds tied up for years to earn more interest. Your financial experts can advise you better if you specify when you will need the principal returned from any investment.

4. *What is your temperament with respect to taking chances with your money?* Investing in federally insured savings accounts and Treasuries is not likely to keep anyone awake at night worrying about the safety of her money. However, for some people, investing in stocks and bonds and mutual funds is a scary venture. Ask yourself if you are the type of person who becomes anxious and fearful about the daily ups and downs of the stock market or, rather, a person who finds it exciting and stimulating. If the changing value of your portfolio would cause you to lose sleep almost every night, then you may want to consider investments in which your principal does not fluctuate.

If you generally understand how investment objectives apply to your own situation, then you are ready to work with a professional financial advisor. Even though with time you may eventually become quite sophisticated about financial affairs, we suggest you continue to work closely with your advisors.

**Phase III— Working with Financial Professionals**

You may now have decided that you want to venture beyond the point of leaving your investments in savings accounts or T-bills. Those choices offer security for your principal, but may not earn enough to keep up with inflation. Women who wish to consider investments other than insured accounts, or who inherited securities portfolios from their husbands, are often overwhelmed by investment choices. At this point the best approach is to work closely with a professional financial advisor such as a stockbroker, certified financial planner, registered investment advisor, asset management advisor or bank trust officer. Do not assume your advisor will make buy-and-sell decisions for you. An advisor usually makes recommendations, but you have to make the final choice. To help you make better decisions, next we explain how to select a good advisor, briefly describe the workings of the stock market, compare stocks and bonds, and list a few investment alternatives.

**Selecting a Professional Financial Advisor**

Financial advice runs the gamut from excellent to poor, depending on whether you were fortunate in inheriting a highly qualified advisor from your late husband or carefully shopped for the best financial professionals you could find, or whether you acted on a hot tip you overheard at a cocktail party. If you are comfortable with the financial advisors you have and you trust their guidance, then stay with them. In Chapter 6 we discuss what to look for in highly qualified financial advisors.

Some women with a sizable sum to invest may want to interview a few financial institutions to compare what would be most suitable for their goals. If you are considering employing new financial professionals, the following suggestions may help you choose a highly qualified individual. Begin by asking your friends and trusted business associates to recommend financial institutions or advisors. If your friends are satisfied, ask why and how long the association has continued. Some firms offer a no-charge initial consultation, with the length of the interview dependent on the amount you have to invest.

1. Consider the general reputation of the financial insti tution as well as any individuals you interview. A well-known, reputable organization is likely to have employees with stronger backgrounds. If you live in a small community with few choices, you may want to consider a long-distance choice. You need not have face-to-face meetings. Small banks often have access to large correspondent bank resources, such as full-service trust depart ments with asset management specialists.

2. Ask the firm for the names of a few references. Do not be shy about calling the references to ask if they are satisfied with the guidance and service they have received. Any good businessman checks out references before signing a contract, and you are now in the business of managing your money. Inquire about the financial institution's fees. Make sure the firm and advisor are registered with the Securities and Exchange Commission.

3. Ask a registered investment advisor, an assets manager and perhaps the bank trust department or trust firm to explain their investment strategies with respect to stocks and bonds.

4. Ask your prospective advisor how long he or she has been with the firm. You want someone with a few years' experience. What is his or her experience and education? You want an advisor who is neither overextended with hundreds of clients nor a begin- ner with only a few clients. You need the best advice you can get. It is not unreasonable to ask how much time your manager will spend on your account. Once you have decided on a firm, ask to see what their written reports look like and how often they will be sent. You may also want to ask how much time should pass before you can effectively evaluate the investment results. The nature of your questions will vary with the type of financial advisor you sel- ect and the nature of your account. Do not be awed by your finan cial advisors. Remember they are working for you and with you.

Widows often inherit their late husband's financial portfolio. **The Stock Market—** Some haven't the slightest idea of what it is all about, and run the **Basics** risk of losing part of their assets. We present a simplified discussion of the stock market, so you can decide if you want to participate either by making your own decisions or by relying on your professional investment advisor.

The stock market is a popular term for an industry in which

public buying and selling of shares of ownership (securities) of listed companies is transacted every business day. The sales transactions are made through organized security exchanges—the New York Stock Exchange (NYSE), American Stock Exchange (AMEX), regional stock exchanges and the Over-the-Counter markets (OTC) found in the financial pages listed under NASDAQ. (National Association of Securities Dealers Automated Quotations). There are other specialized exchanges for commodities and foreign currency. More than 3,000 corporations trade shares on the New York and American Stock exchanges. Because the buy and sell procedures are complex and carefully regulated by the Federal Securities and Exchange Commission, you need to work with a brokerage firm and a broker who understand the system and are registered to use it.

People who are "trading in the stock market" own shares of stock that represent equity ownership in one or more corporations. Stock market investors hope that the companies in which they own stock will perform well and earn a profit that will be distributed to shareholders as dividends, and that the value of their ownership will increase. The "return" on their investments may vary up or down. If the companies do well, other people presumably will want to jump on the bandwagon and buy stocks in those same companies. The idea is that if there are a limited number of shares available to buy and there are more buy orders than shares available for sale, then the price of this relatively scarce product will go up.

Sylvia Porter explains in her *Money Book* what causes individual stock prices to change: "Once a company has sold its original stock to the public and the stock is freely traded in the market, the price of the stock will be set solely by what buyers are willing to pay for it and what sellers are willing to take . . . a classic case of supply and demand in action."[39] Stock market prices in general are affected by worldwide economic and political actions. The overall stock market performance is reflected by the daily movement of the Dow Jones Industrial Average, which refers to the average share price of thirty leading industrial and transportation companies.

OWNING STOCK

Buyers of stock are investors who purchase a "piece of the action" and become part owners of a corporation. Thus equity owners or shareholders share in the ups and downs of a company's business. Generally, people consider purchasing common stocks for two reasons. First they want to realize "income" or earnings from a portion of the company profits distributed as dividends. Many investors also want to realize "growth" or appreciation of their capital when the share price increases. Ideally, investors look for stocks that pay dividends and have a potential for capital gains, giving them two avenues for increasing the worth of their investment.

Companies that may continue to pay dividends or have a potential for increased dividends are those that have established steady and dependable earnings and dividend growth over the years. A company's historical performance is important. Many strong income-producing companies have not missed a dividend payment for decades, or have tended to do well despite general economic downtrends. Historically the utility companies have paid regular dividends. Their sales revenues have continued because people use power and the telephone no matter how the economy is faring.

In considering common stocks for growth, look for companies that offer products and services with favorable long-term growth potential. Look for managements that tend to be aggressive, always searching for new products and growing markets—those, in other words, that emphasize research and new product development.

To get a more in depth understanding of stock ownership, a potential investor should read and study far beyond the brief notes in this chapter. The business sections of bookstores and libraries are continually expanding to accommodate the increasing variety of books dealing with the stock market and other investments. Our Selected Sources lists several well-written books that are appropriate for the beginning investor.

## CHOOSING THE "RIGHT" STOCK

If you choose to invest in stocks, specifically common stocks, there are three important factors to consider. The first of these is picking the "right" stock, or the stock that best meets your objectives. We have previously mentioned the need for diversification among industries and for diversification among companies within an industry. But when you are narrowing your scope to focus on a few companies there are two basic characteristics that may help you make your decisions—quality and earnings.[40]

Quality of common stock is difficult to determine. Perhaps one measure is to consider the overall reputation of the company. You may want to invest in a company that has been around for some time and provides high-quality service, or produces a high-quality product that will continue to be in demand in the future.

Earnings are more easily considered. If the stock has historically shown a healthy growth in earnings per share (the total earnings of the company divided by the outstanding shares), is earnings growth likely to continue? Consider the company's stock price performance relative to the overall stock market performance. Does this stock price tend to fluctuate generally with the market, or is it more volatile?

In determining the right stock to buy, also consider your investment objectives and your temperament. If stock price fluctuations make you nervous, you may want to consider "defensive" stocks, those that remain relatively stable or change slowly in spite of changes in the general economy. (The term *defensive* implies that the investor assumes a protected position, that he or she is somewhat insulated against ups and downs experienced by more volatile issues.) Two industries that have been defensive are the electric utilities and the telephone companies, according to the United Business Service.[41]

A second major consideration for prospective stock market investors, and the essence of investing, is the idea put forth by Benjamin Graham: "For 99 issues out of 100 we could say that at some time they are cheap enough to buy and at some other price they would be so dear that they should be sold."[42] This rather formal-sounding tenet has often been similarly expressed as "Buy low and sell high." A good stock can be a bargain or it can be overpriced.

How does the novice investor begin to act on these obvious truths? How does she determine when a stock price is low in order to buy or when a stock price is high in order to sell? Usually the investor looking for a capital gain wants to avoid buying stocks that have already realized a significant gain and that may have slight chance for additional appreciation.

There are no easy answers or sure-fire techniques for determining when a stock price is high or low relative to your decision to buy or sell. One idea is that a good time to buy at a low price is when a company is still in its early stages of development or if an established company is about to experience a major expansion. A well-established company can fit the criteria for future growth if the company has proven its ability to introduce and successfully market new products or services. Another consideration in timing your buy is to look at the company's current price compared to its price range over the past year. If the current price is at a yearly high, or if this stock is in favor and almost everyone seems to be interested in buying it, then this may not be the time to buy. But if you own shares in a favored company, this may be the time to sell this particular stock!

Deciding when to sell a stock is often difficult. With the notions of earning slow but steady gains, and buy and hold for the long term, it is confusing to know when to sell. Some investors tend to base their sell decisions on the general market downswing, or prevailing market hysteria. A more definitive criterion is to consider changes in the future prospects for a company. Are there new regulations or laws, or have new products been introduced by a competitor? Have expected new contracts been cancelled or not awarded? Perhaps a more structured consideration might be, "Would I still consider this stock a good buy today?" To apply this question practically, you need to return to the "buy" criteria and analysis methods you used to decide that this stock was originally a good buy, plug in some "what-if" higher prices, then repeat the analysis. At some higher price your analysis will show that the stock is no longer a good buy. That is the price you might set as your sell price.

An aptly phrased opinion about deciding whether or when to sell admonishes, "Don't marry your stocks. . . . Even though you subscribe to the 'buy good stocks and hold them long-term' philosophy of investment, there are times when stocks should be sold. You do not do so when you think the market in general will go down, but you do when there is evidence that a company's position is deteriorating, its market is shrinking, its products are becoming obsolete, or some other demonstrable unfavorable situation is developing."[43]

Choosing and buying the right stocks depends on more than quality, earnings and timing. Professional stock analysis services and a number of dedicated individuals put forth a great deal of effort analyzing current political events, economic trends and historical corporate performance in order to try to predict the future actions of the stock market and individual issues. Investors have often used one or more of the following methods to help them decide whether to invest or which stocks to buy.

STOCK ANALYSIS METHODS

Numerous professional analytical services sell newsletters and subscriptions that analyze historical corporate stock performance, to predict what they think the future will hold. To learn about these publications and sources, visit the business department of your local library, enlist the help of the research librarian and review some of the choices to see which ones meet your needs. Your professional financial advisor should be able to suggest some reference material and good books. Your trust officer and stock-broker will also provide investment advice and buy-and-sell recommendations.

Many investors and analytical services generally compare stocks using one or more of the following three techniques.:

• One approach is to look at the company itself in light of the general economy and with respect to the competition within its industry. Questions you may want to ask include: Is this company likely to grow—faster than the general economic situation, or is it headed for a slowdown? Look for a company with a strong financial position, showing more assets than liabilities on its balance sheet. Look for a company that has a strong or higher market position than its competitors within the same industry. And, as previously mentioned, look for a company with an established record of introducing quality products or services and successfully marketing them.

• Once you have narrowed your selection to a few issues, another way to analyze which stock to buy is to evaluate stock performance. Some factors to consider are the price/earnings (P/E) ratio, earnings per share, sales and earnings growth, stock price range, dividends paid (if any) and yield of dividends compared to the price of a share. Many investors rank the P/E ratio as a major feature. This factor, calculated by dividing the stock price by earnings per share, is used to compare a company to itself historically and to compare stock performance between companies within an industry. De-

scribing how to perform and interpret these analyses is beyond the scope of this book. To learn how these factors affect your buy and sell decisions, you will want to read and study some of the references listed in the Selected Sources.
• In addition to the above two analysis methods, some professional analytical services and a few seriously interested and sophisticated investors employ "technical analysis." These technical considerations depend on the creation of charts and the analysis of volumes of data to make statistical predictions. The more sophisticated approaches depend on computer models to analyze the data.

If you invest in stocks, you can risk losing a portion of your capital, earn a hedge against inflation, or realize a substantial gain, depending on your judgment. If you choose to invest in stocks, consider this advice: "Buy for the long term. Buy common stocks for capital growth. Buy them for a rising pattern of dividend growth. Choose your investments carefully and stick with them. Avoid fads. Be content to grow wealthy slowly—but surely."[44]

## LEARNING MORE ABOUT STOCKS—ON YOUR OWN

In addition to relying on the highly qualified professional financial advisors you have employed, you may want to learn more about stocks on your own. Deciding which securities to buy is a critical issue. Prudent investors stick with high-quality stocks and the highest-rated bonds. In any case, there are no guarantees; your investment values can decrease as well as increase. To learn how to analyze which stocks you might want to purchase, start with your professional investment advisor, asking his or her advice about helpful courses and books. Investment firms and community colleges list courses in financial analysis. Private individuals offer stock analysis classes.

## READING THE STOCK MARKET QUOTATIONS

Another direction for the interested student is to learn to read the stock market quotations about any stocks you may own or are contemplating buying. The first point has to do with stock market averages. In general, if the prices for most stocks are increasing, you are more likely to make money in the stock market. There are many measurements of the health of the stock market, but the most widely quoted is the Dow Jones Industrial Average. This is the average stock price of thirty of the largest corporations in America. If the Dow goes up, this does not mean that every stock increased in value, or that the stocks you owned increased, but it does indicate something about the health of the largest companies. To find a broader indicator, you can look at the number of issues that advanced (gained) versus the number that declined, and you can also look at the Standard & Poor's Index. All of these numbers are printed daily on the financial pages of your newspaper.

But you are not primarily interested in averages, you are interested in what has happened to stocks you own. On the financial pages of a recent daily paper, the following information appeared for the Ford Motor Company:

112 5/8   49 1/2   Ford Motor   3.00 3.1   6   17622   98   2 1/8

The first number is the high the stock has been in the last year ($112.62).

The second number is the low for the stock in the last twelve months ($49.50).

The third item is the name of the company.

Fourth is the annual dividend the company has paid on a share of stock ($3.00).

Fifth is the yield (3.1 percent). It is calculated by dividing the dividend by today's stock price.

Next is the price/earnings ratio (6), calculated by dividing the price of the stock by the earnings of the company during the last twelve months.

The following figure indicates the number of shares in hundreds that were traded yesterday. In this case, 1,762,200 shares of Ford were sold.

Next is the price that a share of Ford stock sold at the close of business yesterday ($98.00).

Last is the change in the stock price in trading during the day. In this case, a share of Ford stock cost $2.12 more at the end of business yesterday than it did at the end of the previous day.

Now that you know how to read the financial pages, you can begin to follow some stocks and become aware of what investing means. Some days a stock will go up, some days it will go down.

But the real questions are: Is the general trend higher? Are you comfortable with your investment in this stock?

If you want to do your own research about which stocks to buy, we list several excellent books and publications in the Selected Sources to guide you in evaluating companies. Each of these books offers valuable guidance in "how to" and "what to do" and "don't dos." Ask any bookstore to order the book you want. You can also learn how to invest and analyze stocks through stock market investment clubs, which allow members to pool their resources to buy stocks. Belonging to an investment club lets you learn from two sources—your financial advisor and your peers. Some clubs allow new members to invest as little as $20 per month. Novices are welcome. To find out about investment clubs in your area, write the National Association of Investors Corporation (or NAIC), 1515 East Eleven Mile Road, Royal Oak, MI 48067.

During and after World War II, the government issued Series E Savings Bonds. Typically, people bought them at a discounted price and held them until maturity, at which time they cashed them in or redeemed them for the "face value" (the amount printed on the face of the bond). A $25 bond initially sold for $18.75. If the owner needed the money before the bond was mature, he or she could redeem it at any time after owning it for two months and receive the initial purchase price plus accumulated interest. Nowadays, except for government bonds such as the EE series of savings bonds, the bond market is far more sophisticated and complex.

**The Bond Market—Basics**

A bond is a record of debt issued by a government body or a corporation for a period of a year or longer, up to as long as thirty years. The issuer promises to pay interest on the loan, generally twice a year. It also promises to pay back the face amount or principal at the end of a certain period. Newly issued bonds are usually sold in denominations of $1,000. They can be issued by the U.S. Treasury, by other federal government agencies, by state and municipal governments and by corporations. Bonds differ widely in terms of safety, time to maturity, interest paid and the ease with which they can be converted to cash before maturity. The interest earned on some bonds is exempt from federal or state income taxes.

We discuss bonds in some detail, because some people mistakenly assume that they cannot lose their principal when they invest in bonds. Bonds are often misunderstood, because people think the value of a bond is fixed when it isn't. The only way you can avoid losing some of your principal is to purchase a newly issued bond as the first and only owner, and hold it until maturity. The only risk you take is that the lender might default on it. On most bonds, only *the interest rate is fixed*—hence the term "fixed income." Bonds are also sometimes called "debt securities" or "debt instruments," because a government agency or corporation goes into debt when it borrows money from the investors.

There are three important points to understand about bonds. First, the issuer of the bond is the borrower, and you are the lender. Second, when the bond "due date" or "maturity" date arrives, the owner (lender) expects to be paid back with the full "face" amount of the bond plus any interest that is owed. Finally, you as the lender are trusting the borrower to be able to pay you back on the due date. The borrower's "credit rating" is a major factor in your decision about which bonds to buy. Specialized companies like Moody's and Standard & Poor's analyze and rate bonds by the issuer's ability to repay the debt. The highest quality is Aaa or AAA, ranging to a low rating of C or D, based on the issuer's repayment capability. When you decide to invest in bonds, go to your bank or to a trusted professional within the bond department of a stock brokerage firm. Many people who want to own bonds, but cannot afford to purchase them individually, invest in "bond funds," in which the resources of hundreds of investors are pooled to purchase a variety of bonds with differing maturity and interest rates.

TYPES OF DEBT INVESTMENTS (BONDS)

Bonds issued by states, territories or possessions of the United States or any political subdivisions thereof are called "municipal bonds." These "munis" can be issued by hospitals, schools, tax districts, cities, counties and port authorities, and are normally not taxed by the state in which they are issued. Municipal bonds are issued in different categories—e.g., general obligation bonds, revenue bonds, limited tax bonds, special assessment bonds and others depending on how they are to be repaid. Munis are ususally promoted as a tax-exempt product, but they are not always a tax advantage. Check with your tax advisor to compare whether the lower return on a tax-exempt muni would be more to your benefit than a higher yielding taxable investment. Generally only investors in the highest tax brackets realize a tax break from munis.

"Zero coupon bonds" are bonds that do not pay out the periodic interest as cash, although they do earn interest for the owner. The interest remains with the bond, to compound on the accumulated unpaid interest as well as on the original principal. They are purchased at a "discount" or less-than-face-value amount, and the purchaser receives the face value of the principal and interest when the bond is redeemed at maturity. Zero coupon bonds can be issued by municipalities, by corporations, by the U.S. Treasury as a stripped-of-its-coupon bond, and by banks as zero-coupon certificates of deposit.

Some government agencies sell bonds to implement their various lending programs. "Government guaranteed bonds" or "mortgage backed securities" are offered to finance the lending programs for such corporate instrumentalities as the Government National Mortgage Association (GNMA or Ginnie Mae) or the Federal National Mortgage Association (FNMA or Fannie Mae) as well as others.

Ginnie Mae securities, promoted as a secure investment, are backed by the U.S. government. When investors buy a Ginnie Mae, they are actually buying into a pool of twenty-five- to thirty-year FHA or VA mortgages that individual homeowners have financed through certified banks. The Ginnie Maes are issued in $1 million pools that are bought by brokerage houses and sold to the general public in $25,000 denominations. However, you can participate in the Ginnie Mac market by investing in a brokerage house unit investment trust for a minimum of $1,000.

Ginnie Maes trade actively on the open market and rise and fall in value inversely to interest rate fluctuations. As interest rates go up, the investor suffers price depreciation on the security itself, but is able to invest the monthly proceeds at higher rates. If interest rates drop, the Ginnie Mae appreciates in price, but the owner of the certificate is reinvesting his or her monthly proceeds at a lower rate.

In addition to considering which bonds to purchase and understanding what happens when bonds are repeatedly bought and sold, it is helpful to review the bond jargon used by professionals. In the Glossary we include some commonly heard bond terms such as *par, premium, discounted bond, coupon bond, junk bond, corporate bond* and *callable bond*.

**Stocks versus Bonds**     The beginning investor is sometimes confused by the different features of stocks and bonds. If you have inherited both stock and bond portfolios and are unclear about how they differ, we outline some of the features below. Discuss the fine points with your advisor.

## COMPARATIVE FEATURES BETWEEN STOCKS AND BONDS

| *Stocks—Equity Ownership* | *Bonds—Debt Ownership* |
|---|---|
| The investor is called an equity owner or shareholder. | The investor is called a lender. |
| Part of the company is owned by purchasing shares of its stock. | A loan is made to the government agency or corporation by purchasing its bonds. |
| The owner can share in the profits, which may be paid as dividends or shares of stock. | The lender knows in advance bond face value amount (how much he or she will be repaid) if the bond is held until it matures. |
| The owner may realize a capital gain if the value of his or her shares have appreciated since purchase. | The lender may realize a capital gain over the purchase price if the bond is paying a higher return than other investment choices available at the time of sale. |
| The owner may realize a capital loss if he or she chooses to sell when stock prices have declined. | The lender may experience a loss in bond value if required to sell at a time when other investment choices offer a high return. |
| The owner typically purchases previously owned shares on the secondary market, but may purchase newly issued stock. | The lender often purchases newly issued debt on the primary market, but may purchase previously owned bonds on the secondary market. |
| Shares of stock are highly liquid, i.e., they can usually be readily sold and convert to cash before maturity. | Bonds are moderately liquid, i.e. some special kinds of bonds are not easy to resell before maturity and converted to cash. |
| Sell decisions are under the control of the stock owner. | Redemption (repayment) may occur ahead of schedule if the bond has a "call" feature. |
| The returns earned on shares of stock are uncertain. | The returns earned from the interest on most bonds is usually fixed and certain, or for a few bonds may vary according to certain formulas. |

Whether you are beginning to work with your financial advisor or have been investing for some time, heed the advice given by Adam Smith in his excellent book *The Money Game*: "The first rule of making money is not to lose it."[45] This is important for every investor, but it is especially true for a woman on her own. Your first objective is to preserve your capital, then to figure how to make it keep up with inflation and provide long-term financial security.

As you recover from your grieving and begin to gain a sense of confidence in yourself, you may want to take a more active role in financial decision making. Besides continuing to work with your professional investment advisor, you may choose to invest on your own. When you venture forth, remember, commit only what you can afford to lose without adversely affecting your present or future standard of living. Set long-term goals first, then review your investments after about six months to see if you are proceeding as planned. If not, re-evaluate your objectives and your investment choices. Make sure you have the temperament to withstand the sometimes frightening daily changes in the financial marketplace.

**Taking a More Active Role**

Some investment advisors suggest that unless you plan to invest about $50,000 in stocks through a brokerage firm ($50,000 is considered the minimum to achieve diversification and to get a lower commission rate), you might choose to invest in a mutual fund. Considerations include: What is a mutual fund? How do you find out about them? How do you decide which ones to invest in? In addition to your own research efforts, a financial advisor or broker can help you with mutual fund decisions, just as with individual stocks.

A mutual fund is a financial investment vehicle in which you invest your money in a diversified collection of stocks and bonds selected by professional investment managers. You, along with hundreds of other individuals, buy shares in a mutual fund, which in turn pools the money to buy securities. There are currently more than 1,500 mutual funds. Investment firms that manage mutual funds sometimes offer an assortment of funds called a "family" of funds.

**Mutual Funds**

Once you own shares in any one of the family members, you may switch your investment to another member of the family of funds without a charge.

Generally there are three categories of mutual funds:

• Money market funds,

• Stock funds, which further specialize in income stock funds, growth stock funds, or growth and income stock funds, and

• Bond funds, which include taxable bond and tax-exempt bond funds. Within each of the two bond fund categories there are money market funds and high-yield funds. For example, a tax-exempt money market fund invests only in municipal bonds so that the interest is tax-exempt. If you are in the highest income tax bracket, tax-exempt bond funds may make sense for part of your investments.

*The primary consideration for investing in mutual funds is that the mutual fund objectives match your investment goals.* If, for example, you need strong assurance that your principal will be preserved, you   might want to select a fund that invests in government guaranteed securities.

You can locate mutual funds in the financial pages of major daily newspapers, where the share prices are quoted. Most funds will send you a prospectus (legal description of the fund) plus information on how to invest if you call or write. Many people prefer to buy into a "no-load" fund, which has no up-front sales charge. A no-load fund usually has "NL" listed with the name. However, administration fees are charged in a variety of ways, some as annual management fees, or as "redemption" fees when you sell your shares in the fund.

Deciding which mutual fund or funds to invest in is important for the beginner. You should diversify, as with individual investments made through your broker. For example, a very conservative mutual fund portfolio might include 30 percent invested in a money market fund and 70 percent invested in a growth and income fund. Some Individual Retirement Accounts or qualified retirement plans are invested in mutual funds. If your IRA is already in mutual funds, you may notice that each quarter the value of the shares fluctuates up or down, reflecting the performance of the securities bought and sold by the mutual fund.

To begin your search for a mutual fund, review the most recent August issue of *Forbes* business magazine, which lists the

long-term performance of each mutual fund. Look for a fund that
has consistently shown a positive performance (five or more years)
and still has the same fund managers. Narrow your list to four or
five funds. Then contact the company and order the prospectus or
legal description of any fund in which you are interested. Match
the fund objectives to your financial goals. Once you have carefully studied the prospectus, the purchase decision is up to you.

The following publications will help you assess the performance of mutual funds:

*Business Week, Money, Forbes* and other business magazines
provide rankings of mutual fund performances.

The Weisenberger Investment Company's annual handbook available at many public libraries lists performance data on
most mutual funds.

Private directories that describe fund performance, risk and
fees can be ordered from (a) *Individual Investor's Guide to No-
Load Mutual Funds,* 612 North Michigan Avenue, Chicago, IL
60611, for about $20, (b) *Handbook for No-Load Fund Investors,*
P.O. Box 283, Hastings-on-Hudson, NY 10706, for about $38,
and (c) *Mutual Fund Sourcebook,* 53 West Jackson Boulevard,
Chicago, IL 60604, for about $50.

The advantages offered by a mutual fund include: diversification for the person who does not take time to analyze
individual issues, a possibly lower minimum initial investment
requirement, professional management, liquidity and the variety
(or family) of funds offered by an investment firm. Your success
depends on your ability to select a good fund that will continue to
perform well. Whatever mixture you choose for your diversified
portfolio, you should keep an eye on your investments. Even with
a conservative strategy, you will want to re-evaluate your changing
needs and the changing market conditions.

**Other Choices**

Nowadays almost everyone has heard the terms *commodities,
futures, stock indexes, options, limited partnerships* and *precious
metals.* You have heard the success stories about someone who has
made a "killing" or huge profit investing in these speculative
ventures. You don't hear about the numerous times someone
"lost his shirt." These investments are sophisticated and can be

risky. Don't let your financial advisor or anyone else rush you into an investment you don't clearly understand. Ask your advisor to explain how the following financial products work and what the risks and rewards are. It takes time and training to understand these complex but fascinating financial choices.

The following two lists cover general terms that designate groups of financial products or aspects of the everyday vernacular of the financial world and the volatile investment choices that you may have seen or read about.

## FINANCIAL PRODUCTS

*Debt Instruments.* Generic investment term that refers to bonds
- also called debt securities

*Equity Securities.* Generic term for short- and long-term investments in which the investor buys part ownership in the corporation
- includes common and preferred stocks
- can be purchased through stockbroker
- value of principal investment can fluctuate up or down

*Financial Products.* Broad term referring generally to all choices of investment vehicles
- includes stocks, bonds, life insurance, annuities, futures, mutual funds, unit trusts, money market, government securities, savings accounts, commercial paper, precious metals, gems, oil, etc.

*Fixed Income Securities.* Includes bonds, preferred stock and non-negotiable certificates of deposit
- the rate of interest is specified with definite times this interest is to be paid
- usually lower-risk investment than common stock

*Investment Vehicle.* Broad term that refers to investment opportunities (see Financial Products)

*Money Market Funds.* Mutual funds that pool investors' resources for investment into money market instruments, which include negotiable CDs, commercial paper and government securities

*Mutual Funds.* Professionally managed, diversified portfolios of securities that are actively traded
- a "load" fund charges an up-front or initial management fee and may charge surrender charges, etc.
- a "no-load" fund charges on-going management fees
- funds may be invested in government securities, stocks, bonds, municipals, gold, foreign securities, etc.

*Stocks.* Generic term that refers to shares of equity ownership of a corporation
- includes common stocks, preferred stocks, blue-chip stocks, growth stocks, income stocks and cyclical stocks
- risk that invested principal will decrease in value rather than increase
- popular investment vehicle
- low to high risk, depending on stock

*Tax Exempts.* Bonds on which the investor does not pay federal and sometimes not even state income taxes on the income
- can be purchased through "muni-bond funds"
- also called tax-free or tax-advantaged

*Unit Trusts.* Professionally selected, diversified portfolio of securities
- not actively managed by investor
- also called unit investment trusts or fixed trusts
- can also include real estate investment trusts and Ginnie Maes

## VOLATILE INVESTMENT PRODUCTS

*Commodities.* Generic term for products bought and sold in commerce
- includes livestock, foodstuffs, grain, metals and oil
- bought and sold (traded) as commodities futures

*Futures.* General term that can refer to commodities futures or financial futures
- a contract to purchase or sell a given amount of an item for a given price by a certain date in the future
- highly risky investment products
- requires specialized knowledge to invest in them

*Junk Bonds.* Below-investment-grade corporate bonds that provide higher returns for greater risk

*Limited Partnerships.* Limited partners contribute money to partnership; general partner manages the funds
- illiquid investment
- invested funds are usually tied up for life of partnership
- high risk that value of invested funds can significantly decrease

*Options.* The right to buy or sell a security at a given price within a specific period of time
- requires specialized investor knowledge

*Precious Metals.* Gold and silver
- may be purchased as bullion, shares of a mining company, coins, jewelry, certificates and futures
- sometimes seen as a hedge against inflation

## Life Insurance

Life insurance is commonly thought to benefit only our beneficiaries after we die. However, some types of life insurance allow you to build a "cash value" against which you can borrow money at a low interest rate. Although we discussed life insurance in the preceding chapter, here we reiterate briefly the various investment types. The dual benefit of life insurance as an investment is that it builds savings and also provides benefits after your death. Be choosy about the life insurance company you select; make sure that it is financially sound and will prudently manage your invested premiums. Consult *Best's Insurance Guide* at your local library for the top companies.

    • *Whole life* (also called straight life) insurance provides both protection and a savings or cash reserve. Interest and/or dividends are earned on the cash value. You can borrow against the cash reserve, often at very low interest rates. Any outstanding loan is deducted from the benefits paid out at death.

    • *Universal life, variable life* and *single premium whole life* insurance are variations of whole life insurance, but differ in that the interest earned on the cash reserve varies with the money market rate.

## Annuities

Fixed annuities are investment-oriented contracts, sold by financial investment and life insurance companies, that guarantee the return of your principal as well as a stated rate of return for a number of years. A variable annuity resembles an investment in a portfolio of mutual funds. You bear the risk of earnings associated with the performance of the portfolio. The annuity contract provides that in return for your investment the company will repay you in regular (usually monthly) payments for a period of time in the future. An annuity is commonly used to supplement retirement income.

    The two main benefits of annuities are that earnings are not taxed until monies are withdrawn and, depending on your payout choice, you have control over when payments are distributed and income tax is paid on the funds. Should you decide to purchase an annuity contract, consider the insurance company's size, its A. M. Best rating, and, in some cases, its Standard and Poor's claims-paying ability rating.

    Prudent investors spread their risks by allocating or diversifying their assets into a variety of investment vehicles. Only high flyers who can afford to lose their entire investment should take chances on volatile financial ventures. Widows are not usually in a position to speculate with their assets. Even in the most conservative situation, such as leaving your assets to be managed by professionals, you need to review your financial security to make sure your managers continue to have your best interests in mind. You are the person most interested in your money. You can best take care of those you love if you take care of yourself too. Carol and Charlotte have found a new sense of accomplishment and confidence by taking charge of their own financial affairs. They are earning the income and making the decisions about where to spend and invest their resources. It's a nice feeling!

## Notes

## Conclusion

# *Looking at the New You*

> *Who knows what women can be when they are finally free to become themselves?*
>
> —Betty Friedan (1921–    ), American feminist

Whether you have been a widow only a few months or several years, pause and take a moment to look at yourself. Think back several months, look at yourself now, then think ahead to your future. Sometimes the uncertainty of tomorrow is easier to handle if you can gather courage from the issues you have already confronted. Now is the time to take measure of how far you have come in your widowhood experience. One way to look at your progress is to start with today and, working back through the weeks, mentally note or list each new responsibility over which you now have greater control or each decision that you now feel was the best one you could have made at the time. Perhaps you are now more confident about facing an upcoming anniversary. Perhaps you are now successfully balancing your checkbook. Don't forget the compliments given by caring family and friends about how much better you are looking or how well you seem to be doing. Even though you may continue to feel bereft, their observations indicate that your physical self is healing and that you seem to have more control over your life.

At times, the only way to realize you are making progress in dealing with your grief and managing your life, is to encounter a more recent widow or a newly bereaved person. You may experience a sense of identification and may be able to express your sympathy by saying, "I understand. I've felt this way, too. Let's talk sometime soon." If your recovery has progressed to the point where you can offer a sympathetic ear, you are no longer completely immersed in your own pain, but have a portion of strength to give.

**Looking at Now**   How do you feel about your life today? Have you considered that another way of looking at being alone and feeling lonely is to recognize that now you have a wonderful opportunity for personal freedom? For perhaps the first time you can control your own life. In the smallest of ways you are free to do as you please. For example, you can eat dinner anytime you wish, or skip it altogether. You can indulge in ice cream or pizza for breakfast, if you choose. You can clean house in the middle of the night, or leave the radio turned on all day. You can visit as many museums as you like for as long as you like. If your husband was ill and you had to rush home to care for him, your new-found freedom may feel strange at first, even disquieting. It may even take you a couple of years to feel comfortable with this sense of independence.

This may be the first time you have been in complete control of your financial affairs. You know exactly how much you have to spend and that any purchases made will be solely at your discretion. Knowing how to manage your finances can provide a heady feeling of success.

Feeling confident about your plans and decisions is another indicator of successful coping and getting on with your life. As a widow, perhaps your first decisions focused on how to pay the monthly bills. Now your decisions may have progressed to the finer points of purchasing mutual funds or a good used car. You may finally feel comfortable about planning for annual property taxes and scheduling auto maintenance. You have gained confidence from the successful outcomes of your earlier choices and, although you have probably made mistakes, your decisions work mostly to your satisfaction.

**Looking Ahead**

All of us are on our own when deciding how we are going to live the rest of our lives. We should not try to suppress or forget the past but, rather, to draw upon the lessons learned. With time, the grieving becomes less intense and less frequent. In her work with widows, Dr. Phyllis R. Silverman notes that a bereaved person is never cured of the grief experience, but is changed by it. She describes the process of relinquishing the role of wife to accept the role of widow and ultimately redefining oneself as a woman.[46] The grief never quite departs; instead, it becomes a part of us. Our memories, which make up our personal history, remain in the background and remind us to cherish what we have today. It is up to each of us to gather courage and to build from our past experiences. One way to do this is to remember the good times you had and how you helped make them better. Focus on your personal contributions to the successes in your life. Try sitting in your favorite chair with a cup of tea while you write a list of what you feel are your strong and helpful characteristics. Perhaps you are a thoughtful, considerate person who always remembers the family birthdays on time. Or perhaps you can always be counted on to follow through with a commitment. In this world of change and uncertainty, a positive, sensitive woman is a welcome source of strength and stability to her friends and community.

Your life ahead may not be anything like you once planned, but the direction it will take is up to you. As you look ahead, you will occasionally wonder, "Is this all there is?" Instead of feeling despair, try to feel a healthy anger that will energize you to meet the challenges of living a life on your own. Tell yourself you *can* get out and about, you *can* get involved with life, you *can* control your life. It is up to you to offer some of your time and skills to help other people, perhaps as a volunteer or as an employee. It is up to you to get yourself involved in the mainstream of life.

**Three Success Stories**

Marjorie, at age sixty-four, has been a widow for more than three years. Her life is full and satisfying, but is moderated by a daily awareness of an uncertain heart condition that occasionally puts her in the hospital. Irene, age seventy, has been on her own for thirteen years. This dynamic, enthusiastic woman has never driven a car, yet is rarely at home because she is busy with dozens of friends and volunteer organizations. Marge, at sixty-five, has discovered a freedom to pursue physical activities and sports competitions she never dreamed would be part of her life. Each of these women displays a positive, enthusiastic attitude about life, even though she, like you, is a widow. All three women were widowed relatively quickly when their husbands died after brief illnesses. Their remarkable recoveries didn't happen overnight. At times, the women weren't aware that they were moving forward with their lives, until they compared themselves to an earlier time in their widowhood.

**Marjorie**

Three times a week Marjorie, with the consent of her cardiologist, dashes to her aerobics class to enjoy a new-found sense of well-being. She laughs at her attempts to keep up with the instructor and delights in how well she feels. She is looking forward to improved results on the treadmill test scheduled for her next routine cardiology exam.

Being on her own was a new experience for Marjorie since she, like most young women of her time, married and went from her father's care to her husband's care. In Marjorie's community, husbands traditionally made most major business and money management decisions. Today, Marjorie's late husband, Garland, would be proud of her shrewd, self-taught financial skills in managing the stock portfolio he so enjoyed. Marjorie has never met her stockbroker, who is in a distant city, yet she feels comfortable with their telephone contact. "I think Garland would be pleased with how I've improved our portfolio," she said. "And I can make quick decisions about how to get repairs on the car done."

Marjorie keeps in touch with young people by volunteering two days a week with a local first-grade teacher. She continues to walk about and search for Indian arrowheads and has taught herself to recognize the various tribal markings and cutting styles. "The most difficult thing about being a widow is not having anyone to cook for," she said. "Sometimes I make things just so the house will smell lived in." A few times a year she plans short excursions or longer trips with groups or with a friend. Marjorie's advice to other widows: "Make yourself get out of the house every day and at least talk to someone. If you stay in it gets too lonely. People just don't come by like they used to when your husband was here."

Irene became a widow when her husband, Jim, died suddenly of a heart attack. Thirteen years later, at age seventy, this energetic, cheerful woman greets each day at 5:45 a.m. by walking three miles with a neighbor. Her days are filled with volunteer and group activities. Twice a month Irene helps feed the homeless street people at a soup kitchen. Every week she is off to the hospital, where she works as a volunteer for the pediatric outpatient department. Amazingly, this dynamic widow does not drive a car, yet that doesn't slow her down. When asked how she gets around, Irene answered, "It is not much of a problem. A lot of older women don't like to drive, especially in the mountains, so we pay a small fee to ride in a car pool. I have a two-wheeled cart to tote my groceries and the rest of the time I can take the bus."

When Irene was first widowed, she also had to care for her bedridden aging mother. Resourcefully, she offered free room and board to a nurse in exchange for help in caring for her ailing mother. Irene got some respite and her mother had a new friend, or at least someone to talk to. Irene sees her greatest source of accomplishment as learning how to make household repairs. "My husband was an expert and a perfectionist, and he would be surprised that I took a class and learned to do these things for myself." Irene said the biggest, continuing hurdle is "traveling with our friends as half a couple and just noticing they are still couples."

Irene's advice to other widows: "Make a contribution to yourself while you are contributing to others. We each change from being a daughter to being a wife and mother to being a total person—as ourself. You have to like yourself before others can like you." As a member of the Colorado Mountain Club, Irene has successfully made contributions to herself and to her community. With the new friends she has made there, she attends concerts and the theater. She goes fishing and camping once a month during the summer and helps build parts of a 480-mile hiking trail from Denver to Durango, Colorado. For seven years she has worked as a trail construction crew leader assuming responsiblity for shopping for provisions, planning and cooking meals and wielding a shovel. "There is a lot of satisfaction in leaving a visible mark," she says of her trail-building efforts.

**Marge**

Some women discover previously unknown talents after they become widows. One amazing example of athletic ability was described in a recent newspaper article, reprinted with permission from the *Denver Post*.[47]

Marge Millis, 64, dribbles her basketball down the driveway, weaving quickly through an obstacle course of two Raid cans, a can of Weed-B-Gone and a dying houseplant. She is dressed in sweats and a pair of Nike running shoes, one of five pairs of sneakers she owns.

Her late husband, Scott, wouldn't recognize this active woman. But "he'd get a kick out of it," Millis said. "Two weeks after he died, I had a strange feeling of survival. Either I could lean on my kids and be a martyr or start a whole new, healthy life." That was three years ago. Today, the grandmother of three who never owned gym shoes and did nothing more strenuous than golf or bowling when her husband was alive, is a running long jump competitor in the first-ever National Senior Olympics in St. Louis. Millis dancercizes and belly dances twice a week. She attends ballroom dances. She has learned to spin-cast for accuracy, free-throw a basketball and use a bow and arrow.

The transformation began a few days after Millis had the "survival" talk with herself. She went to the Aurora [Colorado] Senior Center and signed up for swimming lessons. "It was a challenge. But I did it and proved to myself that I could learn new things," said Millis, who has lived in the same Aurora home for 36 years. "My old life was gone so abruptly, that it was important to live a new life."

Millis mastered the sidestroke, backstroke and crawl and learned to dive. Then she found her next challenge: The Rocky Mountain Regional Senior Olympics. "Someone handed me a basketball and I, the mother of three girls said, 'What is it?' But now the three ladies and I go great guns— you should see how fast we go." Millis and her friends practice free throws at the neighborhood high school courts, much to the surprise of the teenage athletes and cheerleaders practicing after school. "At first, they just look. Then, when they get to know us, they say, 'Hey, good for you. We're proud of you,'" Millis said.

Millis has convinced others that it is healthier to get involved in life than watch television all day, yearning for what they have lost. She taught her sister, widowed two years ago, to spin-cast and throw a Frisbee for Senior Olympics events and the pair has gone on cruises together. She also encourages good swimmers she meets in the pool to participate in the regional Senior Olympics.

"If you don't try a new life, you get into a rut. I see so many people my age taking over the baby sitting or locking themselves in their homes after dark. Women say, 'When my husband died, I died.' That's so sad . . ." Millis said. The spunky, youthful woman who now mows her own lawn but rarely cooks or sews has also lost 20 pounds through her new activities.

**Conclusion**

The stories presented here describe three women who have made great personal efforts to successfully adjust to a new phase of living. They never planned to be alone, yet now that they are, they have developed new interests and are interesting women. You may never want to compete in the Senior Olympics, construct mountain trails or manage a stock portfolio, yet the fact that you are looking for guidance in facing your practical and emotional problems shows that you are interested in getting on with your life and gaining control of your life. This is the beginning of the new you.

The suggestions offered in this book are intended for the first two years or so of widowhood, yet we clearly understand that the experience of being widowed will remain with each of us for the rest of our lives. Becoming and being a widow is a searingly painful and poignant event.

In retrospect, for most of us, life was easier when we were wives. It is natural to yearn for what we had and to be apprehensive about our futures. Each succeeding year does not always move forward more smoothly or with more accomplishment. Our first steps on our own are tenuous. Stressful situations can set us back. It is not unusual for a widow, even after several years, to be suddenly caught off guard by tearful memories. The sudden sadness can be brought on by something as simple as a beautiful sunset or by the start you feel when you see a stranger who, for an instant, looks or sounds like your late husband. We feel that it is appropriate to have private times for grief for as many years as you wish. But instead of dwelling on the pain, try to cling to the happy memories and use them as a source of strength from which you can move forward with your own life. Let this book serve as a guide as you move from who you were to who you will become.

# Notes

### Chapter 2. The Funeral
[1] *Consumer Guide to the FTC Funeral Rule* (Washington, D.C.: Federal Trade Commission, Bureau of Consumer Protection, April 1984).

### Chapter 3. The First Days
[2] The Widow's Network, P. O. Box 1041, Danville, CA 94526.

### Chapter 4. Emotional Support During Grief
[3] Elisabeth Kübler-Ross, M.D., *On Death and Dying,* (New York: Collier Books, Macmillan, 1969).
[4] Richard Lewis Detrich and Nicola J. Steele, *How to Recover from Grief* (Valley Forge, Pa., Judson Press, 1983), 41.

### Chapter 5. Enlisting Legal Help
[5] *Money Matters: How to Talk to and Select Lawyers, Financial Planners, Tax Preparers, Real Estate Brokers* (Washington, D.C.: American Association of Retired Persons, 1986).

### Chapter 6. Your Financial Advisory Team
[6] Ibid.
[7] Ibid.

### Chapter 7. Settling the Estate
[8] Don and Renee Martin, *Survival Kit for Wives* (New York: Villard Books, 1986), 25-26.

### Chapter 8. Filing Claims for Life Insurance and Survivor Benefits
[9] For additional information, write to the U.S. Government Printing Office, Washington, D.C. 20402, and request the free pamphlet *A Summary of Veterans Administration Benefits,* VA Pamphlet 27-82-2, Revised June 1984. For $2.25 you can purchase the IS-1 fact sheet entitled *Federal Benefits for Veterans and Dependents.*

### Chapter 9. Social Security, Medicare, Health Insurance and Disability
[10] *Your Medicare Handbook,* (Washington, D.C.: U.S. Government Printing Office, re. no. 1986-491-252/20503).
[11] Faustin F. Jehle, *The Complete and Easy Guide to Social Security and Medicare* (Madison, Wis.: Fraser Publishing, 1987), 125.
[12] Ibid., p. 132.
[13] Ibid., p. 137.

[14] The Consolidated Omnibus Budget Reconciliation Act (COBRA), PL 99-272, was enacted in April 1986 and is effective for health plan years beginning July 1, 1986.

[15] *Group Health Insurance Continuation* (Older Women's League, National Office, 1325 G Street, N.W., Lower Level B, Washington, D.C. 20005, (202) 783-6686, October 1986).

[16] Health Insurance Association of America, 1850 K Street, N. W., Washington, D.C. 20006, July 1984, p. 8.

### Chapter 11. Your Auto and Home—Care and Maintenance

[17] *At-a-Glance Auto Record* (Sheaffer-Eaton Division of Textron, Inc., 1985).

[18] *Reader's Digest Complete Do-It-Yourself Manual* (Reader's Digest Association, Reader's Digest Road, Pleasantville, New York 10570, 1973).

[19] *Fix-It-Yourself Manual* (Reader's Digest Association, Reader's Digest Road, Pleasantville, New York 10570, 1977).

[20] Stephen Mink, *Insuring Your Home* (New York: Congdon & Weed, 1984).

[21] *Money Matters: How to Talk to and Select Lawyers, Financial Planners, Tax Preparers, Real Estate Brokers* (Washington, D.C.: American Association of Retired Persons, 1986).

### Chapter 12. Single Parenting

[22] Jill Krementz, *How It Feels When a Parent Dies* (New York: Alfred A. Knopf, 1986).

[23] Fitzhugh Dodson, *How to Single Parent* (New York: Harper & Row, 1987), 124.

### Chapter 13. Three Widows

[24] "Caregivers Need a 'Care Break'," (*Senior Beacon in Focus for People over 50,* Lakewood, Colo., Vol. 2, No. 2, February 1987), 1-2.

[25] Loren McIntyre, "The High Andes" (Washington, D.C.:*The National Geographic,* April 1987), 426.

[26] Anne-Grace Scheinin, "My Turn: the Burden of Suicide," (New York: Newsweek, February 7, 1983), 13.

[27] Edwin Shneidman, as quoted in *After Suicide: A Unique Grief Process* (Springfield, Ill.: Elnora Ross, Human Resources Division Creative Marketing, 1981), 4.

[28] John H. Hewett, *After Suicide* (Philadelphia: Westminster Press, 1980), 92.

[29] Ibid.

### Chapter 14. Taking Care of Yourself—Getting Out and About

[30] Monica Dickens, "When I Lost My Husband," *Reader's Digest,* March 1987, 116.

[31] Genevieve Davis Ginsburg, M.S., *To Live Again* (Los Angeles: Jeremy P. Tarcher, 1987).

[32] Frances Weaver ,*The Girls with the Grandmother Faces,* (Century One Press, 2325 East Platte, Colorado Springs, Colo. 80909), 72.

## Chapter 17. Taking Care of Those You Love—Estate Planning

[33] "Plan Your Estate as You Would Plan Your Home" (Denver: Colorado Bar Assoc., 1982).

[34] Ibid.

## Chapter 18. Taking Care of Your Money—Finance and Investments

[35] Benjamin Graham, *The Intelligent Investor* (New York: Harper and Row, 1973), 1.

[36] Ibid., 35.

[37] "A Busy Person's Guide to Managing Risk," *Investment Vision* (Boston: Fidelity Investments, Vol. 4, September-October 1987), 1.

[38] Sylvia Porter, *Sylvia Porter's Money Book,* (New York: Avon Books, 1976), 820.

[39] Ibid.

[40] *Successful Investing. An Authoritative Financial Self-Help Book about Investing in the Stock Market,* Staff of United Business Service (New York: Simon and Schuster, 1983), 47.

[41] Ibid., 45.

[42] Graham, op. cit., xv.

[43] *Successful Investing,* op. cit., 40.

[44] Ibid., 13.

[45] Adam Smith, *The Money Game* (New York: Random House, 1968).

## Conclusion: Looking at the New You

[46] Silverman, Phyllis R., M.D., *Widow to Widow,* (New York: Springer Publishing Co., 1986), viii.

[47] Joni H. Blackman, "Athlete Takes Life in Stride" (Denver: Denver Post, June 29, 1987).

# Glossary

**Administrator**—A person appointed by a court to administer or manage the estate of a person who dies without a will (intestate).

**Agent**—A person authorized to act for another. Examples include a stockbroker, a real estate salesperson or an insurance agent.

**Annuity**—A contract between an insurance company and an individual (the annuitant), in which the company agrees to provide an income, which may be fixed or variable in amount, for a specified or indefinite period in exchange for a stipulated amount of money.

**Asset**—Anything owned that has monetary value such as physical properties or intangibles.

**Beneficiary**—A person designated to receive the death proceeds or death benefit accruing under a life insurance policy or an annuity, or a person who is to receive the income or principal of a trust or estate.

**Blue Chip (Company or Stock)**—A blue chip company is known nationally for the quality and wide acceptance of its management ability, products or services, and its ability to make money and pay dividends. A blue chip common stock is highly esteemed as an investment based on continued earnings through bad as well as good times, a long history of consistently paying cash dividends, established leadership within an industry, and with solid expectations for continued success.

**Bond**—A promissory note (debt instrument) of a corporation, a municipality or the U.S. government that promises to pay the lender a specified amount of interest for a specified period of time, with the principal to be repaid on the maturity date.

**Broker**—An agent who, for a fee, executes the public's orders to buy and sell securities, commodities or other property. (See also Real Estate Broker.)

**Callable Bond**—A bond containing a provision that allows the issuing agency or corporation to "call" back or redeem it before the maturity date, if certain conditions are met.

**Capital Gain or Capital Loss**—Profit or loss from the sale or exchange of capital assets, such as securities or real estate, subject to special tax treatment when certain conditions are met.

**Cash Flow**—In personal finance, cash flow refers to a comparison of income ("cash flowing in") to expenses ("cash flowing out") for the same period.

**CATS**—Certificates of Accrual on Treasury Securities (a Salomon Brothers brokerage firm product) are zero-coupon U. S. Treasury certificates sold at a discount that carry a locked-in interest rate when held to maturity. The coupon portion (interest rate) and principal are sold separately.

**Certificate of Deposit (CD)**—Evidence of a deposit in a financial institution for a specified time that earns a specified rate of interest.

**Churning**—Unjustified and excessive trading in a customer's securities or commodities account to generate additional brokerage fees.

**Codicil**—A document that changes or adds to a will.

**Collateral**—Security pledged for the repayment of a loan.

**Commission**—A broker's fee for executing buy and sell orders for securities or commodities.

**Common Stock**—Securities which represent an ownership interest in a corporation.

**Community Property**—Property acquired during a marriage and held to be equally owned by husband and wife under the laws of states providing for such ownership. In theory it means that half of what either the husband or wife earns while married belongs to the other. Upon the death of one, the value owned by the deceased becomes subject to disposition by his or her will.

**Compounding**—Allowing the total investment principal amount plus any accrued interest earnings to be accumulated and kept with the original investment, making more total dollars available for earning interest in the future.

**Corporate Bonds**—Bonds issued by corporations to secure loans that vary in maturity dates, rates of return and safety. Some corporate bonds are secured by specific assets of the issuer, while others are unsecured debt. Most pay interest semiannually.

**Coupon Bond**—A bond that has interest coupons (pieces of paper) attached to it. To claim the interest, the owner must clip the coupons as they come due and take or mail them to a registered payor.

**Debt Securities**—Bonds.

**Decedent**—A deceased person, especially one who has died recently.

**Discount** —The amount by which a bond or preferred stock may sell below its par value.

**Discount Broker**—A broker who charges a lower commission for executing buy and sell orders than a full-service broker and who typically does not offer investment advice.

**Dividend**—A payment (usually the net earnings) designated by the board of directors of a corporation to be paid to its stockholders. For preferred stock, dividends are usually fixed; and with common shares, dividends vary with the fortunes of the company.

**Equity**—The value of a person's ownership in real property or securities. In home ownership, equity is the current market value of the home, less principal owed on the outstanding mortgage. Equity in securities is the ownership interest of common and preferred stockholders in a company.

**Escrow**—Money (or documents) held by a third party until specific conditions of a contract or agreement are met.

**Estate**—The real and personal property owned or possessed by a person. At death the estate is distributed to the heirs according to the decedent's will or, if there is no will, by a court ruling.

**Estate Administration**—The management of an estate, including inventorying the assets, taking care of the assets, accounting to the court, and distributing the assets to creditors and other legally entitled recipients.

**Estate Plan**—An expression of a person's desires and objectives for the ownership, management and preservation of his or her property during his or her lifetime and his or her desires for its disposition upon death. Generally designed to incur the least possible taxes and other costs.

**Estate Tax**—A tax is imposed by a state or the federal government and paid on the right to transmit property from the estate of a deceased person to living beneficiaries. The executor of a decedent's estate arranges for payment out of the assets of the estate itself. Estate taxes may be levied by the federal and state governments.

**Exclusive Agency Contract**—In real estate, a type of contract to sell a home in which the broker receives a sales commission only if he or she or any other broker finds the buyer. If the seller finds the buyer, no selling commission is owed.

**Exclusive Agent**—In real estate, a broker with exclusive right to sell a property within a specific period of time.

**Exclusive Right-to-Sell Contract**—In real estate, a type of contract in which the broker receives a sales commission no matter who finds the buyer, including the seller.

**Executor**—The person and/or institution designated to carry out the provisions of a will. A female executor is an "executrix." In some states the executor is called a "personal representative."

**Face Value**—The value of a bond that appears on its face, unless the value is otherwise specified by the issuing company. Face value is ordinarily the amount the issuing company promises to pay at maturity. Face value is sometimes referred to as "par value" and is not an indication of market value. With life insurance, the face amount is stated on the face of the policy and is paid at death, less any outstanding loans or withdrawals made.

**Federal National Mortgage Association FNMA (Fannie Mae)**—A privately owned corporation that provides a secondary market for federally guaranteed or insured mortgages. It issues a number of different mortgage-backed securities.

**Fiduciary**—A person (or institution) acting in a position of trust with respect to management of assets for the benefit of another. The fiduciary is bound by a legal duty to act in good faith. Examples of fiduciaries are executors of wills, trustees such as banks or trust institutions, and administrators of estates.

**Fiduciary Income Tax Return**—An income tax return filed by a person acting as a fiduciary on behalf of an estate or trust. This return may be required by both the federal and state governments.

**Gift Tax Return**—A return filed annually by the donor to report any gifts in excess of the annual exclusion amount for one recipient even if no tax is payable. It may be required when settling an estate, as gift taxes are imposed by some states and the federal government on an individual's lifetime transfers of money or property by gift.

**Ginnie Maes**—Securities issued by the Government National Mortgage Association (GNMA), which are backed by the U. S. government. When investors buy a Ginnie Mae, they buy into an approved pool of approximately fifteen to twenty-five individual homeowners' mortgages that were financed through certified banks.

**Gross Estate**—The value of all property in which a person possesses an interest at the time of his or her death. Includes the value of personal belongings; amounts on deposit in savings and checking accounts; stocks, bonds and other securities; debts owed to the estate by others; real estate; partnership interests; interest in a retirement plan; interest in an IRA; the value of any annuity that will continue to be paid to a beneficiary after the owner's death; value of jointly held property excluding what is owned by a living spouse; and the value of trust property over which the person possesses a general power of appointment.

**Group Life Insurance**—Insurance coverage offered on a group basis by employers, unions and other organizations to their employees or members. The premiums are often lower than those of individual or private policies.

**Health Maintenance Organization (HMO)**—A type of health insurance provider, most often subscribed to by groups, in which preventive health care is emphasized and the subscribers are treated by staff physicians.

**Heir**—A person who is entitled to inherit a portion of the estate of a person who died without a will.

**Inheritance Tax**—A tax levied by most states on the right of a beneficiary to receive a particular share of an estate. The tax is based on the amount received and the recipient's relationship to the deceased.

**Interest**—A fee or payments that borrowers must pay lenders for the use of their money.

**Intestate**—Dying without a valid will. (As opposed to dying with a will or being "testate," from the phrase *last will and testament.*)

**Investment**—The use of money for the purpose of making more money, to gain income or increase capital, or both.

**IRA**—An Individual Retirement Account is a personal pension plan with tax advantages. An IRA permits direct investment in stocks and bonds through stockbrokers, or through intermediaries such as mutual funds, insurance companies and banks. Interest accumulates tax deferred until the funds are withdrawn beginning at age 591/2. Early withdrawals are subject to a penalty.

**Joint Tenancy**—A way of owning property, either real estate or personal property, in the names of two or more people. When one dies, the survivors become the sole owners. The interest (value of ownership) of the deceased owner passes directly to the surviving joint tenants without probate court proceedings. The last surviving joint tenant obtains title to the entire property.

**Junk Bonds**—Corporate bonds with investment-grade ratings, greater risk of default and sometimes higher yields.

**Keogh Plan**—A tax-favored personal retirement program that can be established by a self-employed individual. A Keogh plan is also known as an "H.R. 10 plan."

**Liabilities**—For personal estate planning or credit applications, liabilities are the total value of all a person owes to others.

**Lien**—A debt on property, such as a mortgage, back taxes or other claims.

**Limited Partnership**—A partnership formed to pursue a financial venture, composed of a general managing partner and limited partners whose liability is limited to the amount invested. Examples of limited partnership investments include oil, gas and real estate ventures.

**Listing Contract**—In real estate, the contract or agreement that employs a real estate agent to sell a particular piece of property. "Listing" generally refers to the property itself.

**Load**—The sales charge payable when certain mutual funds are purchased.

**Marital Deduction**—For federal estate tax purposes, the value of any property that passes from the decedent to the surviving spouse, which may be deducted in calculating the estate tax due.

**Market Price**—The price actually paid for property, usually referring to real estate or securities.

**Maturity**—The date on which a loan or bond comes due or is redeemable and is to be paid off.

**Money Market**—A market where short-term debt instruments (also called money market securities) such as Treasury bills, short-term federal agency issues, large certificates of deposit, corporate commercial paper and banker's acceptances are traded. Usually only professional dealers trade in the money market. A private individual can participate in the money market by purchasing T-bills or by investing in mutual funds that specialize in money market securities.

**Money Market Account**—A money market deposit account may be offered by banks, credit unions and savings and loans. A minimum amount, often $1,000 may be required to open the account. Money market accounts have limited check writing privileges and are insured by the FDIC, FSLIC or credit union insurance company. The interest earned may be more or less than the rate earned by a money market mutual fund account. The funds are liquid—that is the depositor may withdraw his or her funds without penalty.

**Money Market Fund**—A mutual fund whose investments are in high-yield money market instruments such as federal securities, CDs and commercial paper. Its intent is to make such instruments normally purchased in large denominations by institutions available indirectly to individuals.

**Multiple Listing**—An agreement that allows several real estate brokers to share information on "for sale" properties. Commissions from a sale are split by mutual agreement between the listing and selling brokers.

**Multiple Listing Service**—The MLS is the local office that supervises the printing and distribution of listings of properties for sale to the members of the local Board of Realtors.

**Municipal Bonds**—"Munis" are debt obligations (bonds) issued by states, municipalities, or state agencies or authorities that pay interest that is exempt from federal income taxes for owners who reside in the state in which they are issued.

**Mutual Fund**—An investment company that pools and professionally manages shareholder funds for investment purposes.

**NASDAQ**—The National Association of Securities Dealers Automated Quotations is an automated information network that provides brokers and dealers with price quotations on securities traded over the counter(OTC).

**Net Worth**—In personal finance the value of a person's assets minus the value of liabilities owed.

**New York Stock Exchange**—The largest organized securities market in the United States, founded in 1792. The Exchange itself does not buy, sell, own or set the prices of securities traded there. Prices are determined by public supply and demand. The Exchange is a not-for-profit corporation of 1,366 individual members, governed by a Board of Directors consisting of ten public representatives, ten Exchange members or allied members, a full-time chairman, executive vice chairman and president.

**Open Enrollment**—During the annual period of "open enrollment" in organizations (employers) that offer more than one health insurance carrier, currently insured employees are allowed to switch health insurance carriers without evidence of insurability.

**Ordinary Income**—Income earned from salaries, wages, tips, interest and dividends that does not receive special tax considerations (as opposed to capital gains income).

**Over the Counter**—The OTC market for securities is made up of securities dealers who may or may not be members of a securities exchange. The over-the-counter market is conducted over the telephone and deals mainly with stocks of companies without sufficient shares, stockholders or earnings to warrant listing on an exchange. Prices for many OTC securities are reported daily in the newspaper under the NASDAQ listings.

**Par**—With respect to securities bonds, especially the value or amount printed on the face of the bond. The interest paid on bonds is calculated on the bond's par or face value.

**Permanent (Whole) Life Insurance**—A type of life insurance that pays a lump sum at death, with a cash value that can be borrowed, used as collateral or withdrawn when the policy is surrendered.

**Personal Property**—Generally, any property or assets owned by a person other than real estate.

**Personal Representative**—In some states, the executor of a will or the administrator of an estate.

**Points**—In real estate, a point is 1 percent of the face value of the mortgage loan. Points are charged by lending institutions when real estate is purchased.

**Portfolio**—Holdings of securities by an individual or an institution. A portfolio may contain bonds, preferred stocks, common stocks and other securities.

**Preferred Stock**—A class of stock that receives preference over the common stock of a corporation with respect to payment of dividends and distribution of assets in the event of liquidation.

**Premium**—The amount by which a bond or preferred stock may sell above par or its face value. May also refer to the redemption price of a bond or preferred stock if it is higher than face value.

**Price-Earnings Ratio**—The price of a share of stock divided by its annual earnings share. The P/E ratio is used as a way to compare the prices of different stocks. For example, a stock selling at $35 per share and having an annual earnings per share of $3.50 has a P/E of 10.

**Principal**—In finance, the capital or main body of money in a holding, to be distinguished from the interest or revenue from it. In real estate, principal is the amount of money owed or the amount borrowed.

**Probate**—The process of establishing the validity of a will.

**Probate Estate**—The assets of a decedent that are distributed to other persons through the probate process and under the jurisdiction of the probate court. Life insurance proceeds are not usually part of the probate estate.

**Real Estate Agent**—Generic reference that includes real estate salespeople, real estate brokers and Realtors (a registered trademark term).

**Real Estate Broker**—A real estate salesperson who has passed the state licensing examination for brokers and who represents others in real estate transactions. A broker may have his or her own real estate agency.

**Real Estate Investment Trust**—An REIT is a professionally managed portfolio of real estate holdings and/or mortgages in which investors purchase shares.

**Real Estate Salesperson**—A state-licensed real estate sales representative who must work under the supervision of a real estate broker.

**Real Property**—Land, buildings and anything permanently attached to them.

**Realtor**—A real estate broker who is a member of the National Association of Realtors. (Realtor is a registered trademark word and is always capitalized.)

**Redemption Price**—The price set by an issuing company at which a bond may be redeemed before maturity.

**Refinance**—In real estate, to pay off on a loan by taking out another loan on the same property.

**Revenue Bond**—A type of municipal bond whose repayment and interest are based on the receipts from the project rather than from general taxes.

**Securities**—Written evidence of ownership or creditorship, especially stock certificates. Generally refers to stocks, bonds or notes.

**Stocks**—The capital that a corporation raises through the sale of shares entitling the holder to dividends and other rights of ownership.

**Tax Exempt**—Refers to kinds of income that are not subject to income tax, such as interest earned from municipal bonds issued in the same state in which the owner resides.

**Tenancy by the Entirety**—A form of joint ownership, recognized in some states, that allows ownership of property (usually of real estate) to be shared by husband and wife. Neither spouse can sell his or her ownership alone, and when one spouse dies the other automatically takes ownership as the survivor.

**Tenancy in Common**—A form of co-ownership of real estate or personal property in which two or more persons are entitled to possession at the same time and any owner may sell or otherwise transfer his or her portion. Upon the death of any owner his or her interest passes to the heirs or beneficiaries. On a securities account owned by two tenants in common, for example, if one owner dies then 50 percent of the account continues to belong to the other owner and 50 percent of the account goes to the estate of the deceased.

**Term Life Insurance**—A type of insurance that covers a specific period of time or "term." Death benefits are paid when the death of the insured occurs during the term in which the policy is in force.

**TIGRs**—Treasury Investors Growth Receipts (a Merrill Lynch brokerage firm product) are zero-coupon U.S. Treasury certificates sold at a discount that carry a locked-in interest rate when held to maturity.

**Treasury Bills**—T-bills are short-term debt obligations of the U.S. government. New issues are sold at a discount and mature to face value in thirteen, twenty-six or fifty-two weeks. The discount is the difference between the purchase price and the maturity value, and equals the interest.

**Treasury Bonds**—The U. S. government debt obligations with maturities of usually ten to thirty years that pay interest semiannually and are issued in minimum denominations of $1,000.

**Treasury Notes**—U.S. government debt obligations that mature in one to ten years and pay interest semiannually.

**Trust**—A legal arrangement whereby title to property is given to one party (the trustee, who may be a surviving spouse or another person or a corporate trustee) who manages the property for the benefit of a beneficiary or beneficiaries.

**Trust Deed**—An instrument used in place of a mortgage in some states, with a third party trustee (not the lender) holding title to the property until the loan is repaid or defaulted.

**Trustee**—An individual or institution named to hold, manage and distribute the assets of a trust.

**Unified Tax Credit**—The federal estate tax and federal gift tax rates were "unified" or combined by the Tax Reform Act of 1976. Generally, depending on which year a death occurs in a specific value of the decedent's estate and lifetime gifts are excluded from federal estate taxes. If a death occurred in 1987, for example, the first $600,000 of the estate may be excluded from the federal estate tax.

**Unit Investment Trust**—A limited portfolio of bonds or other securities in which investors may purchase shares. A UIT is not continually managed.

**Universal Life Insurance**—A form of whole life insurance that allows savings and deferred taxes on earnings. The premium amount and payment schedule are flexible.

**VA Loan**—A Veterans Administration-backed mortgage loan, also called a "GI Loan." Widows of veterans who died of a service-connected disability may qualify for this low- or no-down-payment loan.

**Warranty Deed**—In real estate, the warranty deed guarantees good title to a property.

**Will**—A legal declaration of a person's wishes concerning what shall be done about the disposition of his or her property and the administration of the estate following his or her death. It is revocable during life, inoperative until death and applies to the situation that exists at the time of death.

The clauses or articles that comprise a will vary from state to state, but may include:

- The person's name, address, and a provision for a revocation of former wills,
- Funeral arrangements,
- Instructions for payment of inheritance taxes,
- Specific money gifts to legatees,
- Bequests of personal property and household items,
- Disposition of real property (Real estate is "devised" to beneficiaries.),
- Disposition of the residue (remainder) of the estate,
- Description of trusts and administrations,
- Description of guardians if necessary,
- Names of executors and trustees,
- Treatment of spouses and grandchildren,
- Description of who will succeed as executor or trustee if the first named cannot perform (fiduciary succession),
- Testamonium clause that affirms who is making this will as of this date,
- Attestation clause that includes the witnesses' signatures, and
- Signature clause that validates the will.

**Yield**—Sometimes also called "return." The interest or dividends paid on a particular security and expressed as a percentage of the purchase price or of the current price.

**Zero Coupon Bond**—A bond on which no periodic interest payments are made, but on which the interest earned accrues to be paid at maturity. Zero coupons are often sold at deep discount.

# Selected Sources

(The following books and support organizations are presented as a sampling of resources available for grieving persons.)

**Books for Widowhood and Grieving**

Caine, Lynn. *Widow*. New York: William Morrow & Co., 1974.

Grollman, Earl. *Concerning Death: A Practical Guide for the Living*. Boston: Beacon Press, 1974.

Kushner, Harold S. *When Bad Things Happen to Good People*. New York: Avon, 1981.

Nye, Miriam Baker. *But I Never Thought He'd Die: Practical Help for Widows*. Philadelphia: The Westminster Press, 1978.

O'Conner, Nancy. *Letting Go with Love: The Grieving Process*. Apache Junction, Arizona: La Mariposa Press, 1984.

Parkes, Colin Murray. *Bereavement*, 2nd Edition. Madison, Connecticut: International Universities Press, 1987.

Pincus, Lily. *Death and the Family: The Importance of Mourning*. New York: Pantheon Books, 1974.

Shuchter, Stephen R. *Dimensions of Grief: Adjusting to the Death of a Spouse*. San Francisco: Jossey-Bass Publishers, 1986.

**Books for Spiritual Healing**

Detrich, Richard and Nicola J. Steele. *How to Recover from Grief*. Valley Forge, Pennsylvania: Judson Press, 1983.

Kuenning, Delores. *Helping People Through Grief: When a Friend Needs You*. Minneapolis: Bethany House Publishers, 1987.

Landorf, Joyce. *Mourning Song*. Old Tappan, New Jersey: Fleming H. Revell Company, 1974.

Marshall, Catherine. *To Live Again*. New York: McGraw-Hill Book Co., Inc., 1957.

Peale, Norman Vincent. *Not Death at All*. Englewood Cliffs, New Jersey: Prentice Hall, 1979.

Swindoll, Chuck. *For Those Who Hurt*. Portland: Multnomah Press, 1977.

Westberg, Granger E. *Good Grief*. Philadelphia: Fortress Press, 1971.

**Books for Recovery and Rebuilding**

Caine, Lynn. *Lifelines*. New York: Doubleday & Co. Inc., 1978.

Ginsburg, Genevieve Davis. *To Live Again: Rebuilding Your Life After You've Become a Widow*. Los Angeles: Jeremy P. Tarcher, Inc., 1987.

Loewinsohn, Ruth Jean. *Survival Handbook for Widows (And for Relatives and Friends Who Want to Understand)*. Washington, D.C.: American Association of Retired Persons and Scott Foresman and Company, Glenview, Illinois, 1984.

Martin, Gail M. *Help Yourself to a Midlife Career Change*. Reprint from Spring 1981 issue of Occupational Outlook Quarterly. Washington, D.C.: U.S. Department of Labor: Superintendent of Documents, U.S. Government Printing Office, 1985. Publication No. 0-477-128.

Nudel, Adele Rice. *Starting Over: Help for Young Widows and Widowers*. New York: Dodd, Meade & Company, 1986.

Stearns, Ann Kaiser. *Living Through Personal Crisis*. Chicago: The Thomas More Press, 1984.

Tatlebaum, Judy. *The Courage to Grieve: Creative Living, Recovery, and Growth Through Grief*. New York: Harper & Row Publishers, 1980.

Weaver, Frances. *The Girls with the Grandmother Faces*. Colorado Springs, Colorado: Century One Press, 1987.

Wylie, Betty Jane. *Beginnings: A Book for Widows*. New York: Ballantine Books, 1977.

## Books for Single Parents

Atlas, Stephen L. *The Official Parents Without Partners Sourcebook*. Philadelphia: Running Press, 1984.

Dodson, Fitzhugh. *How to Single Parent*. New York: Harper & Row Publishers, 1987.

Furman, Erna. *A Child's Parent Dies: Studies in Childhood Bereavement*. New Haven, Connecticut: Yale University Press, 1974.

Jewett, Claudia L. *Helping Children Cope with Separation and Loss*. Harvard, Massachusetts: Harvard Common Press, 1982.

Schaefer, Dan, and Christine Lyons. *How Do We Tell the Children? A Parents' Guide to Helping Children Understand and Cope When Someone Dies*. New York: Newmarket Press, 1986.

Vogel, Linda Jane. *Helping a Child Understand Death*. Philadelphia: Fortress Press, 1975.

## Books for Children

Grollman, Earl A. *Talking About Death: A Dialogue Between Parent and Child*. Boston: Beacon Press, 1976.

Jackson, Edgar. *When Someone Dies*. Philadelphia: Fortress Press, 1971.

Krementz, Jill. *How It Feels When a Parent Dies*. New York: Alfred A. Knopf, 1986.

LeShan, Eda. *Learning to Say Good-by: When a Parent Dies*. New York: Macmillan Publishing Company, 1976.

Rofes, Eric E., and the Unit at Fayerweather Street School. *The Kid's Book About Death and Dying*. Boston: Little, Brown and Company, 1985.

Bolles, Richard Nelson. *The 1985 What Color Is Your Parachute?* Berkeley, California: Ten Speed Press, 1985.

Windy Boy, Betty. *Women's Job Search Strategy or . . . How to Keep the Wolf Away from the Door.* Denver: Arrowstar Publishing, 1987.

**Books for Employment**

Barker, Becky. *Answers.* New York: Harper & Row, 1986.

Harl, Neil. *Farm Estate and Business Planning.* Skokie, Illinois: Agribusiness Publications, 1983.

Martin, Don, and Renée Martin. *A Survival Kit for Wives: How to Avoid Financial Chaos Before Tragedy Strikes.* New York: Villard Books, 1986.

*Reader's Digest Family Legal Guide.* Pleasantville, New York: The Reader's Digest Association, Inc., 1981.

**Books for Estate Settlement and Estate Planning**

Jehle, Faustin F. *The Complete and Easy Guide to Social Security and Medicare.* Madison, Wisconsin: Fraser Publishing Co., 1987.

*The Woman's Guide to Social Security.* Social Security Administration, Publication No. 05-10127, July 1985.

*Your Medicare Handbook.* Washington, D.C.: Superintendent of Documents, U. S. Government Printing Office, 1986. Publication No. 491-252/20503.

**Books for Social Security and Medicare**

Hewett, John. *After Suicide.* Philadelphia: The Westminster Press, 1980.

Ross, Elnora. *After Suicide: A Unique Grief Process.* Springfield, Illinois: Creative Marketing, 1981.

**Books for Survivors of Suicide**

Brown, Judith N., and Christina Baldwin. *A Second Start: A Widow's Guide to Financial Survival at a Time of Emotional Crisis.* New York: Simon & Schuster, 1986.

David, Walter W. *The 50-Plus Guide to Retirement Investing.* New York: Dow-Jones, 1987.

Fowler, Elizabeth M. *Every Woman's Guide to Profitable Investing.* New York: American Management Association, 1986.

Gatov, Elizabeth Smith. *Widows in the Dark.* Bolinas, California: Common Knowledge Press, 1985.

Goodman, George J. W. (Adam Smith). *The Money Game.* New York: Random House, 12th Printing, 1968.

Graham, Benjamin. *The Intelligent Investor.* New York: Harper & Row, Fourth Revised Edition, 1973.

Klott, Gary L. *The New York Times Complete Guide to Personal Investing.* New York: New York Times Books, 1987.

Passell, Peter. *How to Read the Financial Pages.* New York: Warner Books, 1986.

**Books for Finance and Money Management**

Perkins, Gail, and Judith Rhoades. *The Women's Investment Handbook*. New York: A Plume Book, New American Library, 1983.

Porter, Sylvia. *Sylvia Porter's New Money Book for the '80s*. New York: Avon Books, 1979.

Quinn, Jane Bryant. *Everyone's Money Book*. New York: Delacorte, 1979.

Siegel, Joel G., and Jae K. Shim. *Investments: A Self-Teaching Guide*. New York: John Wiley & Sons, Inc., 1986.

Tobias, Andrew. *The Only Investment Guide You'll Ever Need*. New York: Harcourt Brace Jovanovich, 1978.

United Business Service. *Successful Investing*. New York: Simon and Schuster, 1983.

**Support Organizations for Widows**

*Families of Homicide Victims Program*
c/o Victim Services Agency
2 Lafayette Street
New York, New York 10007
(212) 577-7700
Provides counseling for the surviving spouses of murder victims.

*National Association for Uniformed (Services) NAUS*
5535 Hempstead Way
Springfield, Virginia 22151-4094
(703) 750-1342
A national organization for all members of the military family, including widows and widowers. Offers numerous benefits for members ranging from grief counseling to travel and group insurance programs for life, health, home and auto.

*Older Women's League*
730 11th Street NW, Suite 300
Washington, D.C. 20001
(202) 783-6686
National organization, working through local chapters, that lobbies to resolve older women's problems with low income and health insurance.

*Recovery, Inc.*
802 N. Dearborn Street
Chicago, Illinois 60610
(312) 337-5661
International organization of 1,000 groups in the United States, Canada, England, Ireland, Wales and Puerto Rico. Assists persons in dealing with anger and depression. Groups led by trained volunteers.

*Society of Military Widows*
5535 Hempstead Way
Springfield, Virginia 22151
(703) 750-1342
This branch of the National Association of Uniformed Services provides support
for widows of active duty or retired military men of any rank or branch of
the armed services.

*THEOS (They Help Each Other Spiritually)*
1301 Clark Building
717 Liberty Avenue
Pittsburg, Pennsylvania 15222
(412) 471-7779
The THEOS foundation provides nondenominational spiritual and educational
programs for the widowed and their families. The main objective of
THEOS is "to help widowed persons make the transition into singlehood
by helping them rebuild their lives with Christ as the foundation."

*Widowed Persons Service (WPS)*
American Association of Retired Persons
1909 K Street, N. W.
Washington, D.C. 20049
(202) 728-4370
Offers guidance in coping with grief, understanding financial matters, making
decisions, finding employment and setting up programs for widowed
persons.

*Widows' Network*
3483 Golden Gate Way, Suite #2
Lafayette, California 94549
(415) 283-7174
A California based organization run by volunteers, who are also widows,
provides bereavement counseling, workshops for management skills,
travel programs and social events.

## Support Organizations for Parenting
*Business and Professional Women's Foundation*
2012 Massachusetts Avenue, N.W.
Washington, DC 20036
(202) 293-1200
BPW provides information on child care, pensions, flextime, job sharing and
parental leave.

*Child Care Action Campaign*
99 Hudson Street, Room 1233
New York New York 10013
(212) 334-9595
The Campaign comprises a coalition of leaders from organizations that seek to
inform the public about child care problems, and about solutions and
services that may be attainable through the efforts of government, corporations and individuals.

*Parents Without Partners*
International Headquarters
7910 Woodmont Avenue, Suite 1000
Bethesda, Maryland 20814
1-800-638-8078
An international organization providing discussion groups for single parents,
    whether widowed or divorced, and sponsoring some social activities.

**Resources for**        *Catalyst*
**Career Changes**        2150 Park Avenue South
New York, New York 10003
(212) 777-8900
Catalyst is a national not-for-profit organization that works with corporations and
    individuals to develop career and family options. The Catalyst Network is
    a group of independent resource centers that provide career and educa-
    tional counseling and programs. All have a particular commitment to
    meeting the career needs of women.

*The Displaced Homemakers Network*
1010 Vermont Avenue, N.W., Suite 817
Washington, DC 20005
(202) 628-6767
The Network is an umbrella organization that links people around the country
    who are concerned about the problems of displaced homemakers.

**Support**                *American Association of Suicidology*
**Organizations for**      2459 South Ash
**Survivors of**           Denver, Colorado 80222
**Suicides**               (303) 692-0985
Call or write for nationwide referrals to support groups and for professional
    assistance for survivors of suicides.

*Survivors of Suicide*
Suicide Prevention Center, Inc.
P. O. Box 1393
Dayton, Ohio 45401-1393
(513) 223-9096
Write or call for their directory of nationwide support groups for survivors of
    suicide.

# Index

# Notes

## Notes

**Notes**

# Notes

# About the Authors

**Charlotte Foehner**

After the death of her husband, Charlotte Foehner moved her family across the country, changed careers and began to learn financial investment strategies and tax preparation. She now makes her home in Denver, Colorado.

**Carol Cozart**

Carol Cozart was a traditional housewife and mother who devoted her life to her family. When she lost her husband, she was forced to redefine herself. She had to search for a new career and has recently begun her first full-time job. She is a resident of Colorado.